ISBN: 9781313485920

Published by:
HardPress Publishing
8345 NW 66TH ST #2561
MIAMI FL 33166-2626

Email: info@hardpress.net
Web: http://www.hardpress.net

BL
1245
V36
S39

CORNELL
UNIVERSITY
LIBRARY

Date Due

MAY 4 - 1954 H S'		
SEP 19 1956 CU		
NOV 22 1953		
DEC 3 1958 K R		
INTERLIBRARY LOAN		
SEP 1975 S		
Interlibrary Loan		
SEP 23 1977 F		

Cornell University Library
BL 1245.V36S39

Chaitanya and his age /

3 1924 022 952 695

CHAITANYA AND HIS AGE

Chaitanya and His Age

(Ramtanu Lahiri Fellowship Lectures for the year 1919 and 1921)

By
Rai Bahadur Dinesh Chandra Sen, B.A., D.Litt.,

Fellow, Reader, and Head Examiner of the Calcutta University, Associate Member of the Asiatic Society of Bengal, Author of History of Bengali Language and Literature, the Vaisnava Literature of Mediæval Bengal, Chaitanya and his Companions, Typical Selections from Old Bengali Literature, Folk Literature of Bengal, the Bengali Ramayanas, Banga Bhasa-O-Sahitya, etc., etc.

Published by the
UNIVERSITY OF CALCUTTA
1922

PRINTED BY ATULCHANDRA BHATTACHARYYA AT THE CALCUTTA
UNIVERSITY PRESS, SENATE HOUSE, CALCUTTA

Dedicated

To

The Hon'ble SIR ASUTOSH MOOKERJEE,

Kt., C.S.I., M.A., D.L., D.Sc., Ph.D.,

F.R.A.S., F.R.S.E., F.A.S.B.

Vice-Chancellor of the Calcutta University,

whose resolute and heroic attempts

to rescue our Alma Mater from destruction

at the hour of her great peril

may well remind us

of the famous line of Jayadeva

" प्रलयपयोधिजले धृतवानसिवेदं "

with the sincere gratitude of

the Author

"Hail thee O Chaitanya—the victor of my heart,
Mark the rhythm of his mystic dance in lofty
      ecstasy—quite alone.
Merrily sounds the tabor and the cymbal's
      note keeps time.
The joyous band following him sing and
      dance merrily—merrily;
He steps a pace or two onwards in his
      dancing gait,
And knows no rest—intoxicated with his
      own over-flowing joy.
Oh my heart's Lord, how can I express the
      love I have for thee?
Saha Akbar craves a drop from the sea of thy
      piety and love."

Song by Emperor Akbar
(Translated from Hindi)

PREFACE

The first 190 pages of this book embody my lectures as Ramtanu Lahiri Research Fellow for the session 1919, and the remaining portion is meant as my lectures for 1921. The subject chosen for 1920 was "The Bengali Prose Style from 1800 to 1857." As this subject was to be studied by the students of the Indian Vernaculars in our University for their examination, the urgency of its treatment required me to stop the Chaitanya topics and deliver a course of lectures on the prose-style last year. These lectures were delivered and published early in 1921. And, I next hastened to revert to my half-finished lectures on Chaitanya. There are some points in this book which are a repetition of the things said in my other books, but this could not be helped. As I have attempted to give here a complete and consistent story of the great hero of my memoir I had to include all noteworthy points of his life in a short compass. There are of course many things in this book not dealt with elsewhere and I have always tried to present the incidents of Chaitanya's life in a new light. It is hoped that the sketch herein presented will, by its comprehensive character, satisfy the curiosity of all students who want to have a clear account of Chaitanya, his religious views and of the sects that follow his religion. Everything said in this book is based on old authority, though I have not given references in all cases, as it would make the book heavy with foot-notes and more or less mar its popular character. The readers will find one and all of such references in the works mentioned in the bibliography given on pages 97-98 of this book.

One thing has struck me in regard to the recognition of the Vaisnavas by the Hindu society in general. The Goswamies of Khardah and Santipur—the descendants of Nityananda and Adwaita respectively—not only enjoy the highest social rank amongst the Vaisnavas but have quite a respectable standing amongst the lay Brahmin community. My idea was that they created this position outside their own society, even after they had broken stringent caste-rules, through the sheer dint of their noble sacrifices and high spirituality. But quite lately a book named "Sri Nityānanda-vamsāvali-O-Sādhanā" written by Pandit Kshirodbihari Goswami—a direct descendant of Nityananda—has disillusioned me on this point. I now find that the descendants of Nityananda and Adwaita had very nearly become outcastes in the primitive stages of the promulgation of the Chaitanya cult. They redeemed themselves, however, in the eyes to the Brahmin community, outside their own ranks, by contriving to enter into frequent matrimonial alliances with the 'kulin' Brahmins of the mother society, often by satisfying large pecuniary demands of the latter. This alliance with a large number of 'kulins' has gradually made their position secure in the Hindu society. This shews that the caste-rules amongst the Hindus is a factor of so great an importance that though the efforts of a prophet may for a time succeed in unloosing its hold upon our people, it reasserts itself with all its rigidity, a short while after. And, however mighty the enemy, it is only by manœuvres, tactics and bribes that he can expect to gain his lost position in society—not by open war. The Sahajiyas disregard the caste-rules at night, fearing exposure in daylight. It is for this reason that some of them have compared themselves with bats (p. 380).

I take this opportunity of expressing my hearty thanks to Dr. Sylvain Levi, the distinguished Orientalist, who has kindly written a fore-word for this book in the form of a letter. The high compliments that a scholar of his world-wide fame has given me, have been very gratifying to me, as indeed they would have been to any Indian. There can be no question as to the sincerity of his appreciation, though I feel that there may have been a friendly bias. I regret, however, that my presentation of Chaitanya does not appear to be sufficiently indicative of the greatness of his character, and Dr. Levi will not give him a place in the ranks of the world's greatest men. He refers to Chaitanya's religion being restricted to a narrow geographical area contrasting it to that of Buddha. The universal recognition of the Buddha and a few other greatest leaders of the world in the spiritual domain is chiefly due to political causes, the advantage of which Bengal of the 16th century could not evidently possess. Vaisnavism of Bengal is, besides, the youngest of the world's reputed creeds, so it is perhaps premature to pass a judgment now on Chaitanya's work. Regarding the view that the theology of Chaitanya lacks originality, the codes of all religions of the world may be traced to earlier sources; and a complicated code of Ethics is not, in my humble opinion, always the true criterion of the greatness of a faith. The infusion of life into the universal truths and their presentation in the most attractive form are, I submit, a far truer test. I cannot follow the reason that love for God is a peculiar or local feature of Indian religions, which cannot be appreciated outside India. The difference, I think, lies in the fact that Europe has not yet transcended the ethical limits, beyond which lies the domain of mystic felicities. Chaitanya did not ignore mankind; he tried to lead men to the dizzy heights of paradise, which my learned friend, following the limitations of Christian theology, speaks of as "forbidden." I agree with him so far that Chaitanya cannot have a universal recognition in this materialistic age. But I verily believe that when this age will be followed by one of spiritual awakening all over the world, he will be differently judged. He brought to the doors of ordinary men the highest spiritual bliss of divine love, which like the stream of the holy Ganges, lay entangled in the meshes of Indian religious philosophy, more knotty than the matted locks of Siva. I hope, my esteemed friend will not take me amiss. As a Bengali, it is natural for me to be prejudiced in favour of my Bengali apostle. But love always sanctifies the soul. If I have been blind to the defects of Chaitanya's religious system, I do not regret it. I would in that case only crave my friend's forgiveness. Speaking for myself, my heart, more than to any logic, responds to the couplet first sung by Nityananda :

"One who admires Chaitanya and sings praises of him, is dear to me as my life."

I hold myself fully responsible for the numerous misprints and errors which will be found in this book, and do not accuse anybody. I am not a good proof-reader and that is all that I can plead as my excuse.

7, VISWAKOSH LANE,
    CALCUTTA.   } DINESH CHANDRA SEN.
The 15th April 1922.

FOREWORD

BY

Dr. Sylvain Lévi.

Mon cher ami,

Vous m'avez demandé une préface pour votre livre : " Chaitanya et son époque." Je n'ai guère de compétence sur ce domaine ; ce que j'en connais, je le dois essentiellment à vos ouvrages : depuis le jour où j'ai lu avec une émotion inoubliable votre " Histoire de la Langue et de la Littérature Bengalie " j'ai suivi avec un intérêt qui ne s'est jamais ralenti votre activité si féconde, et 'cest ainsi que, grâce à vous, le Bengale du temps de Chaitanya m'est devenu familier. J'avais eu pourtant l'occasion d'effleurer le sujet il y a très longtemps, au début de mes études. Je commençais à recueillir des matériaux en vue de ma thèse sur le Théâtre Indien ; j'avais trouvé à la Bibliothèque Nationale à Paris, un vieux manuscrit en écriture bengalie qui contenait le traité de Rūpa Gosvāmin sur l'art dramatique (nāṭya) ; je fus frappé par la ferveur de cet écrivain qui greffait sur un recueil de definitions banales une longue suite d'hymnes enthousiastes à Krishṇa ; ce fut pour moi l'occasion de m'initier au mouvement inspiré par Chaitanya. Je lus ensuite, avec une surprise et une admiration que je retrouve encore après tant d'années, le drame original et puissant où Kavikarṇapūra met audacieusement en scène Chaitanya et ses compagnons. J'ai longtemps rêvé d'en donner une traduction parallèlement à celle du Prabodhachandrodaya, pour mettre en contraste l'ingéniosité raffinée de l'un et la fougue passionnée de l'autre. J'ai traduit le Prabodhachandrodaya, et jai dû m'en tenir là, faute de temps. Je sais gré à votre livre de me ramener vers le héros que j'avais trop négligé, et de me le montrer dans une intensité de lumière qui laisse par instants les yeux un peu éblouis.

Vous possédez à un degré extraordinaire le don capital de l'historien, qui est de projeter la vie sur le passé mort. C'est un don de poète autant que d'historien, et vous êtes si essentiellement poète que votre style oscille entre l'épopée et le lyrisme. Ce besoin de vie que vous portez en vous ne vous permet pas de vous arrêter à ces froides combinaisons de possibilités qui sont partout le fond de l'histoire et dans l'Inde plus que partout ailleurs. La pénurie des documents positifs y laisse à chaque instant l'historien embarrassé pour rattacher dans une continuité provisoire la série des faits connus. Vous ne pouvez pas vous résigner à cette attitude d'expectative. Vous faites résolument la part de l'impossible ; mais cette discrimination une fois opérée, le possible glisse aisément au probable, et le probable au certain.

C'est là un effet fatal de votre imagination fougueuse. Pourtant vous n'êtes pas sans connaître ni reconnaître les exigences de la plus sévère critique, vous épuisez tous les documents avec la patience d'un érudit, et vous pressez vos étudiants avec une éloquence pathétique de rechercher les documents encore inédits. Si j'étais plus jeune, j'aurais voulu vous suivre et je ne doute pas, pour l'honneur du Bengale que vos appels soient accueillis avec empressement par la jeunesse studieuse. Une figure comme Chaitanya mérite les hommages d'un pays entier ; il est juste que les savants lui consacrent leurs veilles, comme les paysans lui consacrent leurs chants.

Je suis assez disposé (et j'ai tort peut-être) à faire bon marché de sa theologie qui m'apparaît plutôt indifférente et de seconde main, sans puissance d'invention ou de système ; ses autres qualités, d'orateur, de poète, de linguiste, etc., n'auraient pas suffi à le mettre hors de pair. Mais ce que donne à sa personnalité un relief unique, c'est le don d'amour qu'il a su porter jusqu'à l'extrême limite des possibilités humaines, en le tournant tout entier sur Krishna, et qui s'est associé spontanément chez lui à la beauté créatrice de l'art. Sa conception de la danse, appliquée à la propagande de l'amour divin aurait séduit l'esthétique délicate de la Grèce ; elle aurait sans doute placé Chaitanya à côté d'Orphée. Qu'il y ait eu, dans ses transes mystiques, un élément maladif, vous ne le contestez pas ; vous citez un de ses propos où il parle lui-même de ses attaques d'épilepsie. Mais cette faiblesse même me plaît ; elle est la part de la " bête," pour reprendre les termes si expressifs de Pascal, chez un être où la part de " l'ange " est si belle. Je sens, chez ce *sannyási* ivre d'amour, la sourde lutte sans cesse déchaînée, et qui le jette à terre, écumant, au milieu des visions qui lui découvraient un monde interdit.

Vous avez vous-même, en plus d'un passage, évoqué par comparaison la figure du Bouddha, cet autre héros indien de l'amour universel. Mais j'ai peur que votre passion dévote et presque fanatique pour Chaitanya vous ait rendu un peu injuste à l'égard de son grand rival. Vous aimez à insister sur l'œuvre sociale de fraternité humaine courageusement poursuivie et en partie réalisée par le missionnaire de Krishna ; vous vous plaisez à montrer les Musulmans ou les Musulmanisés admis dans son église, et vous glorifiez l'esprit de " catholicité " qui anime sa prédication. Ici, je le déclare franchement, je ne puis vous suivre. Vous pourrez mettre en cause, et peut-être avec raison, mes préventions d'Occidental ; mais le respect absolu du sens établi pour les mots qu'on emploie est la condition primordiale d'une discussion, si on la veut loyale et utile, et dans le cas présent, comme partout et toujours, la justesse du mot est solidaire avec la justesse de l'idée. Le terme de " catholicité," quand il ne désigne pas par excellence tous les fidèles de l'Eglise Catholique, garde le sens qu'il tient de son origine grecque, indépendamment du suffixe latin qui s'y est accroché ; il signifie à peu près l'universalité, le monde pris " dans son ensemble " (καθ' ολον). Dans l'immensité presque infinie de l'histoire religieuse de l'Inde, si riche en personnalités et en créations, le Bouddha est uniquement et exclusivement le seul à propos de qui on puisse employer ce terme. Que sa notion personnelle de l' homme ait dépassé les frontières de l'Inde pour s'étendre aussi loin que celle d'un Socrate ou d' un Jésus, rien ne nous permet soit de l'affirmer, soit de le nier. Mais le fait est que l'Eglise née de son inspiration a converti la plus grande partie de l'Asie. Aucune autre croyance originaire de l'Inde, orthodoxe ou hérétique, n'a connu ce succès. Vous avez recueilli pieusement de légers indices qui vous permettent de supposer que l' influence de Chaitanya a dépassé les frontières du Bengale, Orissa compris ; en réalité le mouvement de Chaitanya est régional, très loin d' être " catholique", autrement dit : universellement humain.

L'Inde, à coup sûr, a le droit de se complaire dans son "splendide isolement," comme d'autres peuples se sont flatés de le faire ; mais elle doit alors loyalement accepter les restrictions qui en découlent. Le génie hellénique et le génie hébraïque ont conçu l' homme universel, l'un dans l'ordre philosophique, l'autre dans l'ordre religieux : ils out tendu de tous leurs efforts à le réaliser, et ils y ont prodigieusement réussi. L'Inde a prétendu limiter son horizon au cadre nettement défini de ses frontièrs naturelles, elle a délibérément ignoré le reste du monde. Elle s'est façonné, elle a maintenu un type d' organisation religieuse et sociale qui vise à l'exclusion rigoureuse de l' étranger. La faillite ultime du bouddhisme dans l'Inde est le triomphe suprême du nationalisme hindou ; les seuls liens qui rattachaient l' Inde à la grande communauté humaine étaient définitivement anéantis. Chaitanya peut être un des plus grands voyants de l'Inde ; l' humanité ne le réclame pas comme un de ses grands hommes ; elle ne le reconnaît point, parcequ'il l'a méconnue.

Katmundu,
Nepal, 29 Juin 1922.

FOREWORD

BY

DR. SYLVAIN LEVI.

(Translated from French by Captain J. W. Petavel, R.E., Retired, Lecturer on the Poverty Problem, Calcutta University and Principal, Maharaja of Kasimbazar's Polytechnic Institute.)

Dr. Dinesh Chandra Sen.

DEAR FRIEND,

You have asked me for a preface for your book "Chaitanya and his Age" but I am hardly qualified to give it, for what I know of the subject I owe mainly to your works. From the day when with feelings I shall never forget, I read your History of Bengali Language and Literature, I have followed your fruitful activity with a degree of interest that has never diminished, and thus, thanks to you, Bengal of the time of Chaitanya has become familiar to me. I had, however, skimmed through the subject a long time ago in the early days of my studies, when I was collecting notes for my work on the Indian theatre. I had found in the 'Bibliotheque Nationale' an old manuscript in Bengali script that contained the treatise of Rupa Goswami on dramatic art (Natya). I was struck by the enthusiasm of the writer who grafted on a compilation of commonplace definitions a long series of fervent hymns to Krishna.

That put me first into touch with the movement inspired by Chaitanya. Subsequently I read with a degree of surprise and admiration that I experience again after these many years, the original and powerful drama in which Kavi Karnapur boldly brought Chaitanya and his companions on to the stage. I long cherished the ambition to give a translation of it by the side of that of the Prabodh Chandrodaya, to emphasise the contrast between the refined ingenuity of the one and the passionate ardour of the other. I managed to translate Prabodh Chandrodaya but was compelled to stop there as I had no time to do more. I must be thankful to your book for having brought me back towards the hero I have neglected, and for having shown him to me in intense light that at times dazzles one's eyes.

You possess in an extraordinary degree the capital gift of the historian which is to make the dead past live. It is a poet's gift as much as a historian's, and you are so essentially a poet that your style alternates between the lyric and the epic. This instinctive desire to make things living that is characteristic of you, does not allow you to be stopped over the cold study of possibilities that is everywhere the foundation of the historian's work, and especially so in India. The lack of authoritative documents leaves the Indian historian constantly puzzled to link known facts together in some degree of continuity. You cannot resign yourself to the expectant attitude. You resolutely make the best of an impossible situation, but once your choice made, speculation glides unperceptibly into probability, and probability into certainty. This is the inevitable result of your fervent imagination. Nevertheless you do not fail to appreciate and to recognise the requirements of the most severe criticism (you do not lose your critical faculty). You examine all the documents with the perseverance of the patient scholar, and appeal to your students with touching eloquence to seek for manuscripts still unpublished. If I were younger, I would have wished to follow you, and I have no doubt that, for the honour of Bengal, your appeal will be taken up enthusiastically by her studious youth. Such a figure as Chaitanya deserves the homage of the whole country. It is right that the learned should honour him by burning their midnight oil studying him, as the peasants honour him by consecrating their songs to him. I am quite inclined (though perhaps I am wrong) to think less of his theology, which seems to me rather indifferent and second-hand not showing power of invention or method. His other qualities as an orator, as a poet, as a linguist, etc., would not seem to me sufficient to make him without an equal. But that which marks him as an outstanding personality is the gift of love that he has been able to carry to the extreme limits of human capacity centering it entirely upon Krishna, and which his disposition caused him to associate spontaneosly with the creative beauty of art. His conception of dance applied to the propaganda of divine love, would have appealed to the fine æsthetic sense of the ancient Greeks and would no doubt have given Chaitanya a place by the side of Orpheus. That there was in his mystic trances an abnormal element you do not contest. You indeed quote one of the passages where he himself speaks of his epileptic fits. But even this weakness is pleasing to me. We see in it the manifestation of the "animal-side" of man, to use Pascal's expressive language, in a being in whom the manifestation of the "angel-side" is so beautiful. I feel that silent strife going on incessantly in this *sanyasi*, intoxicated with love, and occasionally throwing him down foaming at the mouth in the midst of his vision that has revealed a forbidden paradise to him.

You have yourself, in more than one passage, compared him to the Buddha—this other Indian hero of universal love. But, I am afraid, your passionate and somewhat fanatical devotion to Chaitanya has made you a little unjust towards his great rival. You like to insist on the social work of human brotherhood courageously pursued, and partly realised, by the missionary of Krishna. You delight in showing the Musalmans or converts to Islam admitted into his church, and you glorify the " catholic " spirit that characterises his preachings. Here I frankly declare that I cannot follow you. You may urge, and perhaps justly, my limitations as a Westerner, but an absolute regard for the accepted meanings of words that one uses is the primary condition of frank and useful discussion, and in the present case, as everywhere and always, the accuracy of the word is one and the same with the accuracy of idea. The word catholicity, when it is not used to designate the followers of the Catholic Church, keeps its meaning derived from the Greek origin, independently of the Latin suffix that has been attached to it. It signifies almost universality—the world approximately as a whole. In the almost unfathomable depths of India's religious history, so rich in personalities, both real and imaginary, the Buddha stands alone, as the one in connection with whom the term can be used. There is nothing to justify us either in affirming or denying that his particular conception of mankind has passed the limits of India to extend as far as the ideas of Socrates or Jesus extended. But the fact is that the church that his inspiration brought into existence has won the greater part of Asia. No other faith originating in India, orthodox or heterodox, has ever succeeded in doing that. You have carefully gathered together and treasured slight indications that allow you to think that the influence of Chaitanya has passed the limits of Bengal and Orissa. As a matter of fact, the Chaitanya-movement is local, far from being " Catholic," *i.e.*, in other words, universally human. India has certainly the right to take pride in her splendid isolation, just as, indeed, some other countries have chosen to do. But then she must frankly accept the limitations which accompany such an attitude. The genius of the Greeks and of the Hebrews conceived humanity as a whole; the former conceived man in the domain of philosophy, and the latter in that of religion. They tried with all their efforts to realise that ideal, and attained prodigious success. India has had the ambition of limiting her horizon within clearly defined natural boundaries. She had deliberately ignored the rest of the world. She created for herself, and has maintained, a kind of religious and social organisation the object of which is strictly to exclude foreigners. The ultimate failure of Buddhism in India is the supreme triumph of Hindu nationalism. The only links that connected India with the rest of the great human family were finally destroyed. Chaitanya may be one of the greatest seers of India. Humanity, however, does not recognise him as one of its great men. He did not recognise mankind. So mankind does not recognise him.

KHATMUND,
27th June, 1922.

Contents

CHAPTER I.

Condition of Bengal before the advent of Chaitanya (pp. 1-57).

(*i*) Vices brought on by reaction against Buddhist asceticism (pp. 1-14); (*ii*) Chandidas as precursor of Chaitanyaic age (pp. 14-31); (*iii*) the influence of the Bhagavata and other sacred works (pp. 31-37); (*iv*) Vaisnavism in Bengal before Chaitanya (pp. 37-52); (*v*) the political condition of the period (pp. 52-57).

CHAPTER II.

A historical review of the biographical works of the Vaisnavas—their claims to reliability discussed (pp. 58-98).

(*a*) Murari Gupta's Chaitanya Charitam (pp. 58-67).

(*b*) Narahari Sarkar's songs (pp. 68-73).

(*c*) The Chaitanya Bhagavata (pp. 73-77).

(*d*) The Chaitanya Charitamrita (pp. 77-81).

(*e*) Lochan Das's Chaitanya Mangal (pp. 81-85).

(*f*) Govinda Das's Karcha (pp. 85-89).

(*g*) Jayananda's Chaitanya Mangal (pp. 89-91).

(*h*) Prembilas, Bhakti Ratnakar and songs on Chaitanya (pp. 92-93).

(*i*) Summary (pp. 93-97) Bibliography (pp. 97-98).

CHAPTER III.

Ancestry, birth and childhood (pp. 99-108).

CHAPTER IV.

Birth and boyish frivolities (pp. 109-112); education and founding of a Tôl (pp. 113-119); the defeat of the Scholar Keshub Kashmiri (pp. 119-121).

CHAPTER V.

Marriage (pp. 121-124); Tour in Eastern Bengal (pp. 124-127); Return to home (p, 127); Visit to Gya (pp. 128-130); Trances (pp. 130-135); Closing of the Tôl (pp. 135-138); The Sankirtan parties (pp. 138-153); Reformation of Jagai and Madhai (pp. 153-156); Srikrishna play (pp. 156-167); His resolve to turn a sannasyi (pp. 157-163).

CHAPTER VI.

Chaitanya's Sannyas (pp. 164-167); His tour and visit to Santipur (pp. 167-176); The incidents at Puri (pp. 176-189); His resolve to go to the Deccan (pp. 189-190).

CHAPTER VII.

Govinda Das's account of his travel (pp. 191-194); Reformation of Sinners—Naroji, Bhilapantha and Bara Mukhi (pp. 194 to 208).

CHAPTER VIII.

Visit to Travancore and other places (pp. 209-212); Reception at Puri (pp. 212-216).

CHAPTER IX.

Proposed visit to Brindavan (pp. 216-218); Interview with Sanatan and Rupa—their Sanyas (pp. 219-323); Private tour,—Baladev's account (pp. 323-326); Stay at Brindavan—on his way back—meeting with Bijli Khan (pp. 227-229).

CHAPTER X.

Chaitanya at Benares,—discussion with Prakasananda (pp. 230-233); Tour in Bengal, (pp. 233-234); At Puri (pp. 234-250).

CHAPTER XI.

Reveries and ecstasies gradually increasing (pp. 251-259); His passing away (pp. 259-265).

CHAPTER XII.

Chaitanya as a teacher (pp. 266-319).
Love—its various phases in the Spiritual plane (pp. 266-276); Service to fellowmen and

compassion for the depressed castes (pp. 276-283); Social reformation—Vaisnava jurisprudence (pp. 283-290); His commanding personality, many-sidedness of character and scholarship (pp. 290-295); Spiritual emotion, love for mother, influence on the Vaisnava poets (pp. 295-319).

Supplement

CHAPTER I.

Chaitanya's religious views—the Dwaita-dwaitabad (pp. 320-323); Rules of conduct, theory of devotion (pp. 324-327); The fivefold *rasas* of the Vaisnavas (pp. 327-333).

CHAPTER II.

The Sahajias (pp. 334-341); The various sects (pp. 341-351); The Buddhist elements (pp. 351-356); Their philosophy of love (pp. 356-361); Durgaprasad Kar—the Sahajia Sadhu practising love (pp. 361-366); Their love-ideal derived from the Buddhists (pp. 367-370); The Madanotsava (pp. 370-372); The Radha-Krishna cult (pp. 372-373); The wickedness of the Sahajias exposed in the novel Charu-Darshan (pp. 373-389); The Sahajia songs (pp. 389-397).

CHAPTER III.

The duty of the Research-students in the field of the Sahajia literature (pp. 398-403).

Chaitanya and his Age

From Old Records

CHAPTER I

CONDITION OF BENGAL BEFORE THE ADVENT OF CHAITANYA

(*i*)   Vices brought on by reaction against Buddhist asceticism.
(*ii*) Chandi Das as precursor of Chaitanyaic age.
(*iii*) Influence of the Bhāgavata and other sacred works.
(*iv*) Vaisnavism in Bengal before Chaitanya.
(*v*)   The political condition of the period.

(*i*) *Vices brought on by reaction against Buddhist asceticism.*

If we take a bird's-eye view of the religious aspects of Bengal from the eleventh to the twelfth century, we shall be in a position to ascertain the causes that have led to the development of the *bhakti*-cult in this province.

Chaitanya's advent has produced a far-reaching effect on the religious and social history of Bengal, and in order to judge and explain how this could be possible, a review of the condition of the religious life and of the social evolution that was going on in this country, prior to the advent of Chaitanya, is essential from many points of view. We shall chiefly restrict ourselves, however, to the evidences that have been found in Bengali literature for arriving at our conclusions.

Religious condition of Mediæval Bengal.

The Nath-cult which originated with Mina-Nath and Goraksha Nath had already an extensive literature in Bengali in the thirteenth century, and there was the Dharma-cult also, probably co-eval with the Nath-creed and having many points in common. The Dharma-cult was a degraded form of Buddhism, and Nathism was a compromise between Saivism and Buddhism. The followers of both the sects believed in 'Niranjan' and 'Dharma,' though the Nath-cult seems to have adhered more closely to Siva worship. Both believed in miracles, and in the supernatural powers of the Siddhas. Kalipa, Haripa and Kanupa, are spoken of in terms of high esteem in the literatures of both the cults, and are held in higher regard than even the gods of heaven. But we are not

The Nath and Dharma-cults.

The common features.

at present concerned with the details of the respective creeds.

Nathism contributed largely to our Vernacular in its primitive stages, and chief among these contributions are the Maynamati songs presented to us from different parts of Bengal in manifold forms. These songs originated in Eastern and Northern Bengal and were spread by the propounders of the Nath-cult over all parts of India. If the reason is asked as to why these songs are to be included in the Nath-literature, I should say that they relate mainly to the glories of Goraksha Nath, the Nath-leader, and of Harisiddha and Maynamati, his two Bengali disciples. There are many incidents described in these songs, but the keynote to them is struck in the panegyrics bestowed on the power of the Siddhas of the Nath-cult. The form in which these songs have come down to us has been considerably modernised by the rhapsodists of the later ages, but the original framework is of the 11th and 12th centuries, and evidences of this lie strewn over the whole range of this lyrical literature.

But though the Maynamati songs traverse by far a wider field, the most strikingly significant note, however, of the Nath-cult is to be found in the Goraksha-Bijay itself—

<small>Goraksha Bijay.</small> a Bengali work which contains an account of how Goraksha Nath redeemed his *guru* Mina Nath from his great spiritual

degradation. This book is sometimes called the 'Mina-Chetana' or restoration of Mina Nath to spiritual consciousness. The tone of the poem is elevated and calm, and a quiet philosophy and spirit of stern asceticism pervade the work. The doctrines of Yoga as practised by the Naths are discussed here in the '*Sandhya-bhasha*' or 'the language of twilight' as it has been called by some scholars, in which the Buddha-Doha-O-Gan and many other works were written.

In this literature of the Nath-cult we find asceticism of a high order based on an observance of moral virtues. An unimpeachable sexual integrity is aimed at, and preserved among many temptations by the heroes of these poems, and chief amongst them Goraksha Nath, the prince of the Yogis, rises to our view surrounded by many mystic and legendary tales, resplendent in his vows, like the peak of a mountain, when sunrise is just dispelling the mist around it. He sets at naught all the temptations that a man ever faced from a woman, and saves Mina Nath from the moral pitfall to which the latter had unheedingly fallen.

The high moral tone.

In the songs of Maynamati also we find Prince Gopichandra facing temptations and becoming glorious by overcoming them. Hira, the wealthy harlot, to whose fascinations a hundred youths of noble lineage had succumbed, proved powerless before our hero. In the Dharma-literature Prince Lou Sen conquers passions like a Yogi. Women renowned for their beauty and accomplishments try him, but he proves invincible. Not only unimpeachable in sexual morality, the principal characters are endowed with virtues of truthfulness and integrity which hold to light some of the great features of Buddhistic moral tenets. Where could we find a greater martyr at the altar of truth and loyalty than Kalu-Dom, the general of Lou Sen? Harihara Baity's struggle for overcoming the temptations of worldly prosperities on the one hand, and fears of grim persecution on the other, resulting in his ultimate triumph, invests him with a solemn grandeur which commands our admiration. The Dharma-mangal songs and those of Maynamati have certainly a crude humour and are spotted with the blemishes of style of illiterate people. But the great idea is there, the idea of unstinted morality, of loyalty and devotion to the king, which sets all dangers at naught; of adherence to truth, knowing the result to be confiscation of property and death. The characters are often no doubt drawn by clownish hands; there is a forest of wild legends, which almost stifle the breath of the readers with their incredibleness and prolixity; the crudeness of descriptions and their monotony are often tiresome to the extreme. But these do not diminish at all the lustre of faith that illuminates the pages,—faith in the great moral virtues which truly ennoble a race.

But at this very time when stern asceticism and strength of character were being glorified, we find another side of the picture in which the forces of reaction are clearly indicated. Vaisnavism of old school and Tantricism are shown on the reverse of the picture. We find the people of rustic villages, amongst whom the practice of Yoga and Tantric culture had been current in those days, revolting against all rigour of asceticism and yielding to profligacy and sexual pleasures. We find the courts of kings steeped in these vices, and favouring libertinism in the name of religion by a quite royal indulgence in sensuous pleasures. We find *tantrics*, originally imbued with the object of attaining a high spiritual goal, sinking low in debauchery. Men and women sat freely around the Chakra or the *circle* where all moral laws were set at naught. King Ballala Sen (1100-1169 A. D.) had a mistress of the Chandal-caste named Padmini whom he openly raised above the status of his chief queen, and obliged many of his noblemen to eat the food served by her. " वङ्गालस्यानदोषेण " is a line which we frequently come across in our genealogical records, accounting for the loss of social status of particular members of our community, and the

<small>Reaction.</small>

title স্বর্ণপীঠী is a contemptuous epithet by which our social leaders branded those who obtained rewards from the king, for taking food prepared by Padmini. It is said that this woman was very handsome and was brought by the king to his palace for helping him in *tantric* practices. The inscriptions openly praise Lakshman Sen for intriguing with the beautiful Kalinga women.[1] Abhiram Goswami born in 1095 A.D., a devout Vaisnava, kept a mistress named Malini and this woman is publicly applauded in the Vaisnava traditions.[2] Jayadev himself counts it a point of glory to mention the name of Padmavati in his songs. She was a "sevadasi" of Jagannath temple, and Shekha Subhodaya says that she used to dance in the court of Lakshman Sen, and several authorities confirm that she had been at first dedicated to the Puri temple from where Jayadev picked her up.[3] Jayadev glories in calling himself "পদ্মাবতী-চরণ-চারণ চক্রবর্ত্তী" implying that she danced, while he used to play upon some musical instrument to keep time. The poets of this period sang panegyrics of their patrons the kings, for their licentiousness ; and the copper-plate inscriptions

---

[1] "যস্য লক্ষ্মণসেনস্য কৌমারকেলিঃ কলিঙ্গাঙ্গনাভিঃ" I.A.S.B., Dec. 1909, p. 473.

[2] See Abhiram Tattwa, Abhiram Patal and Abiramlilamrita (published by Bhupaticharan Goswami and Atulchandra Goswami).

[3] See Bhaktamāla by Chandra Datta and Joydeva Charitra by Banamali Das.

also unmistakably indicate the tendencies of the age by describing the situations of Siva and Parvati in close embrace, in a language not quite becoming or decent according to modern taste.[1] On the door-ways of the Puri and Kanaraka temples are found many human figures in bas-relief, which are grossly vulgar. In the ground-floor of the Sahitya Parisat buildings, an image of Siva embracing Parvati is preserved in the gallery of statues ; this image of Siva is shockingly vulgar and evidently belongs to the age of which we have been speaking. The lays of Jayadev which sometimes rise to great spiritual heights are indecent in many places and the same should be said of the Pavana-duta by the poet Dhoi of Lakshman Sen's court. This country is prone to indulge in religious speculations and there is no lack of subtle interpretations attempting to glorify what a moralist would justly condemn. But when for three centuries beginning from the 12th, we find our art, architecture and poetry all dominated by the same spirit of indecency, we must admit that during the decline of Hindu power, the standard of morality had become low amongst our people, due, as I have already said, to a spirit of reaction against the stern attitude of the Buddhist and Nath ascetics towards materialistic life. This indecency and predilection for sensuous

---

[1] See I.A.S.B., Dec. 1909., p. 471, and Epigraphia Indica, Vol. I, p. 307.

life are manifest in popular literatures of the Krishna and Siva cults. In the Siva songs we have vulgar tales of the Great God's gallantry, amongst the low class women of the Kuchni and Dome castes. The evil-eyed jealousy of Parvati described by Rameswar and other poets has undoubtedly some very gross humour in it. In one of the poems we find her complaining that though she had tried to keep Siva at home, at night by tying the edge of her *sari* to his tigerskin, it proved of no avail, as the Great God ran away to meet the Kuchni-women as soon as she fell asleep. To the songs of Manasa Devi these Siva songs are found prefixed as prologues, and in the Krishna Kirtan of Chandi Das we find the same vulgar taste, which has given rise to an animated discussion amongst scholars, some of whom, familiar with the highly refined and platonic songs of the great poet, have expressed a doubt as to the genuineness of the book. In Rangpore, Cooch-behar, and indeed in many parts of North Bengal, Krishna *dhamalies* are still sung in which Krishna as a rustic cow-herd in clownish humour pursues Radha for an embrace or a kiss, and greater the vulgarity in these songs, the greater is the fun enjoyed by the farmers and the artizans of the country-side. However greatly these songs may have been modernised in their language, their origin should no doubt be traced to the thirteenth and fourteenth centuries and our readers will find that Chandi Das, being a poet of that age, was at first an exponent of the popular poetical sentiments, which, intense in their enjoyment of sensual life, were also vulgar to the extreme. It was the prevalent fashion in that age to be addicted to a woman other than one's own wife for *tantric* practices. And amongst the Buddhist of the latter-day Mahayana school and among their *bhikshus* and *bhikshunis*, the Sahaja Dharma became associated with illicit love. In the Buddha-Gan-O-Doha we have many passages in which this sexual love is used as symbolic of the Sahajia concept of bliss. Chandi Das says that at his time Sahajia love was a mania with young men, and that many noble-minded youths started their career of love with the avowed object of reaching a spiritual goal; this, however, often proved inaccessible to them, and in their attempts to scale the height, they fell down to the lowest pit of vices, rolling in the mire of sensuous pleasures. The poet says that it is a dangerous game for young men to play, as one in a million, and not two, may conquer flesh and find the true spiritual heaven in woman's love. The *tantrics* not only became steeped in sexual vices but were dreaded for inhuman cruelties committed in the name of religion. We have it in the Narottama Bilasha that a sect of vicious *tantrics* offered human sacrifices to Kali and danced with swords in hands before her image in horrid ecstasy and no passer-by was safe, if unfortunately he happened to walk by the side of the temple at the time. "Even Brahmins are then seized and sacrificed before the goddess."[1] In the Chaitanya Bhāgavat we have an elaborate description of the robbers who worshipped Kali on the eve of an expedition for plundering the house of an innocent citizen named Hiranya Pundit.

The Hindu Renaissance had just commenced among the lay people of this province, but they were still a prey to those vices which *tantricism* and vitiated Buddhism had brought on during the decline of spiritual forces that had originally inspired those noble creeds and their rituals. We find drunkards, who spurned all rules of Hinduism, ate beef and ham, though they were Brahmins.[1] We find widows of higher classes eating meat and fish and people spending enormous sums in making clay idols for worship.[2] They sang songs of Siva or Manasa Devi, and of Pal kings for whole nights. These songs, however, generally speaking, related to pastoral life with all its crude love-makings; and faith in gods they worshipped was but half-expressed in the imperfect popular dialect not yet fully developed for literary composition. "Religion" laments Brindaban Das, "was reduced to a

---
[1] Narattom Bilash, Canto VII.
[2] Chaitanya Bhagavata, Madhya, Chap. XIII and Jayananda's Chaitanya Mangal.

mere form and there was no faith in men."[1] Many people worshipped Jaksha, the lord of wealth, with offerings of wine and meat.

Pantheism, generally speaking, was the religion of the learned during this period. When Chaitanya's followers sang aloud the name of God many people of Nadia condemned it saying "Who is the god for whom all these frenzied uproar is meant? Man is his own saviour and his own god. Where could be any God outside this human frame?"[2] Chaitanya travelled through the whole of Southern India and met Dhundiram Tirtha of Tungabhadra, Mathura-nath of Tripadi, Bhargadev of Tripatra, Bharati Gossain of Chandipore, and many leaders of Sannyasis, who were staunch supporters of pantheism. Vasudeva Sarbabhouma, a great Sanskrit scholar of Bengal, was himself one such. He did not believe in a personal god and never took the *mahaprasad* of Puri temple before his conversion to Vaisnavism later on.

Pantheistic views amongst scholars.

Chaitanya-chandrodaya Natak gives us a faithful account of the sort of religious life that was around. It speaks of Sannayasis who remained with closed eyes as if lost in deep meditation, but when they heard the jingling sound of

False Sannyasis.

---

[1] Chaitanya Bhagabat, Adi.
[2] Chaitanya Bhagabat, Adi, Chap. II.

BENGAL IN NEED OF A SAVIOUR

bracelets, indicating the approach of women, they slowly opened their eyes and looked with lust; of pantheists who believed in no other gods than their own selves; of Kapalikas, both Buddhists and Sivaits, who were false Tantrics, of men who were given to visiting shrines for mere curiosity without any spiritual object; and of Sannyasis whose pride was as great as their haughtiness of temper.

Thus we see that the grandeur of moral virtues upon which Buddhism had been founded was wellnigh reduced to atoms. Nagarjuna's school, greatly depraved and confused with crude superstitious beliefs expounded the worship of tortoise and owl (*ulluka*) with curious speculative theories about the origin of the Universe. Their temples held rustic festivities and though a glimmer of faith was occasionally seen in them, the Mahayana had spent its best energies and could no longer elevate the people. The *tantrics* vainly strove with the help of human corpses, wine and women to attain a religious goal; and the pantheists in their self-sufficiency and pride of scholarship were far off from that humility and spiritual meekness which may alone lead to the growth of true faith. The Islam, moreover, with its great energy and appeal to personal God knocked, about this time, at the gate of Bengal declaring that One Great God was the supporter of the virtuous as He was the

<small>The impetus received from Islam.</small>

supporter of the world. Their vehement faith was irresistible and led the Hindu mind involuntarily to the old Aryan faith in a personal God as the many speculative and philosophical theories on religion current in the country could no longer satisfy their growing spiritual need. Our province specially was in need of a saviour, of one who would prove that the true well of spiritual bliss sprang from faith and not from intellectual subtleties, and that moral law and a sense of brotherhood were the concomitant forces of love which could alone bring the Incomprehensible One within human realisation.

Chandi Das.

At this juncture, when the cries of the Mahayana Buddhism for the cause of moral virtues were becoming less and less audible with the gradual disappearance of that faith from the Gangetic valley—when Tantricism was losing strength as a religious force and leading men to revel in debaucheries—when the temple and the court, poetry and art delighted in sensuousness,—there appeared on our religious and literary horizon a great poet who representing the glow and ardour of impassioned love—the significant feature of the past school—became the harbinger of a new age which soon after dawned on our moral and spiritual life and charged it with the white heat of its emotional bliss.

CHANDI DAS

We cannot give any accurate date as regards any incident of Chandi Das's life. There is of course an enigmatic verse which has been construed into implying that in the year 1403 A.D. Chandi Das had composed 996 songs. But the mysterious writing will not, I am afraid, stand the test of historical scrutiny and we cannot use it as evidence of any value.

There are some anonymous verses in which it is stated that Chandi Das and Vidyapati met on the banks of the Ganges, that during the interview one Rupanarayan—Raja of Mithila—or whoever he might have been, was present, and that the poets enjoyed each other's company and discussed their favourite topic of love from many different points of view. These anonymous songs are undated, and are to be found in the Padakalpataru compiled in the middle of the 18th century. Babu Nagendranath Gupta, the learned editor of Vidyapati's poems, does not attach any historical value to this tradition, though he does not support his views by any reason. But we cannot summarily reject a tradition to which some of our early writers have subscribed; the details of conversation between the two poets as given by these writers may be called in question, but the interview itself may be accepted as a historical incident.

Interview between Vidyapati and Chandi-Das.

But all the same, we do not possess any definite evidence as regards the time when Chandi Das lived. We may, however, make an approximate guess from certain facts. Narahari Sarkar, one of the most intimate friends of Chaitanya and born not later than 1465 A.D., sings an eulogistic song about the poet in which he says that Chandi Das's poems had literally flooded the country at his time, that Chandi Das was as remarkable a musician as he was a poet, and that he was a learned scholar whose songs were inspired by love for Rami—the washerwoman. It is well-known to all that Chaitanya chanted the songs of Chandi Das night and day. None of the historical works written about Chaitanya or his followers gives any firsthand information about the incidents of Chandi Das's life though many lyrical songs of the 15th century and of later periods are prolific in their praise of the poet. Ishan Nagar, who wrote a biography of Adwaita in 1560 A.D., refers to an interview which the latter had with Vidyapati probably in the year 1454. Had Chandi Das been alive about this time, there is no doubt that some of the Vaishnab apostles at least, all of whom were great admirers of Chandi Das, would have visited the great Bengali poet who lived at Nanoor in the Birbhum District. But we are not aware of any record relating to such an incident. So the natural surmise is that Chandi Das must have died at a period earlier than the middle of the 15th century. How far earlier, that is the question now and let us

Evidences regarding Chandi Das' time.

discuss it here. We find that one Deva Sarma, a Brahmin clerk, copied the Kavyaprakas in November 1398 by order of Vidyapati. In one of the songs of this poet we find mention of Gyasuddin who died in 1373 A.D. So Vidyapati no doubt had already made his mark as a poet before 1373. If we accept the statement of the anonymous writers about his interview with Chandi Das to be true, that event probably took place when the latter was already in the prime of his youth and Vidyapati had just begun to be known to fame. I cannot altogether reject, as I have already stated, a tradition which has long prevailed in the country, unless it is upset by proper historical evidence.

At this stage of our investigation Mr. Basantaranjan Ray brought the Krishnakirtan to the notice of scholars. Expert calligraphic opinion asserts that the handwriting of the copy could not be of a date later than the end of the 14th century. This work of Chandi Das must have attained a certain celebrity before others could think of copying it out. Hence we believe that Krishnakirtan could not have been written later than the middle of the 14th century. The Krishnakirtan of Chandi Das belongs to that class of love-songs which is called Krishna Dhamali and which is current even now in the backwoods of North Bengal. The poem describes the amours of Radha-Krishna in many different phases. The rustic element, however, predominates in these juvenile writings of Chandi Das. Krishna here is a simple village lad who runs after the pastoral queen of his heart—the pursuit is conducted with an intense ardour, amidst the gay natural scenery on the banks of the black-watered Jamuna, amidst market places and groves resounding with the songs of birds ; no condition however low, no situation however hard, daunting the love-stricken rustic lad who wears the mask of a god. This passionate ardour of the flesh need not be condemned in the poetry of mediæval school as it supplied inspiration to many of the greatest poets of that age. Towards the end of Krishnakirtan the poet strikes a higher note which becomes loudly audible in his later songs. So this work marks the transition of Vaishnab poetry from the sensuous to the idealistic. The earlier songs throb with somewhat gross human instincts, the later songs burst into melodies of finer idealism, the characteristic of the later Vaishnab school. If we read the account given by the poet himself as to how he fell in love with Rami, the problem how this transition came over the spirit of his songs will be solved. But we shall come to it later on.

The Krishna-dhamali to which we have already referred was once the craze of whole Bengal, but which now survives being driven into the borders of Northern Bengal, where the old things of Hindu life have not yet altogether

Krishnakirtan.

DEATH OF CHANDI DAS

perished. Chandi Das greatly embellished that rustic mode of treating Krishna-topics by freely indenting treasures of lyrical wealth from Jaydev. Scholars have come forward to brand Krishnakirtan as a piece of daring literary forgery. But I have met their arguments in my previous course of lectures. In my mind there is absolutely no shadow of doubt as to the genuineness of this work. Now accepting the expert opinion about the date of the copy of Krishnakirtan I find that the book could not have been written by the poet later than 1350. I shall show that Chandi Das died a most tragic and shocking death that has ever befallen the lot of a poet, between 1383 and 1385 A.D.

The latest discovery about Chandi Das is this sad and tragic tale of his death. Some years ago, I referred in a note supplied to the editor of Krishnakirtan to a tradition extant in the neighbourhood of Nanoor, the native village of Chandi Das, that the Begum of a Nawab had fallen in love with the poet, and that the result of this ill-fated passion was the punishment of a cruel death inflicted on him. The Sahityaparisat library of old Bengali Mss. has lately come in possession of a few pages, the handwriting of which is referred to a date about 250 years back, substantially confirming the tradition mentioned by me several years ago. Alas! the tale is a harrowing one. It was the Emperor of Gour and not a Nawab of the locality, as I said in my note, who punished Chandi Das with death. He had invited the poet to his court having heard of his great fame as a musician and poet. Rami, the washerwoman, is herself the writer of this historical account. She laments the day when Chandi Das visited the court of the Moslem Emperor. His queen heard Chandi Das sing some of his masterpieces. They were so sweet that the very trees and the sky seemed to be rapt in silent admiration. The queen was beside herself with joy and felt a passion for the poet. How this passion developed and the matter attracted the notice of the autocrat is not known. Rami skips over details; but she says that the queen when asked, made a bold front and confessed all to her royal husband. The Emperor ordered that Chandi Das should be tied to the back of an elephant and led from place to place and scourged in such a manner that his flesh, sinews and nerves must be torn till he bled to death. The queen interceded and said, "You do not know the sterling merit of the man. In the whole world there does not breathe another soul as warm as his." For mercy she pleaded, but in vain. The infuriated monarch was the more enraged. Rami writes that she saw him glance at her from the back of the elephant with tender love, as the last moment drew near. His clothes lay all

<small>The tragic death of Chandi Das.</small>

UNDER ELEPHANT'S FEET

drenched in blood and looking at her steadily all the time as the elephant moved on, the great poet of Bengal closed his eyes without uttering a moan.

The elephant was often made an instrument in those days for punishing offenders of high rank. Ferdausi was ordered to be placed under the feet of an elephant and trampled down to death, but the poet succeeded in effecting an interview with Sultan Muhammad and averting the punishment. We find Jehangir contriving to set an elephant against Sher Afgan, the husband of Meherunnisa, though that Chief could hold his own by his superior tact and unmatched physical strength. The animal after a ferocious attack took to heels and fled, terror-struck by the blow inflicted on it by the Chief. The Muhammadan history of Western Asia is replete with instances of punishment of death inflicted on men of rank by placing them under the feet of elephants.

Thus died Chandi Das by the capricious orders of the Gour Emperor. He could not have been possibly more than forty years of age at the time of his death. For in the East a woman seldom falls in love with a man above that age. The sad tale of this tragic affair has not been all told. The Begum's end was as tragic, if not more glorious. Repentance was natural to her in the matter, for she felt that if she had not made the confession, the king's anger would not have possibly reached such a climactic point.

There is nothing in the account to show that the queen had been guilty of anything dishonourable. It was her great admiration for the poet which led to a romantic feeling of love, and there is a hint in the account that the poet reciprocated her sentiments. Overwhelmed with repentance for her confession which she had made relying on a generous spirit of appreciation and indulgent pardon from her husband, but which led to the unfortunate catastrophe, she was shocked at the Emperor's attitude, and when the cruel scene was enacted before her eyes, she fainted away unable to bear the sight. She never recovered from that swoon, for the beating of her heart had stopped as she saw the horrible torture and death of her lover.

Rami says that as the queen lay dead she hurried to clasp her feet with tearful eyes. Here ends her verses.

Who this Emperor of Gour was, cannot be definitely ascertained, but if we take into account the fact that Chandi Das wrote his juvenile work—the Krishnakirtan—about 1350 and that he could not have been, as already mentioned, more than 40 years old at the time of his death, we are led to suppose that it was the Emperor Shamsuddin II who probably passed this horrible sentence upon one of the most glorious of Bengal's sons. From 1342 to 1385 five monarchs ruled Bengal. Shamsuddin Bhengara from 1342 to 1358, who was " much respected and beloved by his people"; Sultan Gayasuddin (1359 to 1373) was a patron of poetry who had sent an invitation to Hafiz to come to Bengal and settle as his court-poet and about whom Vidyapati wrote an eulogistic verse. The next Emperor Assulatwin ruled for ten years peacefully and was a very popular monarch. About the next Emperor Shamsuddin II, Stewart says, " on the death of Sultan Assulatwin, the nobles raised to the throne his adopted son, a youth of very inferior talent, who took the title of Shamsuddin II. For little more than two years he enjoyed a tranquil reign, but at the expiration of that period, Kanis, the Zemindar of Vetoria, rebelled against him, and the youth being unsupported by the Muhammadan Chiefs was defeated and lost his life in the year 1385 A.D." He was so unpopular that even the Muhammadan Chiefs did not support him though a Hindu Zemindar killed him and secured the throne for himself. May we not imagine that the cruel punishment of death on the greatest poet of Bengal was probably one of the reasons which had made his rule very unpopular in the country ?

We can expect no historical clue to this matter from the records of the Vaishnabs themselves. They skip over anything that is melancholy or tragic. Their conspiracy of silence in regard to Chaitanya's passing away is well known. Nor had they, while writing elaborate memoirs, described when and how Sachi Devi or

Bishnupriya died. So we should not be surprised at the fact that none of the Vaishnab historians has written anything about the tragic end of Chandi Das. In Jayananda's Chaitanya Mangal we come across a hurried line stating that Gadadhar Pandit had burned himself alive to escape from Muhammadan oppression, but the details are not given. It is curious to note that many points in the career of Gadadhar Pandit, one of Chaitanya's best friends, are to be found in all authoritative books of Vaishnabs, save this most important point of his horrible death. It is true that the Vaishnabs do not at all regard Jayananda's Chaitanya Mangal to be a book of any worth, because he cared not to follow their canons; he has not only referred to the tragic death of Gadadhara but given us historical information about how Chaitanya passed away, as no other writer has done; and we instinctively feel that his accounts are quite reliable, however much he might have disregarded the delicate feeling of the Vaishnab community in the matter.

We have already referred to the fact that love for Rami brought on a change over the spirit of Chandi Das's poetry. It was certainly an epoch-making event in his life. He was a worshipper of Basuli and was piously afraid of any romantic feeling for a woman. But the heart runs out of control. The poet's strength fails him. Look how he falls prostrate before Basuli and laments himself! The holiness of his vow has gone for naught! Night and day he prays, but the glimpses of the glorious form of Rami half-revealed through her blue *sari* in the temple-courtyard, maddens him inspite of his vow of self-dedication to Basuli. His heart is exactly in the same state as a flower fallen in the tide that flows irresistibly like fate. "Alas! mother," he laments before Basuli, "You could not preserve your child from these unworthy feelings for a woman of low caste! My austerities and efforts, my secret vows could not save me!"[1] But not long after, Basuli's voice he heard, as if in a dream—it said, "Love this woman, my son, it is your fate that you should do so—nay, this love will sanctify you; neither I nor hundreds of gods and goddesses like me will be able to give you a glimpse of that higher life which this woman's love will teach you."[1]

<small>Remorse.</small>

Chandi Das arose—wonder-struck. In his heart of hearts he had worshipped Rami. Only a conventional sense of immorality, a consciousness of his difficult social environment had filled his mind with remorse and fear. Now Basuli's mandate was clear. Conventions and fears were set at naught. Each time he saw her, he found her

<small>He worships Rami.</small>

---

[1] Chandi Das's edition, published by the Sahitya Parishat of Calcutta, Supplement, p. 4.

beautiful and lovely as a flower, holy as a goddess, a thing to be placed on the head like a gift dropped from the hands of Basuli herself.

He says, "Though I am a Brahmin and you are a washer-woman, you are to me holy as Gayatri."[1] He rises above caste-prejudices, and sees good in love far more than in his Brahminic blood or in the scriptures. He declares Rami to be as adorable as Parvati, the giver of fortunes, as Lakshmi, the giver of luck and as Saraswati, the goddess of fine arts and learning. Thus he raises his love to the status of legendary goddesses, and this no Brahmin had, I suppose, done before him.

So the traditional Brahminic superiority, sacredness of scriptures and the unapproachable dignity and sanctity of gods all fell to the ground. Chandi Das saw one temple in the whole universe, that was the cottage of the washer-woman near Basuli's courtyard, and he became the high priest there. His love was not limited by any conventional idea. He calls Rami his *pitri matri*—"father and mother." No lover ever spoke such a language. Love to him was a homogeneous and undivided whole. Among

<small>Love defined not in a limited sense.</small>

rivers one is called the Ganges, another Godavari and another Jamuna, but when they come down and fall into the ocean, they loose their

---

[1] Chandi Das's edition, published by the Sahitya Parishat of Calcutta, Supplement, p. 333.

individual names and are called by one common name. So our paternal affection, brotherly feelings and nuptial love, even friendship, in the highest degree of intensity, become one and are designated by the same name. No poet outside India has signified the stages of this one homogeneous idea and classified it so beautifully. The *dasya, sakhya, batsalya* and *madhuryya* of the Vaishnabs indicate degree and not quality. The old poet Valmiki was the first to put this truth in the mouth of Dasaratha in his appreciation of Kausalya in the following lines :—

"यदा यदा च कौशल्या दासीवच्च सखीवच ।
भार्य्यावद्भगिनीवच्च मातृवच्चोपतिष्ठते ॥"

रामायणम्, अयोध्याकाण्डम् ।

But no other poet than Chandi Das has said this so forcibly in respect of his lady-love. "Thou art to me my parents." This indicates absolute dependence and resignation. But look from the worldly point of view ! An orthodox Brahmin speaking in that irreverent and sacrilegious way not only trampled upon all conventions of Hinduism about caste and religion, but also gave a rude shock to the fundamental sense of social morality. For no lover in the Hindu community or in any other community would call his lady-love his parent, that would be blasphemous. Was it not meet that for such profane speech he was outcasted and proclaimed fallen from the Brahminic order by the beat of drum? But though his own men treated him so, he did not lose his faith in man and he saw no god as high as man. He says, "Hear me, brother man, Man is the highest, none higher than he." He certainly saw divinity in the human form before him more than elsewhere. He would believe in no ill from one whom he loved. Radha in one of his songs says to Krishna, "I am not accustomed, dear, to see your happiness and mine apart from one another, what delights you delights me also." So the lover may show all sorts of cruelty, but cannot hurt the soul wearing the armour of this love, and Chandi Das says again, "One who loves and breaks, does not attain the spiritual goal."[1] A lover is bound to retain his love for the person whom he has once loved. However much he may suffer, spiritually he will gain by his devotion. Divorce therefore is not recognised in the law-book of Chandi Das. Did Christ forsake his people because some of them had crucified him? It is the flower's love, tear off its petals, crush it cruelly, it will have a smile for you still. At this stage only a step further and one attains love divine. Says Chandi Das, "One who is unseen and beyond all comprehension, will be perceived by him alone who has loved."[2]

---

[1] Chandi Das's edition, published by the Sahitya Parishat of Calcutta supplement p. 337.

[2] *Ibid*, p. 340.

And we know that before Chaitanya was born, Chandi Das had felt this love, and been lifted to the plain from which he had already visions of his God. Love human had taught him love divine. Otherwise where in the ordinary romantic poems of love, do we so frequently come across lines which charged with spiritual meaning bring us to the threshold of the mystic world?

<small>Love human leading to love divine.</small>

Radha fasts " বিরতি আহারে, রাঙ্গা বাস পরে " when love for Krishna has dawned on her heart; she wears the ochre-coloured cloth of a *yogini* and recites the name of Krishna, till like a Vaishnab apostle she is beside herself with joy. The advent of Chaitanya is presaged in the account Chandi Das gives of Radha as prostrating herself at the feet of every one who speaks of Krishna. And did not Chaitanya do the very same thing? He too like Chandi Das's Radha fainted at the sight of the dark-blue clouds which brought to his memory the lovely colour of Krishna.

Chandi Das not only frees himself from the grip of religious and social conventions, but from the bonds of Poetics and in fact from all sorts of rules laid down by scholars. He was himself a great scholar. Even if we had not his brother Nakul's testimony on that point, supported half a century later by a statement of Narahari, the numerous slokas in Sanskrit that adorn his Krishnakirtan and his closely literal and yet felicitous translation of some of the lays of Jaydeb evidence his erudition and learning. But he rejects all Sanskritic high-sounding words in his later compositions, though in Krishnakirtan they are plentiful. He rejects the rules of Sanskrit Poetics that eternally lay down the bee to be a lover of the flower. The flower, he says, does not go to the bee when the latter does not come. The moon cannot be a lover of the lily, as we find in the Poetics, for when the latter dies in frost, the moon smiles from heaven. Thus freeing himself entirely from all religious, social, and literary thraldom, Chandi Das brings in a new era in Vaishnab poetry and in Vaishnab religion, which in the next period trampled down all conventions and orthodoxy.

He frees himself from all conventions.

The sensuous element becomes gradually idealised in Chandi Das's later writings. His Krishnakirtan shows him at first as one with the poets of an earlier epoch, a faithful disciple of Joydev, scholarly and gorgeous in his description of the objects of senses. At this stage he is not without spiritual meaning in occasional verses, and is an exponent of the popular sentiment, the echo of which is still found in the Krishna Dhamalis. His language is aglow with impassioned rural poetry that draws no line of demarcation between decency and indecency. But suddenly by the grace of Basuli and love for Rami we find him at a later stage throwing off the mantle of sensuousness as the tree puts off its bark, and displaying the blossom of spiritual love and felicitous emotions which reached their flowering point in the trances of the great apostles of Vaishnavism.

The influence of the Bhagavata and other Sacred Works.

A century before Chaitanya was born, the Bhagavata and the Gita had begun to be widely read in this province, as also in other parts of India. We find Govinda Das, Chaitanya's companion, during his tour in Southern India in 1510-11 A.D. recording that at Poona there was a regular craze for the study of the Gita and the Bhagavata.[1] When Chaitanya was there, an illiterate Brahmin was found studying the Gita with a zeal which was laughed at by the scholars. For that diligent student of the sacred book neither understood nor correctly recited the slokas with which he kept himself engaged day and night.[2] The lays of Jaydev and

The study of the Gita and the Bhagavat.

---

[1] এই স্থানে বহুলোক নিপুন বিজ্ঞায়।
শত শত চতুষ্পাঠী মধ্যে শোভা পায়॥
ভাগবত যেই জন করে অধ্যয়ন।
তাহারে পণ্ডিত বলি মানে সর্ব্বজন॥
গীতা আর ভাগবত যেই নাহি জানে।
তাহাকে পণ্ডিত বলি কেহ নাহি মানে॥ p. 134.

[2] Govinda Das's Karcha, p. 100.

Chandi Das, based on the Bhagavata, were sung throughout this province, and we know it on the authority of Narahari that these songs, at his time, filled the whole world[1];—this world was no doubt Bengal and Orissa. The Chaitanya-bhagavata (1573 A.D.) says that the Gita and the Bhagavata were widely read in the country before Chaitanya, though the author regrets that right interpretation of the sacred books was missed by the scholarly pandits in their enthusiasm to display erudition. Our Dharmamangal poems, which give us glimpses of the Hindu courts before the advent of Islam record that the Bhagavata was studied there regularly, and that the kings at their leisure-hours listened to discourses on that scripture from their court-pandits. The 10th Skanda of the Bhagavata, however, formed the subject of special study of the Bengalis. The 11th Skanda treats matters in a philosophical spirit. Bengal being a pastoral country, its inhabitants delighted in pastoral poetry and pastoral religion more than in anything else, and the 10th Skanda embodies these in a way which has perhaps no parallel in world's literature.

<small>The tenth skanda of the Bhagabat.</small>

The sports of Krishna as a boy are described in the tenth Skanda in such a fascinating manner that it has a special appeal for an emotional race

---

[1] Chandi Das published by Sahitya Parisat, Supplement "ক."

THE SPORTS

like the Bengalis. These sports on the sunny banks of the dark-watered Jamuna are richly detailed in the canto. The boys sometimes run pursuing the shadows of birds that fly in the sky. They mimic the apes by showing their series of small teeth,—they catch the monkeys by their tails and often jump from bough to bough pursuing them. They cover their bodies with striped blankets and crawl on hands and knees and become bulls and cows themselves amongst their own bulls and cows. Sometimes one of them shuts his eyes and becomes blind and tries to find out his way in that condition. One dances in imitation of peacocks, and another jumps over a small stream imitating the frog. One takes fancy for becoming a crane and covering himself with a white cloth sits amongst cranes ; while another shrinks and trembles in fear as if he has seen a tiger, where there is nothing of the kind. One hums with the bees, whilst his comrade imitates the sounds of a cuckoo or walks with the geese moving to and fro as those birds do.[1] Krishna and Balaram, when five or six years old, do all these merry-makings with other gay boys of the Vrinda groves. The brothers sometimes pull a small cow by the tail and, when the latter runs forward, it carries the struggling boys behind its heels to the amuse-

The sports of the boys.

---

[1] See Bhagavata, Skanda X, Chap. XII, Verses 6-12 Chap. XVIII, Verses 9-16.

ment of the elderly people who witness these sports.

That Krishna is God incarnate is of course in evidence everywhere. While playing a hundred games in this way, he now and then unfolds his divinity to his bewildered comrades by suddenly killing great giants like Bakasura, Trinabarta and Aghasura, and crushing under his feet the mighty crest of the snake Kaliya. There is a genial breath of affection and emotional tenderness in the whole environment and specially in the house, for fond Jasoda dotes on young Krishna and promising evermore in her mind not to beat him for the mischief he does almost every hour, she sometimes loses her temper very justly. For what mother could bear to see that during her short absence, the child had broken her milk-pitcher, her vessels full of curd and butter, and after having eaten a small part of the contents himself, the marks of which were on his mouth and teeth, was detected in distributing the remainder amongst a host of monkeys that had gathered round him,—he looking like the very prince of them! Jasoda was a milk-maid and these pitchers and vessels were articles of her trade. Now she pursues the mischief-making imp, who with many sprightly leaps evades his mother and at last, caught by her, submits to the punishment of being bound with ropes; but these fall short by a few inches, each time she adds to them by bringing in fresh ropes, so that she cannot tie them in a knot. The surprised mother looks with wonder and fear. Is it a child or what? At this stage she sees in the child a manifestation of divinity and is filled with confusion. When the mother is thus confused and frightened, the child-god withdraws the manifestation of his divinity, and once more appears as a little thing extremely playful and lovable, whom the mother kisses and calls her own. Sometimes the rainy season, the dark night and the lonely forest-paths are made a background from which his plays and love-makings are shown with a singular effect. The whole pastoral country responds as it were to the call of his flute from this background, the irresistible music of which makes the women of the Gokul come out of their homes and surrender themselves unto His love.

The pastoral plays and a thousand attractive incidents of pastoral life have a special charm for the Bengalis, and if one examines a library of old Bengali manuscripts, one will certainly be surprised to see what a large number of these contain the Bengali versions of the 10th Skanda of the Bhagavata. The whole country became literally flooded over by these versions, and, as I have already stated, this liking for the Bhagavata-lore had commenced long before Chaitanya came to the world. In the Krishna-kirtan of Chandi Das there are many passages which read like free versions of the 10th Skanda of the Bhagavata. This Skanda was translated later on by Maladhar Basu in 1480 A.D. or 6 years before the birth of Chaitanya.

The biographies of Chaitanya show that in his childhood he played with his comrades all the plays that Krishna had played according to the Bhagavata. These sports of Krishna had indeed become the craze with the children of Bengal at that time; some one of Chaitanya's comrades became Baka or Aghasur and fought with another who played the part of Krishna. In these Chaitanya was generally the leader. In the Chaitanya Bhagavata we find Nityananda as a child playing Krishna-plays with his playfellows at Ekchaka. The breaking of the cart and the killing of Kansa were of course the familiar subjects; he sometimes wore false whiskers and beard and played the part of Narada. The juvenile poems of Chandi Das illustrate how platforms were raised, where players robed themselves in pastoral dresses and played the parts of Krishna and his little companions. Sometimes they played all the parts of the various incarnations of Vishnu,[1] and Chaitanya himself in his childhood followed the foot-prints of birds, or covered himself with a striped cloth to appear as a bull after Krishna.[2]

Ramananda born in 1299 A.D. (according to Sir R. G. Bhandarkar) and fifth in apostolic

---

[1] Chandi Das, published by the Sahitya Parisat, pp. 14-20.
[2] Chaitanya Bhagavata, Atul Goswami's edition, Adi, p. 40.

succession from Ramanuja worshipped both Krishna and Rama and made no distinction between them as they were both held to be incarnations of Vishnu. In Bengal too we find Murari Gupta and others following the footprints of that great Vaishnab apostle of Southern India and showing devotion to Rama and Krishna alike. Murari composed many beautiful hymns in Sanskrit in praise of Rama, and Chaitanya was so delighted to hear these that he gave Murari the title of Ramadas.[1] The episodes of Rama's life were acted by Bengali children along with those of Krishna; and Nityananda had played them all long before he first met Chaitanya in 1508.[2] The emotion which inspired the players was great, and rose to a frenzy of excitement which sometimes produced tragic results. It is said in the Chaitanya Bhagavata that a Brahmin playing the part of Dasarath was so greatly overpowered by grief at Rama's exile that he died in course of the play on the platform.[3]

Player dying in course of play.

(iv) *Vaishnavism in Bengal before Chaitanya.*

Vaishnavism was already firmly planted in Bengal by the endeavours of Sen kings who had come from Southern India. For we find

---

[1] Chaitanya Charitamrita, Bangabasi edition, p. 169.
[2] Chaitanya Bhagavata, Atul Goswami's edition, p. 65.
[3] Ibid, p. 66.

stone-images of the god, popularly called Vashudev, from every part of this country, traced from the time of these sovereigns. Some of the Pal kings of the later times also became devoted worshippers of this deity. With a slight change in the form of this god he takes a different name. He has four arms, holding the shell, the disc, the mace and the lotus. If by the first arm he holds the mace he is called Vashudev; but if by that arm he holds the disc he is called Pradyumna. In this way he takes the different names of Sankarsana, Aniruddha, Keshava, Narayana, Madhava, Govinda, Vishnu, Madhusudana, Tribikrama, Vamana, Sridhara, Hrishikesha, Padmanava, Damodara, Purushottama, Achyuta, Krishna, Hari, Adhaksaja, Upendra, and Janardana, simply by changing the sacred emblems of divinity from one hand to another. The iconography of this god popularly known as Vashudev is minutely given in the Chaitanya Charitamrita. For the sake of convenience, however, we will follow the popular name Vashudev in designating this god. As all these different names imply the same deity, it is of no use to enter into intricacies of names which concern those worshippers only who have to perform different rituals in regard to the different names. This deity Vashudev, however, was originally no god of Bengal, for there is no

The different names of Vashudev.

Vashudev is not a Bengali deity.

tradition of the god to be found in the works of our earlier potters and sculptors who made images of our gods. In the old sculpture of Bengal we find Krishna with his flute, but nowhere is this deity in evidence to prove that Vashudev had been worshipped here before the Sen kings became dictators of the religion under the Brahmanic renaissance.

But nevertheless the figure of this deity caught the imagination of the Bengalis in later times, for in almost every village of importance throughout this province we find images of Vashudev recovered from tanks and underground. He was certainly imported into Bengal by the Sen kings from Southern India. We find these Vashudevs disfigured by the hands of iconoclasts lying in largest numbers in Eastern Bengal, specially Bikrampore, the reputed seat of the Sen kings.

These images were generally made of black stone. They often show a remarkable tenderness and grace in execution inspite of being wrought out in hard stone. The lips, the nose and the cheeks are so soft that they seem to be made of clay or wax rather than hard black stone. The dark blue tint of this stone lends a lovely interest to the images, so that when they were mutilated, destroyed and removed from the temples, the helpless worshippers associated the colour with divinity. They began to be fascinated by the sight of the dark ranges of clouds, of the dark Jamuna and of everything that had a dark bluish colour. In the songs and poems of the Bengali Vaishnabs we often meet with panegyrics of the dark colour which is Krishna's, but though Krishna's dusty colour is well-known, nowhere outside our province is so much stress laid upon the beauty of the dark colour in popular songs. The people had shed their blood in their attempts to save the temples from the hands of the ruthless destroyers, and when they failed they could not look upon anything dark without being reminded of their god. Hence long before Chaitanya this colour had become the craze with the Vaishnabs. Chandi Das makes his Radha throw away the floral wreath that adorned her dark braids, so that she might revel in an undisturbed sight of the dark colour of her luxuriant hair. She gazed with wild emotion of joy at the dark-blue neck of the peacock, and when she saw the dark clouds in the stormy sky, she fell into a trance, and her eyes moved not from the sight which brought on a mystic vision.[1]

The dark-blue colour.

The first great Vaishnab apostle of Bengal, Madhavendra Puri, had shown this strange liking for the dark colour in the 14th century. Chaitanya Bhagavata describes him as fainting away at the sight of clouds. Smitten with

---

[1] Chandi Das, Sahitya Parisat edition, p. 30.

THE MADDHI SECT

a love for this colour Chaitanya himself at a later age embraced the *tamal* tree with its dark blue foliage mistaking it for the god of his vision and passed into a trance.[1] The dark waters of a river brought the vision so often that the reader will be at no pains to find instances of the wonderful fascination exercised by the colour on his mind.

Chaitanya belonged to the Maddhi sect of Vaishnabs. The originator of this sect was Madhyacharya born in 1191 A.D. The special feature of worship of this sect was the recognition of other gods also than Vishnu in the temples, where Shiva, Parvati and Ganes are worshipped along with that deity. One of the nine rituals practised there by the worshippers is song and dance. And in the temple of Uditi founded by Madhyacharya, music forms one of the important features of service. It will be seen that though Chaitanya belonged to the order of Madhyacharya, he deviated from it in some of the main aspects of their creed. Madhyacharya preached an uncompromising dualism; but Chaitanya's doctrine was *dwaitadwaitavada i.e.*, dualism and undualism both. According to this creed dualism at a certain stage reaches non-dualism. Chaitanya and his sect did not lay stress upon the omnipotence—the *aiswarya*—of

---

[1] Govinda Das's Karcha, p. 120.

God-head, but on His captivating power by which He draws the soul of man to Him. Madhyacharya emphasized *aiswarya* or manifestation of divine power. It will be remembered that Chaitanya insisted on Rupa's drawing a clear line of demarcation between the *braja lila* of Krishna and his *mathur lila*. In the former he is a cowherd playing pastoral games with his companions. But in the latter he plays the part of a king. The Vrinda groves with their tales of pastoral affection and romance had a special charm for the sect founded by Chaitanya, in preference to the manifestations of his power as Almighty God, recorded in the legends of Mathura where he wielded the royal sceptre.

But though Chaitanya belonged to the sect of Madhyacharya, he seldom mentions the great apostle.

Madhavendra Puri.

In fact I find no reference to Madhyacharya in any Vaishnab work written in Bengali prior to Bhaktiratnakar, compiled at a much later period, in the 18th century. All praise is bestowed on Madhavendra Puri, the reputed founder of the Bhakti cult in Bengal, latterly developed by Chaitanya. Chaitanya Bhagavata holds him as the Guru of the Bhakti-cult in Bengal[1] and Narottam Das one of the Vaishnab leaders in the 17th century sings a hymn in praise of

---

[1] Chaitanya Bhagavata, Atul Goswami's edition, pp. 68-69.

Madhabendra, Puri calling him the pioneer of faith amongst the Vaishnabs of Bengal.

Indeed this man, some of the episodes and legends about whose life have been described in my previous lectures, was a great saint who sowed the seed of that emotional religion of which the harvest was reaped in Bengal in the 16th century. He was a Bengali and this I have proved elsewhere. He was an idealist in love and had no care for the material life. Chaitanya Bhagavata describes how he often passed into trances at the sight of the dark clouds.[1] Chaitanya Charitamrita states that he would not seek any help from anyone. In this respect he was like the tree described by Chaitanya Charitamrita; for even though it may dry up it will never seek a drop of water from any one. Madhav was thoroughly resigned to the will of God; he never cared for the morrow, nor even for to-day. If any one gave him anything to eat, unsought for, he ate, if none gave, he fasted; for he would never beg anything from any one. Perhaps this ideal was before Chaitanya when he said to Barmukhi the harlot "Do not touch me, I am untouchable—as I beg alms from house-holders." The two beautiful legends about Madhavendra, described by me in my previous lectures, prove the devotional spirit of the saint.[2] In the Vrinda-groves Krishna himself is said

---

[1] Chaitanya Bhagvata, Atul Goswami's edition, p. 69.
[2] Mediæval Vaishnava Literature.

to have appeared before the saint and fed him, as he was fasting, forgetful of all physical pain—merged in his trances and love for the god. At Remuna Krishna is said to have stolen thickened milk for his devoted follower. In the religious literature of the mediæval world, such legends are common. Whatever may be their value, there can be no question as to Madhav's having been a highly religious soul, worthy of popular veneration; for in India such legends are only told of those men whose saintliness of character and spirituality are much above the level of average men. Madhav always tried to avoid worldly fame. When crowds in great numbers, filled with admiration came to offer him their tribute of respects at Remuna, he fled from the place, but, says the Charitamrita, "Fame follows the man of worth who does not seek it, and when Madhav came from Remuna to Puri, he found himself already a renowned man there, sought for by the king and all the nobility of Orissa." Madhavendra Puri was a good poet himself, and wrote many Sanskrit verses some of which are to be found in the Padavali compiled by Rupa Goswami.

Madhavendra's disciples were already many in Bengal, noted amongst whom were Keshav Bharati, Ishwar Puri and Adwaita who instructed Chaitanya in the ways of Bhakti. Another of his disciples was Pundarik Vidyanidhi of Chittagong who was held in great reverence by Chaitanya.

MADHAVENDRA

Nityananda, in the course of his religious tour all over India, visiting her various shrines, met Madhavendra Puri at Sri Parvat, somewhere near Bankot in the Madras Presidency. He clasped the feet of the saint and exclaimed "Here is the reward I have at last got for visiting all the shrines. I see, Sir, to day your inspired love which sanctifies my soul." We also find Madhavendra paying a visit to Adwaita at Santipur. Madhavendra had died before Chaitanya was born or when the latter was a mere child. So he could not see the great Vaishnab apostle; but he was so fervently impressed with all that Madhavendra had done in inculcating the Bhakti-cult, that evidences of his extraordinary regard are to be met with in many Vaishnab works. Chaitanya Charitamrita refers to the incident in Master's life where he recites the stanza, beginning with অয়ি দীন দয়ার্দ্র নাথ written by Madhavendra, and declares in enthusiasm that as the Kaustuva is the finest of all diamonds, so is the stanza the most beautiful of all world's poems. He becomes lost in ecstatic joy as he recites the *sloka* till tears choke his voice, and he can no longer recite the full *sloka* but merely says "অয়ি দীন অয়ি দীন" and then passes on into a trance.

The Bhakti cult had thus already secured a firm footing in Bengal and secured considerable number of adherents before Chaitanya came to the field. Madhavendra was the first to inaugurate a a new era in the propagation of this particular form of religion in which emotion was given a higher place than rituals of worship. This band of religionists immediately before the advent of Chaitanya was headed by Adwaitacharya, who born in 1356 A. D. at Laur in Sylhet had migrated to Santipur and settled there in his youth. His doctrine originally was the same as of other savants of the age in India, *viz.*, nondualism. I have already stated that pantheism or more properly *adwaitavada* was favoured by all Indian scholars of the age, but Adwaita gradually felt the need of a personal God,—

Adwaita.

with his grace and love. He found that nondualism had made people little better than sceptics; it had increased pride in them and made them fond of logical arguments and a display of scholarship, while the fountain of spirituality and love had gradually dried up. At this stage, he began to preach the Bhakti-cult and some of his disciples, one of whom was a Mahratta Brahmin, were so disgusted with his emotional propaganda, that they refused to accept his doctrines and deserted him. Though led away to pantheism when he became a scholar in his youth, he had in his childhood shown a liking for Vaishnavism and emphatically refused to believe in caste and rituals of worships. As a child he is said to have declared to his mother :—

"মাতঃ শ্রীকৃষ্ণপূজায়াং পাত্রভেদো ন বিদ্যতে, দীক্ষাদি-নিয়মোঽপি ন বিদ্যতে।"[1] (Mother, in the worship of

---

[1] Valya-lila-sutra by Krishna Das, Canto IV.

ADWAITA AND HARI DAS

Krishna all rituals such as initiation and taking the sacred thread are quite unnecessary, every one is free to worship and caste is no barrier.)

At Laur, when a mere boy he could by no means be led to bow before Kali and suffered much persecution for his refractory conduct.

Adwaita's father Kuver Pundit was the minister of the Raja of Laur. The latter became a disciple of Adwaita in after years and took the name of Krishna Das and wrote Adwaita's biography in 1409 Saka (1487 A.D.) when Chaitanya was a baby, a little more than one year old. Adwaita was the title; the real name of the saint and scholar was Kamalakshya. He was 52 years old when Chaitanya was born. It is stated in the Vaishnab works that Chaitanya came into the world owing to the constant prayers and appeal from Adwaita to the Most High to send one who would redeem the world from the sceptical tendencies of the age.

A band of enthusiastic *bhaktas* gathered round Adwaita at whose house frequent meetings were held for devising means to inculcate the *bhakti* cult. Of these men Hari Das was one of the most noted. He was born at Buran in Jessore and was a Mahomedan; though later writers have tried to prove that he had been originally of Brahmin extraction, and was merely brought up by a Mahomedan, older authorities, however, are unanimous in saying that he

Hari Das.

was a Mahomedan by birth. The later writers have tried to prove his Brahmanic blood for the simple reason, that with the growing idea of orthodoxy amongst the Vaishnabs, it was thought degrading that he who had originally been a Mahomedan should be recognised as a leader of the Vaishnabs, claiming Brahmin disciples. The devotion of Hari Das to Vaishnab faith was, as you all know, heroic and worthy of a martyr. He was asked by the Kazi to renounce the faith of the Kafirs:—"It is a great fortune that you have been born as a Mahomedan; how degrading that you should accept the religion of the Kafirs,"[1] he said. But the convert replied, "Though you cut me piece-meal I shall not cease to recite the name of Hari."[2] He was led through 23 market-places at each of which he was mercilessly whipped by the Kazi's order. The by-standers observed this punishment with great indignation. Some said, "This country will be destroyed by God's wrath; some cursed the emperor and his ministers; others actually took recourse to force to save Hari Das and some fell at the feet of the officers and said, 'Give him a few mild strokes only, as it is your duty to punish him, and we will pay you money.'" Hari Das took shelter in the name of God, and such were his faith and joy in the recitation of the

---

[1] Chaitanya Bhagavat, Atul Goswami's edition, p. 118.
[2] *Ibid*, pp. 118-121.

holy name that he was unconscious of his physical pain." A fuller account of his life will be found in my "Chaitanya and his companions." Hari-Das was for a time a guest of Adwaita at Santipur.

The third noteworthy name as exponent of the *bhakti* cult was Srivas of Nadia, who living a life of pleasure in his early years, suddenly heard God's mandate in a dream cautioning him against the sort of life that he was leading. An ascetic at this stage of his life called on him and prophesied that the span of his life extended to a year only. This so much enervated him that he thoroughly changed the course of his life and latterly became steeped in the emotional felicities of a mystic.

<small>Srivas.</small>

There were also several other men who joined this glorious band, such as Bhugarva and Gadadhar, Narahari and Mukunda Datta, Sriman Pandit and Sreedhar, and a few others. One very curious personality was Pundarik Vidyanidhi; he belonged to this new school of the *bhakti*-cult. It is stated of him that he usually wore the costume of a prince indulging in all sorts of luxuries. He slept on a highly polished brass bedstead; his food was served on gold plates and he travelled in State-palanquins. He was rich and handsome and was therefore always

<small>Other men who joined.</small>

<small>Pundarik Vidyanidhi.</small>

taken for the type of men quite different from ascetics and saints. But this outward appearance did not indicate the man truly. He was a devotee and ascetic at heart, though outwardly he seemed to indulge in luxuries. There were moments when he could not put up with this mask of worldliness and threw away all the rich articles he used, and beggar-like sought the grace of God. At such moments he looked like the very prince of ascetics that he really was.

The Kirtan band was already at work at Nadia. God's name was recited with the sound of tabor, cymbal and dance, and already the scholars and lay people assembled to jeer at this new spirit of Vaishnavism. In the Kirtan parties held by Adwaita at this home, where the famous Ishwar Puri was a frequent guest, Mukunda Datta of Srikhanda sang praises of the Lord; and, says Chaitanya Bhagavata "as soon as Mukunda begins to sing his sweet emotional songs, some danced for joy and others wept." Ishwar Puri one day listened to these songs and passed into a trance. The people had already raised a hue and cry against this emotional religion. Chaitanya Bhagavata says "they all ridiculed the Kirtan party when they sang their songs. Some said 'their religion is a mere plea, they assemble to eat fine meals.' Others said 'what do all these dancings and uproar mean? They have abandoned the ways of intellectual discussion which truly become learned men, and dance furiously

THE NEED OF A SAVIOUR 51

like savages.' Some said again 'we have diligently read the Bhagavata but find no text in that scripture which recommends such weeping and dance."[1] In this band Gadadhar was already a prominent man. This young man was known for the fervour of his faith when Chaitanya as a young scholar was sceptical in his views.

This had been the religious aspect of Bengal before Chaitanya's activities were put forth for the promulgation of the creed of spiritual love. A field was already prepared by these few men. The learned discussions, the intellectual subtleties, the extensive rituals and the great vanity of learning that characterised the citizens of Nadia early in the 15th century left a gap in the minds of these few men who felt that all this did not point to the right way.

Men needed a Teacher.

The soil was dry, the path was dark; who was to fertilize the soil and illuminate the path? Pantheism had left no room for faith to grow. Who was to bring the message that man was not himself his God and that he needed helplessly the grace and intervention of a saviour? This band of workers weeping cried for divine mercy and prayed Him for sending some one who would wipe away, so to speak, the sophistry of the age by his tears of love, and prove to the sceptical people around and to the ritualists that

---

[1] Chaitanya Bhagavata, Atul Goswami's edition, pp. 212-214.

God was real,—that He might be loved more than a man ever loved his wife and son, and that rituals were of no value unless they inspired *bhakti*.

(v) *The political condition of the Period.*

Hussain Shah, the Emperor of Gour, was at first inspired like all zealots with iconoclasm. During the absence of Raja Pratap Rudra from Orissa in course of his warfare in the Deccan, Hussain Shah raided the country and destroyed hundreds of its picturesque temples and broke and disfigured a large number of images of gods and goddesses. Pratap Rudra, when he returned to his capital wanted to retaliate these wrongs. He was doubt-

Hussain Shah and Pratap Rudra.

less aware of the fact that one of his predecessors had once invaded Bengal and defeated the Pathan force. He prepared a large force for leading an expedition against Gour, but was afterwards counselled not to do so, as it would cause hardship to the Hindu population. The boundaries of the two kingdoms were, however, clearly defined by the terms of peace, and we find the demarcation line marked by tridents and watched over by armed officers on both sides. While Chaitanya was crossing this boundary, Ram Chandra Khan, the officer of Pratap Rudra, took all possible care, so that Chaitanya and his people might escape molestation from the hands of Mahomedan zealots.[1] Another account states that a high Mahomedan official who had the title of Nawab, instead of showing any sign of hostility as had been expected, was greatly impressed by Chaitanya's religious fervour and became one of his staunch admirers. There was a prophecy current at Nadia, the last seat of Hindu kings in Western Bengal, that a Brahmin of that place would drive away the Pathans and become the Emperor of Gour. We find in many Vaishnab works a mention of this prophecy. Jayananda's Chaitanya Mangal says that the inhabitants of Nadia were at this time skilled archers so that Hussain Shah became actually frightened by the prophecy. He ordered a general devastation of Nadia and its locality. There is a small village near Nadia called Pirullya where the Mahomedan army encamped and carried on oppressions in the neighbouring localities, converting Brahmins and other people to Islam by force. " Wherever there stood a Banian tree, held sacred by the Hindus, it was cut to pieces or uprooted. Hundreds of these trees were destroyed. The same fate attended the sacred Tulsi plants. The temples were broken and their gods desecrated. Bathing in the Ganges was prohibited by law." "These

Molestation of Nadia by Hussain Shah.

---

[1] Chaitanya Bhagavata, Atul Goswami's edition, pp. 385-386.

Mahomedans," laments Jayananda, "ruined the noble Brahmin families of Nadia." Many illustrious Brahmins and amongst them Vashudev Sarbabhouma, his father Visarad and brother Vidyabachaspati left Nadia at this juncture. Vashudev went to Orissa where Pratap Rudra honoured him by giving him a golden seat near his throne in his court. Those Brahmins whose caste was destroyed by force, have since been called Pirili Brahmins; for though unclean food was forced into their mouth and thus they were degraded in social scale, they did not accept Islam but remained Hindus. The oppressions done to Nadia were not novel in this province at the time. We find in Bijay Gupta's Manashar Bhashan written in 1494 A.D., and other contemporary works the *modus operandi* of Pathan zealots in oppressing the Hindus and making them converts to Islam. The Brahmins were not allowed to wear sacred threads. If any of them wore a sacred *tulasi* leaf on his head, he was bound hand and foot and brought before the Mahomedan Kazi for punishment. Von Neor's 'Life of Akbar' refers to the law that was enacted by the Pathan administrators that Hindu subjects must open their mouth to receive spitting from Mahomedan revenue collectors, should they wish to spit in course of their discharging public duties. A reference to such spitting and other humiliating punishments are to be found in many of the Bengali works of this period.

THE EMPEROR'S REMORSE

It seems that after having committed all kinds of atrocities upon his peaceful Hindu subjects at Nadia, a spirit of commiseration and repentance came upon Hussain Shah. Chaitanya Mangal ascribes this change in the spirit of his administrative activities to a bad dream in which the goddess Kali is said to have threatened him with death, should he continue such oppression. Whatever it might be, the remorseful emperor passed orders for repairing Hindu temples and otherwise compensating the losses sustained by the Brahmins of Nadia. We find it mentioned in the same Bengali work that there broke out a great famine in the locality of Nadia about this time. But in the spring of 1485 A.D. the agricultural condition of the country changed for the better, and the city becoming immune from Mahomedan oppression once more attained its old flourishing condition. From the account supplied by Brindaban Das we find that there lived a considerable number of millionaires in Nadia at this time. When the sky thus assumed a serene and cloudless aspect, and the city smiled in prosperity, Chaitanya was born at Mayapur, one of its wards, in 1486 A.D.

Nadia becomes once more a flourishing city.

But the dread of the people for Mahomedan oppression had lurked in the minds of the quiet Hindus throughout the reign of Hussain Shah, and however much he professed friendship for them, they could by no means be absolutely sure of his good will. Chaitanya was advised to leave Ramkeli near Gour, " for," said Keshab Basu, deputed by the Emperor to enquire about Chaitanya, " though Hussain Shah seems to be well disposed to you, Sir, there is no faith in this Mahomedan. How can we forget all the wrongs that he did to the Hindus of Bengal and Orissa, by breaking their temples and gods ? There is no knowing when he may change his mind."[1] The fear of the Emperor sending an armed navy against Nadia to suppress the *sankirtan* and oppress its promoters was ever in the minds of the citizens. Whenever they saw a large boat coming by the Ganges, they feared it contained the king's army, and we know how the house of Ramchandra Khan of Benapole was once raided by the royal army and its temples desecrated. Though in his later years Hussain Shah turned sober and even kindly, his cruel nature could not always be suppressed. It is well-known that inspite of his loud professions of regard for Chaitanya, Sanatan, his minister, was sent to jail for no other fault than his willingness to follow Chaitanya. Availing himself of the absence of Hussain Shah from his capital, Sanatan fled from the jail having bribed Mir Habool the jailor with a sum of Rs. 7,000.

Marginal note: People ever in dread of Hussain Shah.

---

[1] Chaitanya Bhāgavata, Atul Goswami's edition, p. 426.

HUSSAIN SAHA'S OLD MASTER

Hussain Shah in his early youth had worked for sometime as a menial servant in the house of one Subuddhi Ray, minister of a former Gour Emperor. It is recorded that one day failing in his duty he was whipped by Subuddhi Ray; the marks of the whip, it is said, could be seen on his body in after years. But save this punishment, he was otherwise very kindly treated by his Hindu master for whom the Shah entertained high respects and gratitude. Many years after when Hussain Shah became the Emperor of Gour, he remembered Subuddhi Ray and treated him with kindness. His queen, however, insisted on his inflicting some punishment on the old man for having once whipped him. The Emperor remonstrated, but ultimately the counsel of the queen was allowed to prevail, and Subuddhi Ray was forced to taste unclean food, so that his caste was destroyed. He sought the advice of stern Brahmin legislators as to how his sin could be expiated, and they declared, "the only way to save yourself from this sin is to throw yourself into fire and be burnt alive." Subuddhi Ray sought an interview with Chaitanya at Benares and when he met him, the Master said, "Go to the Vrinda groves and lead the religious life of an ascetic. This will expiate all sin, if any sin there has been on your part for the cruelty of others."[1]

---
[1] Chaitanya Charitāmṛita, Chap. 25, Madhyakanda.

CHAPTER II

A HISTORICAL REVIEW OF THE BIOGRAPHICAL WORKS OF THE VAISHNABS—THEIR CLAIMS TO RELIABILITY DISCUSSED.

(*a*) Murari Gupta's Chaitanya Charitam.
(*b*) Narahari Sarkar's songs.
(*c*) The Chaitanya Bhagavata.
(*d*) Chaitanya Charitamrita.
(*e*) Lochan Das's Chaitanya Mangal.
(*f*) Govinda Das's Karcha.
(*g*) Jayananda's Chaitanya Mangal.
(*h*) Prembilas, Bhakti Ratnakara and Songs on Chaitanya.
(*i*) Summary.
(*j*) Bibliography.

(*a*) *Murari Gupta's Chaitanya Charitam*.

A vast mass of biographical literature about Chaitanya Dev seems to be based on the short sketch of the Master by Murari Gupta. This book was written in Sanskrit by the venerable author in response to the enquiries made to him by Damodara, a young scholar and an ardent admirer of Chaitanya Dev.

MURARI GUPTA

Murari Gupta knew Chaitanya from childhood up. The former had already reached the zenith of academic renown when Chaitanya was receiving elementary lessons in Sanskrit Grammar. There are many incidents in Chaitanya's boyhood showing how naughty he was. We find him as a child one day standing behind Murari and mimicing the gestures and movements of the veteran scholar, engaged in an animated discussion on Sanskrit logic with another scholar.[1] Later on Chaitanya himself acquired the renown of a great scholar, nay became invincible in debates on Rhetoric and Grammar. Though the veteran scholar and the young prodigy showed almost equal merit and power in their argumentations this time, soon after Chaitanya's superiority became obvious. Having defeated Murari he used to jeer at him, saying, "You are a physician by caste, look to herbs and plants for curing cough and indigestion. The study of the difficult science of grammar will not suit you."[2]

<small>Murari's intimate knowledge of Chaitanya's early life.</small>

In later years Murari became a staunch admirer of Chaitanya, and was so devoted to him that he wanted to put an end to his own life when he heard that Chaitanya would turn an ascetic and leave Nadia.[3]

---

[1] Chaitanyamangal by Lochan Das, Bangabashi edition, Adi, p. 49.
[2] Chaitanya Bhāgavata, Adi.
[3] Chaitanya Bhagavata, Atul Goswami's edition, p. 307.

Murari's scholarship was held to be quite respectable even in the Nadia of that period when the reputed scholars of the city commanded an all-India renown.

All these would make it exceedingly probable that what he wrote about Chaitanya should possess an unquestionable authority. But we are sorry to say that we cannot place much reliance on this biography. First of all let us consider the claim of the printed edition of Murari's Chaitanya Charitam published by the Amritabazar Patrika Press, as a genuine work. The book is regarded as an authority on all questions relating to Chaitanya's life by the orthodox Vaishnabs. The date of composition given in the colophon is 1425 Saka or 1503 A.D., whereas *The latter chapters not genuine.* the book relates to those events also that occurred in 1530 A.D. and even later! So either the date must be rejected or the subsequent account given in the book should be regarded as a spurious interpolation. It is natural to expect that if Damodar made any enquiry about the incidents of Chaitanya's life to the veteran scholar; he must have done so regarding his childhood. For Damodar himself knew much more about the Master's latter life as his constant companion at Puri, than Murari whose knowledge was mainly confined to Chaitanya's early life at Nadia. Lochan Das, a subsequent biographer of Chaitanya, lays stress on the account of his boyhood described by Murari and to this he acknowledges his indebtedness.[1] He says that Murari's Chaitanya Charitam dealt with what Chaitanya did " from his birth to boyhood." But rejecting the latter portion of the book as unreliable, we have still some serious objections to accepting the narrative of Chaitanya's early life as described by Murari.

This book and indeed most of the biographical works of this kind are replete with legendary tales and ultrahuman matters to which we cannot give any credence. We find angels coming down to rejoice at the birth of Chaitanya. Sometimes Chaitanya holds a discourse with Adwaita from the womb of his mother, as St. Paul did with Jesus while in the womb of Mary. These tales have been told so often in regard to the lives and sayings of apostles that their repetition in each case must always be suspicious from a historical standpoint. We find the same thing spoken in regard to Zoroaster who according to Greek historians lived about 6000 B.C. and to whom, the latest European scholars ascribe an age not later than 2000 B.C. We find angels visiting Maya Devi when Buddha was in her

The supernatural element, a common feature in the biographies of all saints and prophets.

---

[1] " জন্ম হৈতে বালক চরিত্র যে কৈল ।
আদ্য অন্তে যেইরূপে প্রেম প্রচারিল ॥"

The second line seems to refer to the love-cult, preached by Chaitanya during his stay at *Nadia*. See Chaitanyamangal, Sutra Khanda, p. 3, Bangabashi Edition.

womb and heavenly messengers congratulating Mary at the advent of Jesus. The same tale is told of Amina Khatun when Mahomed was about to be born. Indeed a wonderful resemblance can be easily detected in the very methods and styles of description of the birth-incidents of world's religious heroes. The sky becomes clear, the air becomes wholesome and the evil spirits cease haunting the air. All these invariably occur at the birth of each of them.

In India there is an unbroken continuity of such legends and tales even up to the present moment. Ramkrishna Paramahansa, who passed away from this world only the other day, has been, of late, associated with legends of similar character. Babu Rajendranath Roy has recently published a book called "Sri Ramkrisna Bhagabata" in which we find all things ascribed to Jesus, Buddha and Chaitanya and a hundred other miraculous things, occurring at Ramkrishna's birth. These things are ever growing in India, and just when I am writing these lectures I know that such things are being incorporated in a biographical sketch of Prabhu Jagatbandhu of Faridpur regarded as a prophet and apostle by thousands who find divinity in him. In view of the same legends being ascribed to apostles ancient and modern, it is vain to discuss any historical questions involved in them. Murari's book chiefly relates to accounts of this character. It has been said of

CHAITANYA AS DIVINE INCARNATION

Jnaneshaur the Vaishnab prophet of Southern India (born in Alandi near Poona in the 13th century) that he made a buffalo recite the name of God, and we find in the Chaitanya Charitamrita, Valadeva Bhattacharyya referring to his having personally seen a tiger reciting the name of Hari at Chaitanya's bidding.

So when one thing, however inconceivably hard to believe, has been said of one saint, it must be repeated in the case of every subsequent saint in order to give him an equal prestige amongst deified men and apostles.

Even when Chaitanya was only 22 years and a few months old, the reputation had gone forth that he was Krishna incarnate. Govinda Das says, when he first visited Nadia to see Chaitanya, "people of the country-side say that God Himself has come down to Nadia as the son of Sachi; this has attracted me to the city."[1] The reputation was natural enough; for Chaitanya in his love ecstasies rose to such an exalted plane of emotion and so thoroughly identified himself with the holy name of Krishna, that people thought him to be Krishna Himself. There is no doubt that all attempts on the part of the people to deify Chaitanya met with a stern rebuff at his hands. But after he had left Nadia for good, the band of his followers found an unobstructed course left to them in their

Belief in incarnation.

---
[1] Govinda Das's Karchā, p. 2.

attempts to deify him, when the controlling hand of the Master was withdrawn. In doing so, they themselves raised their position in the eyes of people. The companions of God were, as a matter of course, acknowledged as divinities themselves. Adwaita became Shiva, Nityananda became Balarama and Murari Gupta figured as the great ape-god Hanuman in popular estimation.

Moreover in those days it was not customary with the Hindus to write biographies of any individual, other than a saint or an incarnation of Godhead. It was not considered becoming to record the events of a worldly man's life, however great he might be from a materialistic standpoint. Hence since the days of the songs of Pal Rajas and of Goraksha Bijay we have not had a single memoir of any great man written in Bengali. The renaissance-literature, mainly speaking, was restricted to legendary accounts of special religious cults. The first biography to be written of a young Brahmin ascetic who lived in flesh and body before the people, needed an explanation. The only explanation which could satisfy them in this respect was a proof of his divinity. Thus we find Murari Gupta striving to explain to Damodara why Krishna incarnated himself in Chaitanya, by quoting chapters and verses from scriptures, —a course which was latterly followed by Lochan Das and other biographers of Chaitanya.

THE NADIA-TALES

These scholars were all zealots and propagandists who did not care much to record historical facts, but strove with all their mediæval learning to find texts for proving Chaitanya to be Krishna himself. Free from all propagandism and vanity of scholarship is the one book, Govinda Das's Karchā, where we find a faithful historical account of Chaitanya's tour for two years. Nowhere in this book do we find Chaitanya declaring that he was God himself. Whereas in the accounts derived from Nadia-sources, we find him receiving tributes of worship from his devotees, as the supreme God of the universe. We have little faith in these stories. It may be that when in his trances he lost all consciousness of his environment some of his followers eulogised him or offered flowers at his feet; and these small incidents were latterly magnified into tales of Chaitanya's himself admitting his divinity. We know that Govinda Das recorded each event that daily occurred during Chaitanya's tour in the Deccan for two years. Therein we find Chaitanya lost in God's love, full of humility, sweet in his discourses and sometimes passing days and nights in mystic vision, unconscious of the material world; and nowhere haughty, proud, calling himself the lord of the universe and assaulting aged scholars as we find him in the descriptions of Murari Gupta and Brindaban Das. In fact this Nadia period of his life is full of wild myths and exaggerated stories which originated from an ardent and enthusiastic desire of his followers to deify him, when he was no longer present there to control the ardour of his Bhaktas. In the more faithful accounts of him, we find him fasting for God's love,—his frequent trances making him lean and pale, so that his friends could scarcely suppress a tear at the sight of his emaciated figure. But we find some of his biographers recording that at Adwaita's house he ate meals which many men could not by their joint efforts. We know how such legends originated. It was due to the ardour of the orthodox souls to prove that he was like Damodara, the infant Kriṣṇa, who could put the whole universe within his stomach —the *brahmandabhandodara* as he was called. In Chaitanya Charitamrita we find Satir mata, wife of Sarbabhoum, making vast preparations for his dinner, this was taken objection to by her son-in-law Amogha who asked why should there be such rich meal for an ascetic. But we are not inclined to credit any account that says that he ate more than human beings could do, as these were evidently manufactured to prove that he was "*brahmandabhandodara*." On page 155 of the Adwaita Prakasa we find a distinct reference, shewing that the devotees wished to prove that their deified hero could swallow the whole universe if he liked, as he was the same as

<small>How wild myths about Chaitanya originated in Nadia</small>

Damodara. But in these works, we find truer descriptions in which Chaitanya's leanness owing to fasts, vigils, his rigid asceticism and refusal to accept any rich food, are frequently emphasized. He was so particular about food that his instructions to the young ascetic Raghunath should be remembered in this connection:—" Don't touch good food, nor wear good apparel."[1] Murari Gupta believed in all the hearsays and stories that grief-stricken Nadia gave rise to, in order to soothe herself by indulging in reveries about the divinity of Chaitanya, after he had deserted the city. We cannot accept Chaitanya Charitam as a historical work. We must always admire the poetic beauty of Murari's descriptions and admit many facts related by him as true, though as a whole it cannot be accepted as a historical treatise. This detracts nothing from our great regard for the author's scholarship and even saintliness of character, though in the light of modern standard it must be said that he was devoid of what is called the historical sense. Amongst these orthodox Vaishnabs it was held sacrilegious to disbelieve any story that was related of Chaitanya for establishing his divinity. This accounts for the extravagant things described by the biographer.

---

[1] " ভাল না খাইবে আর ভাল না পরিবে ।"
" Chaitanya Charitamrita."

(b) *Narahari Sarkar's Songs.*

For some of the earliest materials of Chaitanya's life we must fall back upon the songs of Narahari Sarkar of Srikhanda, some of which are exquisite from a poetical point of view. Previous to the advent of Chaitanya in the field, Narahari had composed many songs about Radha and Krishna.[1] But after 1508 A.D. when Chaitanya had become lost in God's love and attracted admirers—of whom Narahari himself was one of the greatest—he took up the Chaitanya-theme for his songs. He had already achieved renown as a poet before Chaitanya was born; so if we take him to be 25 years old in 1486, the year of Chaitanya's birth, he may be presumed to have been born about the year 1461 A.D. He was a constant companion of Chaitanya at Nadia. We refer our readers to pp. 100-103 of my "Chaitanya and His Companions" for further particulars about Narahari. Unfortunately, however, we cannot attach much historical importance to the songs of Narahari also, though being a close associate of the Master, he was pre-eminently qualified for acquainting us with particulars about his boyhood and early youth. I have already stated that he had composed many beautiful songs about Radha and Krishna before Chaitanya was

---

[1] Goura Pada Tarangini, compiled by Jagatbandhu Bhadra, p. 456.

born,[1] and when Chaitanya was accepted as an incarnation of Krishna, none was more forward than Narahari in preaching the Chaitanya-cult. The amours of Krishna with the Gopis and sports on the banks of the Jamuna had so great a hold upon the imagination of this poet and devotee, that he ascribed all these to Chaitanya, however incongruous this might seem to us—lay people. Chaitanya was a prince of ascetics; his sexual purity and rigid abstinence are well known to all. But Narahari makes the women of Nadia yearn after him just as the Gopis of the old legend are said to have done for Krishna. The poet represents himself as a woman who is over head and ears in love for Chaitanya. The women-folk of Nadia, by whom the poet probably meant the devotees, are spoken of as charmed by Chaitanya's handsome person and attractive manners and they are represented as confessing their love for him in hundreds of songs in the same manner as the Gopis did in the Bhāgavata. Narahari's songs describing the pain of the Nadia women at their separation from Chaitanya are on the lines of the songs of Vidyapati and Chandi Das—sometimes the very words bear a strange and unmistakable resemblance. We know that Narahari suffered

---

[1] "গৌরাঙ্গ জন্মের আগে, বিবিধ রাগিণী রাগে
ব্রজরস করিলেক গান।"

Gaura Pada Tarangini
by Jagat Bandhu Bhadra, p. 456.

intensely from his separation from Chaitanya on his taking Sanyas; and as womanly love symbolised best the yearnings of his emotional nature, he took recourse to this mode in expressing the ardour of his feelings. It is like the emotion of those mystics who accepted Christ as their bridegroom. There were many people amongst Chaitanya's followers who liked these songs in which love for Chaitanya was expressed in the language of women. Curiously in some of these songs Narahari discourses in a mystic language as regards his propriety in attributing love for Chaitanya to the women of Nadia. "Every one," he says, "knows the crystal purity of Nadia women; they are reputed to be virtuous and chaste; at the same time the strict character of Chaitanya who never looks upon a woman with other than very proper feeling, is beyond question. Why then do I write in this strain, one may justly ask."[1] In reply to this he gives a hint at the psychology of those devotees who would express best their tender feelings in the language of women. That many Vaishnabs do still like to adopt not only the phraseology of women, but wear their costumes and ornaments and assuming their names pass for such, is a well-known fact and those

Chaitanya loved by Nadia women as Krishna was loved by the Gopis.

---

[1] See Gaur Pada Tarangini, Padas Nos. 164, 165, 166, 167 and 171, pp. 229-234.

LALITA DEVI AND NOLAK BABAJI

who would like to see such devotees with their own eyes should visit Nadia and see Lalita Devi. Appearances should not confound a visitor; for Lalita Devi by name and dress is to all outward appearances a woman. But this person is a young man of the Brahmin caste and noted for the saintliness of his character. We know that he has been trying to love Krishna as a Gopi, and this dress and all he has adopted to make himself worthy of Krishna's love. Another saint who practises the tenet of Vaishnab creed in this manner is Nolak Babaji, the name by which he is popularly called, his real name being Harimohan Chakrabarty. He had read for a time in the M.A. class in the Dacca College, and while a teacher in a Government school had composed a small poem in English called 'Toy for a boy.' His translation of Gray's Elegy into metrical Bengali had elicited much appreciation from the press about half a century ago. He is now verging on 80 and is an inhabitant of the village Dhamrai in the district of Dacca. This old man dresses himself like a woman, wears bracelets in his hands and a *beshar* in his nose like them and sings the praise of Krishna in the manner of a Gopi. I do not think the Christian people would feel any difficulty in realising how all these could be possible. Tennyson's beautiful song based on a Biblical text—"Too late, too late, thou can'st not enter now" rings in my

Marginal note: Devotees in the guise of women.

ears and shows how Narahari's exquisite songs should be rightly interpreted and understood. Chaitanya is here the bridegroom of the poet-mystic: However much we may appreciate this mode of poetry, there is no doubt that this is not the right way to lead to a comprehension of historical facts. That this mode of attributing a passion for Chaitanya on the part of devotees represented as women, did not commend itself to many readers, will be known from the following passage in the Chaitanya Bhagavata. It refers to the boyish pranks of Chaitanya:—" He indulged in such pranks with all, but he was very careful in regard to women. In this incarnation (evidently in contrast with Krishna) the lord very particularly avoided any touch with women. He studiously kept aloof from the fair sex. So all wise men should avoid mentioning him as a lover; for this is not the right way to sing praises of the lord. Though all kinds of praises may be given him, yet wise men should describe him as he was."[1]

Chaitanya the bridegroom of the poet-mystic.

Those songs not always approved by the Vaishnavas.

---

[1] এইমাত্র চাপল্য করেন সভা সনে।
সবে পরস্ত্রী মাত্র নাহি দেখেন নেত্র কোণে॥
স্ত্রী হেন নাম প্রভু এই অবতারে।
শ্রবণেও না করিলা, বিদিত সংসারে॥
অতএব যত মহামহিম সকলে।
গৌরাঙ্গ নাগর হেন স্তব নাহি বলে॥
যদ্যপি সকল স্তব সম্ভবে তাহানে।
তথাপিও স্বভাব সে গায় বুধগণে॥

Chaitanya Bhagavata,
Atul Goswami's edition, Adi. 10, p. 110.

This is evidently a comment on the songs of Narahari with whom, it is traditionally known, Brindaban Das had a quarrel. This passage distinctly supports the tradition. The fact is the writers often confounded Krishna with Chaitanya in their enthusiasm to establish the latter's divinity and attributed all things of Krishna's legends to Chaitanya, just as some of them ascribed to him a hunger that could not be appeased by eating enormous quantity of food, with a view to putting him on the level of *brahmandabhandodara*.

We find many of these Nadia-tales and legends far away from history. They grew like wild plants everywhere, as the presence of the Master was no longer there to keep the path of Bhakti clear from all such outgrowths. It is often seen in world's religious history that feelings of admiration and love on the part of the followers of a great teacher, however intense they may be, take an uncouth shape when his controlling hand and ennobling personality are removed.

(c) *The Chaitanya Bhagavata.*

Next, we come to a consideration of the Chaitanya Bhagavata, the standard biography of Chaitanya. This book was written in the year 1573 or 40 years after Chaitanya had passed away. The inspiration of this book came from the Nadia-veterans whose imagination was thoroughly charged with the faith that Chaitanya was an incarnation of Krishna. All the wild myths and legends spoken about the Master were readily accepted by Brindaban Das whose own birth was enshrouded by a supernatural tale in which also he believed more than anybody else.

But Brindaban had a power to follow the sequence and chronology of events, like a true historian, though on account of his being brought up in the orthodox circle he shared in the belief of the supernatural and extravagant things ever spoken of one identified in popular estimation with Godhead. It is his perspective that gives us a better glimpse of historical facts. The Master's sketch is itself sometimes blurred by over-colouring. If we look to the subsidiary figures—the attendants of a god or goddess made of clay by our potters for worship, we note that these are often life-like and true to nature, whereas the main god or goddess as the case may be, in compliance with time-honoured traditions, is made ultrahuman and grotesque with eyes that reach the ears and often with more hands and heads than usual. It is just the same thing that we notice in the case of Brindaban Das. When minor events are described incidentally they have all the interest of historical facts, but when he speaks of the Master, the mythical element is allowed to preponderate.

Quite trustworthy in the account of minor things.

KRISHNA AND CHAITANYA

More than Murari Gupta, more than anybody else, Brindaban was eager to prove that Krishna was identical with Chaitanya. All his inspiration comes from the Bhagavata, and in every action of the Master, he finds a repetition of Krishna's doings on the banks of the Jamuna, however inconceivable this may appear to us lay people. Gangadas, the teacher of Chaitanya is called Sandipani who gave lessons to Krishna as a boy. When Chaitanya sits surrounded by his pupils in his *tole*, Brindaban says that he looks like Krishna in the Naimisharanya in the company of the Rishis. The girls of Nadia come to Sachi and complain that Chaitanya, five years old, does all kinds of wicked pranks. They supplement their report by the significant remark—"Your son's conduct is verily of the same kind as we have heard of Nanda's son (Krishna).[1]" A Brahmin guest comes to the house of Jagannath Misra and before beginning to eat, dedicates, as usual with the Brahmins, the food to Krishna. Just then young Chaitanya comes and takes a handful from the meal and thus spoils it; for no Brahmin would eat the remnant of a meal after an outsider had eaten from it. The Brahmin cooks his meal

[Marginal note: Chaitanya the same as Krishna.]

---

1. " পূর্বে শুনিলাম যেন নন্দের কুমার।
   সেইরূপ তোমার পুত্রের ব্যবহার॥"
                                    Chaitanya Bhagavata, Adi.

again and then shutting his eyes as before mentally dedicates the food to Krishna. The imp, who was lurking somewhere near, at this stage reappears and suddenly takes a handful and flies away and this he repeats a third time. Of course he was quite justified in doing so in respect of the food dedicated to Krishna, if we can only believe that he was identical with that god. This is exactly what Krishna did in regard to Garga, the sage who had become his father's guest for a day. All these are no doubt told to prove the identity of Chaitanya with Krishna. A snake is in the room, and Chaitanya as a baby is found to make a bed of this poisonous worm and sleep on it. This will remind the reader of the sleep of Krishna in his Ananta Shayya or the bed formed by the snake Ananta. In the footprints of the young Chaitanya are the marks of divinity discovered by wondering Jagannath, his father, and as the parents move about in the courtyard, they hear the sound of sacred anklets in the room where the baby lies, though he wears no anklets on his feet. A baby of five months, he kicks from near his bed the pitchers containing curd and milk and the parents wonder how such a little helpless thing could do so great a feat, but this is exactly a repetition of the tale of *sakatabhanjana*—the breaking of the cart containing milk and butter-pitchers as related of Krishna in the Bhagavata. I may refer to

Coincidences with the account of the Bhagavata.

further incidents of this nature with which the Chaitanya Bhagavata is replete, but it is not needed after all that has been said. My readers will see that the foremost thought in the mind of Brindaban Das was how he could best prove that Krishna was incarnated as Chaitanya. The Vaishnab Masters at Brindaban considered the book to be thoroughly successful from this point of view and changed its name from Chaitanya Mangal to Chaitanya Bhagavata for like the Bhagavata this book also was regarded by them as an authentic record of Krishna's doings in his incarnation as Chaitanya.

But as I have already stated that barring the account of a supernatural and legendary character chiefly mentioned in regard to Chaitanya, the book contains much valuable historical information about the period it describes, and for this it deservedly occupies a high place in popular estimation.

Much valuable information.

(d) The Chaitanya Charitamrita.

The greatest work on the life of Chaitanya, however, is the Chaitanya Charitamrita of Krishna Das Kaviraj, begun in 1574 and completed in 1581 A. D. Krishna Das lived a life of celebacy in the Brinda groves, and was a scholar and devotee, held in high regard by all. But from the historical point of view we

The Adikhanda full of legends.

cannot rely on the book in its entirety. In writing the first part of the work—the Adi-khanda—he had to depend, as he himself acknowledges, on the accounts of Brindaban Das and other biographers. He accepted the miracles and supernatural tales as they were found in the previous books without exercising any discrimination. He could not help doing so, as being an orthodox Vaishnab, he could not disbelieve the statements of those whom he considered as saints and authorities amongst the Vaishnabs. But his own weak point however lies in the fact that being a great scholar himself he represented Chaitanya mainly as a scholar and the founder of a school of theology, though towards the last Khanda Chaitanya in his descriptions gradually asserts himself as a lover of God. The great love leading to mystic visions and trances gives him a far greater prominence than his scholarship. Chaitanya in this book frequently holds learned discourses and propounds the philosophy of Vaishnab religion to Sanatan, Ramray and others. We no doubt find many of his views in these instructive discourses but cannot vouch for the absolute historical accuracy of some of them. We find in this book that Chaitanya, while discoursing on theology, quotes Bhaktirasamrita Sindhu—a work written long after the time. Similarly at Benares he quotes Haribhaktivilas

<small>The theological discourses attributed to Chaitanya not always genuine.</small>

—a book that was written at a much later date.[1] Numerous such instances will be found in the Chaitanya Charitamrita in which Chaitanya refers in his discussions to passages written by his followers or their descendants in after times. The truth is that Krishna Das Kaviraj was so imbued with the theological ideas propounded by Sanatan, Rupa, Jiva, Kabikarnapur and other followers of Chaitanya, that he went on quoting chapters and verses from the works of these Vaishnab worthies, most of whom were his contemporaries, without remembering in his enthusiasm that Chaitanya could not probably have quoted extracts from their writings. And at the same time it must also be stated that all the theological views of these great Vaishnabs could not be endorsed by Chaitanya for obvious reasons. One fundamental thing should be remembered in this connection. The subsequent Vaishnab theology was based upon the assumption that Chaitanya was an incarnation of Krishna. The theology latterly developed a theory that Krishna incarnated himself as Chaitanya in fulfilment of a promise he had made to Radha. Radha loved him so intensely that Krishna told her once that he would try to requite this great debt of love in his incarnation of Chaitanya—that he would abandon home for her love, and be lost in mystic

---

[1] See Madhyakhanda, Chap. 17.

vision of her and roll in the dust like a mad man singing her name. Radha said, "How shall I bear to see you fall down for the sake of my love on the dusty ground that will hurt you? I will, therefore, cover you with my body in that incarnation of yours so that the ground may hurt *me* and not *you* my beloved, when you will fall down in your trances." So Krishna's dusky colour in his incarnation as Chaitanya lay hidden under Radha's fair colour, bright as that of the Champaka flower. Radha covered him with herself and Chaitanya in the eyes of the orthodox Vaishnabs represents the united figure of Radha and Krishna. These and many such legends which in some cases developed into theology by the scholarship of learned Vaishnabs could not have possibly got any approval from the Master. Another theory that the Vaishnab worthies were incarnations of the Gopies of the Brinda groves formed a part of Vaishnab theology and we find in many learned works an attempt to prove it. The theological school of Chaitanya's followers was founded to a great extent on this theory of incarnation to which Chaitanya was far from giving even an indirect support. So in many points discussed by Krishna Das in his Chaitanya Charitamrita we find his account more of a legendary than historical character. But it must be admitted at the same time that all the orthodox biographers of world's saints and apostles have this tendency to believe in miracles and legends. We have St. Paul, St. John and other writers of the Gospel recording such things. If we do not lose our respect for them, and if we regard the Lalita Bistara and other works of this kind as great authorities, why should we proceed in a fastidious spirit in regard to the writings of Vaishnab saints? Human mind when it comes in contact with extraordinary greatness is carried away by admiration, and indulges in the belief of things which do not belong to this world. We must not assume an attitude of arrogance, and sit in judgment, even on a plea of scientific criticism, over the writings of saintly men and brand all miracles and supernatural events related by them as false; but as ours is a historical treatise we must not put down anything which is against the light of our reason as it is constituted at the present moment.

(e) *Lochana Das's Chaitanya Mangala.*

One of the main objects which inspired Lochana Das in writing his Chaitanya Mangala was evidently to record facts about Narahari Sarkar, whose name was left out by Brindabana Dasa owing to his quarrel with him, to which we have already referred. Following his Guru, Lochana Das cares more for poetry than a strict narration of historical facts. For instance the long description which

11

Lochana gives of the sweet discourses said to have been held by Chaitanya with his wife Vishnupriya on the eve of his leaving Navadwip cannot possibly have any foundation in fact. Call it very exquisite poetry if you like, but it is far from what really occurred. Chaitanya here takes leave of his wife like a lover burning with romantic love, with many a sigh and tear. We know Chaitanya was so maddened by God's love that the romance of sexual love had absolutely no attraction for him. We quote the familiar lines of Brindabana Das in this connection : " to divert her son's mind to wordly pleasures Sachi used to bring his wife, a charming young woman, and made her sit near him ; but Chaitanya did not even do so much as glance at her. ' Where is my Krishna gone ?' he cried aloud, recited slokas and wept."[1] In the Chaitanya Chandrodaya also we find him not taking any notice of Vishnupriya though she was reputed for her beauty and accomplishments. Govinda Das says in his Karcha that when the news of his resolution to take *sanyas* had spread at Navadwip and Bishnupriya wept at the report, Chaitanya

The poetical element shadows the historical facts.

---

[1] " লক্ষ্মীরে আনিয়া প্রভুর নিকটে বসায় ।
দৃষ্টিপাত করিয়াও প্রভু নাহি চায় ॥
কোথা কৃষ্ণ কোথা কৃষ্ণ বলে অনুক্ষণ ।
দিবানিশি শ্লোক পড়ি করয়ে ক্রন্দন ॥ "

Chaitanya Bhāgavata, Adi.

did not show any sign of being at all moved by her tears. This was stoic and even cruel, but this was a fact. Authentic accounts of his *sanyas* given by other writers do also confirm us in the belief that Chaitanya could not give such prolific expressions to romantic love for his wife as described by Lochana Das. The fact is that this writer never misses any opportunity to introduce poetic situations.

<small>Chaitanya's attitude towards his wife.</small> In the present case he gives such details of what was supposed to have passed between Chaitanya and his wife in their bedchamber, as none but one who overheard the long conversation and recorded it then and there, could do. In the description of this episode it is further stated that Chaitanya in order to prove to his wife that he was Vishnu himself showed her his four arms, two of which ordinarily lay hid from mortal eyes. Not only in this poetic description but in many other accounts he indulged in free imagination and often reproduced legendary tales which Nadia people were ever fond of hearing about Chaitanya His animated account of Bibhisana's visit to Chaitanya at Puri is <small>Bibhisana's visit.</small> noteworthy. Bibhisana was a brother of Ravana who had obtained the boon of immortality from Brahma, the Creator, and therefore he lives through all ages and still reigns in Lanka according to orthodox notions. So after thousands of years from the time when the great

war is said to have been fought by Rama at Lanka with his help, he comes to Puri about the year 1530, knowing that Chaitanya was no other than an incarnation of Vishnu and identical with Rama to whom the Rakshasa king was bound to pay his homage. I do not know whose fertile brain first conceived this fable, but it was believed by Murari Gupta, the great scholar, and had been recorded in his Chaitanya Charitam from which Lochana Das no doubt copied it.

What I have said above is more or less true of all other biographies of Chaitanya. The same ardour for believing in the supernatural marks the Chaitanya Chandrodaya Nataka by Kabikarnapura who records the legend of the birth of the heavenly nymph Urbashi, and of how Krishna resolved to incarnate himself as Chaitanya and other such stories which carry us far beyond this physical plane of ours. Lochana states that when Chaitanya in one of his trances proclaimed that he was Godhead, Sachi, his mother, bowed down before him and addressed him a Sanskrit hymn. We find in all these the characteristic excess and prolificness of imagination that mark the Nadia tales. In the subsequent career of the Master we have occasional mention of similar legends, but they are not certainly so extravagant and numerous as those related in regard to that period of his life which he had spent at Nadia. The Chaitanya Chandrodaya of

Kabikarnapura is a masterly work, and though legends and miracles are to be met with in these accounts, they are also store-houses of historical information which we cannot ignore.

Though these authors yielded occasionally to the general tendency of the age, to a belief in the supernatural, they exhibited, however, great industry and enthusiasm, inspired by love alone, in collecting materials on which we must build a historical biography of the Master. Without their aid it is impossible for us to proceed, however greatly we may regret their want of historical sense, judged by the scientific standard of the modern times. And our comment for the purpose of ascertaining historical facts should not be taken as indicating any disrespect for these authors.

(f) *Govinda Das's Karcha.*

The works, referred to above, seem to have been written under the same inspiration. Murari Gupta was the man who held the pioneer's flag in the field, and what he had written was followed more or less closely by other biographers, so far as Chaitanya's boyhood was concerned. All these works are held in high esteem and the authority of these is never questioned by orthodox Vaishnabs. But there are two biographical works which do not belong to this class. They have never been recognised as works of authority by the orthodox people.

Of this the first is Govinda Dās's *karcha*. It was written in the form of notes taken by the author who was a companion of Chaitanya in his tour in the Deccan from 1510 to 1511. The author says that he took notes every day very privately; for the Master would not tolerate anyone recording the particulars of his own life which might lead to worldly vanity. It is the same spirit that actuated Lokenatha Goswami in after-times to request Krishna Dās Kaviraj, the author of Chaitanya Chari-

<small>He seldom describes supernatural things.</small> tamrita, not to mention his name in the work. Govinda Dās's *karcha* is plain history. It holds to us in a vivid light what Chaitanya was. It is not a scholarly work inspired by propagandism. Nowhere in this book is recorded any fact that jars with our historical sense. If the author calls Chaitanya here and there as an incarnation of Vishnu it is the language of common courtesy used by all in that age in regard to him, and indeed in regard to all great saints and *Sanyasis* of that period. There is no mention of six arms shown by Chaitanya to people to show that he was the same that had been Krishna and Rāma in previous *Y gas*, as stated about him in many of his biographies. Nowhere is to be found in this book the extraordinary tale of Chaitanya's sowing mango-seeds, and like a magician creating in course of a few minutes trees with ripe fruits, as recorded in the Chaitanya Charitamrita. Nor

do we find Chaitanya in this work invoking the infallible *chakra*—the divine weapon— to punish the ruffians, and in response the mighty weapon coming through the air, whirling like a fiery ball, as is mentioned in the Chaitanya Bhagavata. Chaitanya does not appear here as the leader of an orthodox community, all attention to laws of conduct as laid down in their jurisprudence. In fact this one book gives a far truer account of Chaitanya than others, showing how he won the hearts of people by his great spiritual force. It is for this representation of him in his true colour, that the orthodox community was startled at the discovery of the book and not finding him as he is sketched elsewhere—the Supreme Deity who could do and undo the universe at his will, they rejected the book saying that it was not authentic. There are of course certain incidents described in this book, evidently in conflict with those to be found in standard 'biographies.' The Chaitanya Charitamrita says that the Brahmin Krishnadas accompanied Chaitanya in his tour in the Southern India. We find, however, in Govinda Dās's *karcha* that Krishna Dās journeyed only a short distance but was required to return, so that Govinda was the sole companion of Chaitanya in this tour. The orthodox Vaishnabs had refused to believe in this statement of Govinda Dās. But all their arguments have been swept away by a flood of evidences that in recent years have come to light. Several very old manuscripts of Jayananda's Chaitanya Mangala confirm that Govinda Dās accompanied Chaitanya in his tour in the Deccan, and a song by the poet Balarama Das who flourished in the 16th century, to be found in the work Gourapada-tarangini, compiled by late Jagabandhu Bhadra, also substantiates this statement. The reason why manuscripts of Govinda Dās's *karcha* are not numerously found is because the orthodox people want to hear that Chaitanya is Krishna himself more than an account of his love. They want to hear that he is identical with the great Hog—the Baraha, an incarnation of Vishnu, and could assume the shape any time—that he was ready to prove himself to be Vishnu by a display of many arms. A simple historical narrative does not commend itself to lay people or make any impression on them. For this reason the book has not been held in that esteem which it deserves ; for simple truths, often the highest, are generally ignored by ordinary people, who love show more than true merit. Yet old MSS. of the work are by no means rare. The one that was 250 years old was in the custody of late Babu Sisir Kumar Ghose, editor of the Amritabazar Patrika, for some time, and from another, about 200 years old, Pandit Jaygopal Goswami of Santipur had collected the first portion running up to the 51st page of

The genuineness of the karcha. Why the orthodox community does not credit it as authentic.

his printed edition. Nowhere in the whole range of the Vaishnab literature is the true greatness of Chaitanya shown with so much force as in this book. The minute description of the places in Southern India visited by Chaitanya will be of great historical interest to students of the topography of the different parts of India. We need scarcely say that in the present memoir of Chaitanya which will follow, we shall depend a good deal on the faithful records of Govinda Dās who was an eye-witness of the events that he describes in his book. The language of the book seems to have been refined here and there by the editor Jaygopal Goswami but there is enough of archaic expressions to be found lingering in its pages.

(g) *Jayananda's Chaitanya Mangala.*

The next work to which orthodoxy refuses to give its support is Jayananda's Chaitanya Mangala, a curious work in which all kinds of legends and fables have been given a place together with statements of facts. But still it differs in some respect from works believed to be authorities according to orthodox Vaishnab notion. It begins with hymns in praise of Ganesh and other gods. In the orthodox works such a thing would not have been possible as their authors would not recognise any god or

<small>The book does not belong to the orthodox school.</small>

goddess except Chaitanya and Radha Krishna. We find many facts in this book not mentioned in other biographies. For instance there is the important discovery made from this book that Chaitanya's ancestors belonged to Orissa. The manner in which Chaitanya passed away from this world is a revelation which we owe to this book alone. The political condition of Navadwip immediately before the birth of Chaitanya, the origin of Pirili Brahmins, the fact of Chaitanya's first wife Laksmi having a maid-servant named Chitralekha and his being attended to as a baby by a nurse named Narayani,—of his meeting at Gaya a great sage named Munindra who had observed the vow of muteness for 12 years,—of Chaitanya's having a dog which he had named Gangadas,—all these and many small details of this nature are to be found in this book alone and not in any other.

<small>It contains much new information.</small> Though Brindabana's Chaitanya Bhagavata had been written a few years before this work, and this Jayananda himself admits, we find the book not based on Murari's Chaitanya Charita, as Chaitanya Bhagavata, Chaitanya Charitamitra and some other works are—I mean as far as the account of the Master's boyhood is concerned. It is a truly independent work differing in some respects from those works in the matter of chronology of events and other particulars. For instance in this book it is mentioned that

Chaitanya was a *bhakta* and lover of God from his boyhood, whereas it is stated in all the standard biographies that a love for God dawned on his soul for the first time on the eve of his paying a visit to Gaya. The latter is perhaps the more reliable account, but whether we accept Jayananda's views or not in regard to various points at issue, there is no doubt that he presents to us facts and incidents not following the beaten track, but independently and this is a great relief to historical students, giving them an opportunity to form an impartial judgment by discussing conflicting statements. And it is exactly for this reason, for Jayananda's asserting himself in his own way in describing his narrative without following Vaisnava canons, that makes the orthodox people reject his authority. Jayananda is some-

<small>Historical account blended with myth.</small> times carried away by emotional poetry and sometimes by faith in supernatural tales about the subject of his memoir, but he furnishes historical side-lights on obscure points and presents to us facts not hitherto known about Chaitanya. For all these reasons and for the fact that his work is original, not belonging to the class approved by the orthodox school, we consider it to be a valuable contribution to the Vaishnab biographical literature. Jayananda's Chaitanya Mangala was written about the year 1575 at the command of Pandit Gadadhara, a favourite companion of Chaitanya during his boyhood and early youth at Nadia.

(h) Prembilasa, Bhaktiratnakara and Songs on Chaitanya.

There remain to be considered some historical works such as the Prembilasa, the Bhaktiratnakara, the Anuragballi and books of this class in which incidentally many events of Chaitanya's life are described. Prembilasa was written about the year 1640. Bhaktiratnakara about 1725 and Anuragballi in 1696. In these books though now and then we come across many new facts in regard to the Master's career, he is represented as God and Saviour with much over-colouring. But we shall use such materials to be found in them, as will help us in making a complete research in this field. The statements made in the different works mentioned by me are sometimes of a conflicting nature. For instance the Bhaktiratnakara says that Chaitanya took leave of his mother on the morning of the 1st of Magh, Sak 1430, and proceeded towards Katwa for Sanyas; but Jayananda's Chaitanya Mangal says that for 3 days the fact of his leaving Nadia was kept concealed from her by his friends. We shall deal with these small questions in their proper place.

Discrepancies.

We have however omitted to speak of one important mine of information about Chaitanya. These are songs about him written mostly by Narahari and Basudeba Ghosh—his

The great value of Chaitanya-songs.

contemporaries. These should not be mistaken for stray lyrical pieces composed by the poets for describing momentary sentiments of devotion or love. They are oftentimes threaded together in such a way as to describe some of the entire episodes of his career. Many of these are masterpieces of poetry. They create pathos of indescribable sweetness, reproducing situations which become bright with the glimmer of poetic light upon them. Having been written by those who had a direct and personal knowledge of the Master's life, they possess all the interest of real history and should not be mistaken for mere products of poetic fancy. Often times Chaitanya appears in these songs like a picture in life-like vividness ; the charm of reality is thus heightened by the touch of poetic hand that drew these sketches. We shall take help from this poetic treasure in the present memoir of the Master as we go on.

(i) Summary.

Now to recapitulate some points discussed in the foregoing pages, we have classified our materials in three groups. Firstly, the anecdotes of Chaitanya's boyhood which were magnified into supernatural tales and sometimes owed their existence to the fancy of the pious people who wanted to prove him to be an incarnation of Vishnu. The most noteworthy works of this class are Murari Gupta's Chaitanya Charitam and the *karcha* or notes by Swarupa Damodara. The writers of standard biographies of Chaitanya—Brindabana Das, Krishna Das Kaviraj and Lochana Das—have put implicit faith in these tales and added to them what they themselves heard from country people, while describing the Master's boyhood and early youth before *Sanyas*, spent at Nadia. In this period of his life the supernatural element predominates in his memoirs, due to an ardent desire on the part of his biographers to make him an Avatar in popular estimation. These tales went on increasing as no one at Nadia and in the adjacent locality had the heart or wish to contradict them for they were meant for the glorification of Chaitanya. On the other hand there was a natural tendency in all of them to credit miracles which would raise Chaitanya to the level of Krishna.

<small>The Nadia legends.</small>

Secondly, the description of the latter part of the Master's life is contained chiefly in the Chaitanya Charitamrita. Here the supernatural element is not at all very prominent but we find Chaitanya in these accounts sometimes reduced to a product of the theological school that latterly arose with its centre in Brindaban, having established theories of incarnation and their necessary corrolaries, which Chaitanya, had he lived at the time, could not have possibly

<small>Vaishava theology of a later school attributed to Chaitanya.</small>

SUMMARY

endorsed. But inspite of this shortcoming the Chaitanya Charitamrita is the most complete and authoritative biography of Chaitanya.

And all these works bearing, as they do, the stamp of a particular theological school of the Vaishnab community, have a special claim to the regard of historical students, as they unfold the various stages of progressive Vaishnavism in Bengal. And let me repeat here that prominent amongst them is the Chaitanya Charitamrita, which for its exposition of Vaishnab Philosophy is perhaps unmatched in the world's theological literature of the 16th century. The Chaitanya Chandrodaya of Kavi Karnapur and Chaitanya Bhagavata of Brindaban Das are both monumental works which should be given a place in the field of Vaishnab theology, next only to Chaitanya Charitamrita.

Thirdly, we have a few works, and it is unfortunate that there are not too many good works of this kind, which do not strictly belong to the Vaishnab school and which do not show allegiance to the rules and canons of any particular theological section. Govinda Das's *karcha* and Jayananda's Chaitanya Mangal are the two books that breathe an air of freedom from convention, and on account of their presenting us with new angles of vision, have a special attraction. It is Jayananda's Chaitanya Mangal, as has been already stated, that has given us the information

<small>Govinda and Jayananda.</small>

that Chaitanya passed away from this earth, being attacked by an inflammatory fever due to a hurt he received on his right foot while dancing at Puri during the Car festivities. All other authors are silent on this point, and their silence lends an indirect support to the popular legend that Chaitanya passed into the image of Jagannath, as his corporal body consisted merely of spirit. There is another tradition current, no doubt created by the priests of the rival temple of Gopinath, associating the same legend with the image of the latter god. One author seems to indicate that this legend is true by saying " we lost him in the temple of Gopinath." When there was nothing to guide us to truth on this point one man at least was found speaking what appears obviously as a fact. Regarding the notes of Govinda Das, we consider them the most reliable though they record events of the Master's life for the brief period of two years only. Though this author was called an illiterate fool by his wife Sashimukhi, we find him possessed of a superior literary talent, developed no doubt by the impetus he received from association with the Master. He is so unassuming that nowhere does he assert himself with his views in the name of Vaisnava religion and following Chaitanya with dog-like fidelity, as he did, he recorded his trances and sayings in life-like vividness. He has not one word to say about his own high character, though from incidental

SUMMARY

remarks we find that he was a conqueror of the flesh like a true Yogi and devoted to the Master as a very few of his followers have ever been. Govinda Das even tries to expose himself to ridicule by showing himself to be a glutton, but one who carefully reads his pages will find him a most instructive companion,—a true guide to the Bengali Vaishnava life of the 16th century.

(I) BIBLIOGRAPHY

For presenting a memoir of Chaitanya in the following pages, I have, among other books, made a thorough historical study of the following old works :—

1. Songs of Narahari, Govinda Ghos, Basu Ghos, Gopala Basu, Narahari Sarkar, Parameswar Das, Nayanananda, Raisekhar and others.
2. *Karcha* by Govinda Das (1509 to 1511 A.D.)
3. Chaitanya Charit by Murari Gupta.
4. Chaitanya Chandrodaya Nataka, and its translation into metrical Bengali by Premadas.
5. Svarupa Damodar's notes.
6. Chaitanya Bhagavata by Brindabana Das.
7. Chaitanya Mangala by Jayananda.
8. Chaitanya Mangala by Lochana Das.
9. Chaitanya Charitamrita by Krishna Das.

10. Balya Lila Sutra by Lauria Krishna Das.
11. Advaita Prakasa by Isana Nagara.
12. Prembilasa by Nityananda Das.
13. Bhaktiratnakara by Narahari Chakrabarti.
14. Narottambilasa by Narahari Chakrabarti.
15. Abhirama Lilamrita.
16. Anuraga Valli.

CHAPTER III

ANCESTRY, BIRTH AND CHILDHOOD

Chaitanya's father Jagannatha Misra removed from Dakha Daksin, a village in the district of Sylhet (Jaypur of the same district according to Jayananda) and settled at Nadia, when he was about 25 years old. This must have taken place at about 1460 A.D.[1] We have references in many works to his marriage at Nadia with Sachi Devi—the accomplished daughter of Nilambara Chakrabarti. He had, therefore, settled at Nadia prior to his marriage. Nilambara Chakrabarti himself was originally a Brahmin of Sylhet. It appears that he and Jagannatha Misra came down and settled at Nadia about the same time. The chief object of these people of Eastern countries for coming to Nadia was of course the completion of their education; for Nadia was one of the greatest seats of learning in India during this period. Says Brindabana Das, "There is no end of scholars in this town. Hundreds of professors and students bathe in the Ganges every day. The enthusiasm

Nadia, a seat of learning.

---

[1] Mr. Underwood in an article in the Calcutta Review says that Sachi Devi was 67 years old in 1486 when Chaitanya was born. For not giving us any reference as to his authority—and for some anomalies which it involves we cannot accept this statement of Sachi Devi's age to be true.

for learning is so great that even a boy will come forward to match his lance with veteran professors."[1] We all know that the school of logic founded there by Basudeva Sarbabhaum and latterly developed and richly contributed to by Raghunatha Siromani attracted pupils to this academic centre from all parts of India. In jurisprudence, the word of Raghunandana who wrote his famous *Astavingsati Tatva* about this time has become the one law for all people of Bengal.

Jagannatha Misra and Nilambara Chakrabarti as also many other scholars of Sylhet were no doubt attracted to Nadia as students for receiving academic laurels from this reputed field of learning. The reason of their finally settling at Nadia was, however, different. Says Jayananda referring to this point :—" There were famine and drought of a terrible kind in many parts of the district of Sylhet at this time. The political condition of the country had grown very unsafe ; robbery and theft had become the order of the day. People fled to different countries at this juncture. Nilambara Chakrabarti and Jagannatha Misra left their native villages and settled at Nadia at this time ; for, in the district of Sylhet no good and honest man could stay for a moment."[2]

Famine in Sylhet.

---

[1] Chaitanya Bhagavata, Adi Kanda.
[2] Chaitanya Mangala by Jayananda,

UPENDRA MISRA

Jagannatha Misra's ancestor Madhukara Misra, a Vaidic Brahmin of Batsayana Gotra, was originally an inhabitant of Jajpur in Orissa. Jayananda tells us that he too had left his native city, for Raja Bhramarabara the king of Orissa, had made it impossible for honest Brahmin folk to live at Jajpur by his capricious administration. Madhukara Misra left his native country about the year 1440.

From Jajpur to Sylhet.

I have appended a table showing the pedigree of Chaitanya in my work "Chaitanya and His Companions" (p. 218). This pedigree was collected from some standard works of the Vaishnavas. Jayananda also gives a pedigree in which he says that Janardana was the grandfather of Chaitanya; but the former was his uncle. In all standard works we find Upendra Misra to be Chaitanya's grand-father. There could be possibly no mistake about the name of Jagannatha Misra's father in such well-known Vaishnava biographies as Chaitanya Bhagavata and Chaitanya Charitamrita. In respect of the pedigree it is always safe to trust the version supplied by the orthodox community; for they were more in touch with the relations of the leaders of their sect than lay men. So the pedigree found in Jayananda's book cannot be relied upon.

Jagannatha Misra was junior by some years to Advaita Acharyya who was born in 1434 A.D.

We find the Misra bowing down before Advaita as a younger Brahmin does to another older than himself. Chaitanya was the last of the 8 issues (9, according to Jayananda) that Jagannatha Misra had by Sachi Devi. Taking Jagannatha to be 48 years old (Advaita was at the time 52) at the time of Chaitanya's birth, we may approximately accept the year 1435 as the date of Jagannatha Misra's birth. We are quite confident that the date is not very far from the actual year.

<small>Jagannatha born about 1435 A.D.</small>

It is stated by all authorities that Jagannatha Misra was a scholar of some renown at Nadia. He had obtained the title of *Purandara* for his learning. But he was a poor man. He once said to his wife "Just see, though I am a scholar I have no money." When Chaitanya neglected his duties as professor owing to his great emotional sentiments and love for God, his old teacher Gangadas reproached him in this way:[1] "it is not proper that you should neglect these

<small>Jagannatha, a learned scholar.</small>

---

[1] Chaitanya Bhagavata, Adi.

" মাতামহ যার চক্রবর্ত্তী নীলাম্বর।
বাপ যার জগন্নাথ মিশ্র পুরন্দর॥
উভয় কুলেতে মূর্খ নাহিক তোমার।
তুমিহ পরম যোগ্য ব্যাখ্যাতে টীকার॥
অধ্যয়ন ছাড়িলে সে যদি ভক্তি হয়।
বাপ পিতামহ কি তোমার ভক্ত নয়॥"

duties. Just remember your father Jagannatha Misra and your grand-father (on mother's side) Nilambara Chakrabarti. They were all learned men. Born of this illustrious family, why should you behave in such an unbecoming manner? If for seeking God, learning is to be eschewed, were not your father and grand-father learned and religious at the same time?" Murari's Chaitanya Charita and Kavikarnapura's Chaitanya Chandrodaya also refer to the great learning of Jagannatha Misra.

But a more positive information is at hand. A copy of the Adiparva of the Sanskrit Mahabharata written in Jagannatha Misra's own hand bearing his signature and the date of copying, is in the possession of Mahamahopadhyaya Ajitanatha Nayaratna of Nadia. The date is Saka 1390 (1468 A.D.) or 17 years before the birth of Chaitanya. The handwriting is beautiful and bold and looks like a thing of yesterday; the ink is bright and its lustre has not diminished after 450 years. The copy is free from errors, and this is a thing not too often found in the copies of Sanskrit works. Curiously, very few Bengalis have any knowledge of the existence of this rare and precious manuscript. A few years ago Lord Carmichael paid a visit to the Pandit's house at Nadia with the object of seeing this sacred book.

Mahabharata copied by Jagannatha in 1468 A.D.

---

[1] Chaitanya Bhagavata, Adi, p. 149. A. G.'s Edition.

This copy of the Mahabharata substantiates the statement made by biographers that Jagannatha Misra was thoroughly learned in Sanskrit; not a single grammatical error or spelling mistake is met with in this large volume. Such mistakes are found in abundance in the ordinary copies of Sanskrit works.

Jagannatha Misra was contented with his poverty. His scholarship only confirmed him in his faith in the fairness of divine dispensation and made him humble and meek. His eldest son Bisvarupa, born in 1465 A.D., adopted the vow of *Sanyasa* when 16 years old and left him for good. It was on his marriage day, that the boy thought that it was not the right thing to marry as he had resolved to pursue a high religious ideal.

The dread of the parents. But he ventured not openly to stand against the wishes of his parents. He crossed the Ganges in the night with the sound of drums and other musical instruments at his house still ringing in his ears. He went far away after having taken the vow of *Sanyasa* but no one yet knows where and how he lived and died. We know, however, that on his joining the order of Sanyasis he took the name of Sankararanya Puri. The feeling of grief that this occasion gave rise to may be easily conceived. Sachi Devi was completely overpowered by her sorrows, but Jagannatha Misra was stern as Job of the Old Testament. He said in almost the very language of the Jewish saint "Krishna has given and Krishna has taken. May his will be fulfilled." Though he took this philosophical view of life like Job, his firmness of character gave way for a time. And we can well sympathise with this miserable Brahmin who had to fight continually with an untoward fate. Seven daughters had died; the promising son who was to be the supporter of his parents in old age was lost for ever, yet he continued in his resigned faith to suffer without a murmur. But when Chaitanya only five years old had acquired the alphabet within two or three days and showed a wonderful cleverness, the father said "no, he must not go to school any more." The medieval learning inspired young learners with monkish ideas of renunciation and asceticism. Jagannatha Misra said to Sachi Devi " if this boy becomes a scholar, he will feel a contempt for worldly pleasures and leave home as a Sanyasi, it is no good educating him. Let him be illiterate, but let him remain at home." Chaitanya grew to be a wild boy being thus freed from the hands of the village schoolmaster. He began to do all wicked things in the company of the mischief-making imps of the locality. This became intolerable to a degree, and the honest neighbours who had to suffer for the child's wicked acts appeared in a body to Jagannatha Misra and requested him not to allow the child to go astray in that way but to send him to a school. They all reproved him for his foolish fears that education would make his boy turn a Sanyasi. Jagannatha Misra felt the force of their argument and sent young Chaitanya to school again. Jagannatha died of fever in 1506 A.D. when Chaitanya was only 20 and had not yet completed his education. Sachi Devi, as has been already said, was a daughter of Nilambara Chakrabarti, originally a native of Sylhet. Govinda Karmakar describes her as "of a quiet temperament and of a very short stature." As a doting mother she had a great dread for Advaita Acharyya's teachings to which, she imagined, her young sons listened with attention and confidence. He had no doubt imparted some of his philosophical views to Bisvarupa, Chaitanya's elder brother, and Sachi held him responsible for turning the head of Chaitanya also. We find her openly charging Adwaita with putting the idea of *Sanyasa* in the head of her son Biswarup. " Bright as the moon," she said, "was that boy of mine, and Advaita's council turned him out from home as Sanyasi. And not satisfied with doing so he is now bent on leading astray this young boy of mine and ruining all happiness of my life. The lad spends his whole time with the old man and never looks at my

<small>Advaita Acharyya held responsible by the mother.</small>

daughter-in-law."[1] Then with a pun on the word Advaita (lit. professing the pantheistic faith) she said "who calls him Adaitya? He should rather be called a Daitya" (lit. a demon) and she habitually called the veteran scholar by the latter name. It is related in the Chaitanya Bhagavata, Bhaktiratnakara and other books that she was afterwards made to apologise to Advaita for doing so.

Her quietness of temperament, referred to in Govinda Das's *karcha*, is proved by the fact that she finally gave her permission to Chaitanya to follow his resolve of taking *Sanyasa*, however much she suffered for it. She was a very sensible woman and when Chaitanya eloquently described what Indian mothers had suffered in the past for righteousness and truth,—how Kausalya had given permission to Rama for going to the forest and how Aditi and Daivaki had made their natural feelings of love and affection subservient to their sense of duty when their sons

---

[1] "অদ্বৈত সে মোর পুত্র করিল বাহির"
ছাড়িয়া সংসার সুখ প্রভু বিশ্বস্তর।
লক্ষ্মী পরিহরি থাকে অদ্বৈতের ঘর॥
না রহে গৃহেতে পুত্র হেন দেখি আই।
এহো পুত্র নিল মোর আচার্য্য গোঁসাই।
সেই দুঃখে সবে এই বলিলেন আই
কে বলে অদ্বৈত, দৈত্য এ বড় গোঁসাই;
চন্দ্র সম এক পুত্র করিয়া বাহির
এহো পুত্র ঘরে না রাখিল করি স্থির।"

Chai. Bha., p. 319.

were called away from them, she could not resist the noble appeal though she had argued with him for a while saying "what is that religion that condones cruelty to parents? You want to explain to the world the truth of religion. How do you think yourself fit for doing so when you fail to do your duties to your old mother?"[1] Though she was persuaded to give the permission at last, she became thoroughly overcome by grief for the time being. The Chaitanya Bhagavata says, she fasted for twelve days after Chaitanya had left Nadia. The interview between Chaitanya and his mother shortly after the former's *Sanyasa* at Santipur is one of the most pathetic episodes described in his biographies. At her house deserted by Chaitanya she lived a wretched life of sorrow. One day we find her weeping over a particular meal that she had prepared to be served to the family-god. She wept and said: "He liked this sort of meal. Who is there now left to eat it now?"

---

[1] " ধর্ম্ম বুঝাইতে যদি তোর অবতার ।
জননী ছাড়িবা ধর্ম্ম কোন বা বিচার ॥
তুমি ধর্ম্মময় যদি জননী ছাড়িবা ।
কেমতে জগতে তুমি ধর্ম্ম বুঝাইবা ॥
বিবর্ণ হইলা শচী অস্থি চর্ম্ম সার ।
শোকাকুলী দেবী কিছু না করে আহার ॥"

Chai. Bha., p. 389,

CHAPTER IV

BIRTH AND BOYISH FRIVOLITIES, EDUCATION, AND FOUNDING OF A *TOL*. THE DEFEAT OF THE SCHOLAR KESAVA KASMIRI

Birth and Boyish Frivolities.

Chaitanya, according to all Vaishnava biographers and historians, was born on the full moon day of Falgun, 1407 Saka, corresponding to the 18th February, 1486, at 6 P.M. There was a lunar eclipse at the time, and just when the planet came out free, bright in its full majesty, and the people as usual in this country after an eclipse, cried aloud God's name on all sides, Chaitanya came to the world amidst this general jubilation and recitation of the holy name. According to Jayananda the nurse who took charge of the baby was one Narayani. It is stated in the several standard biographies that Sita, the wife of Advaitacharyya, and Malini, the wife of Sribasa, paid a visit to the house and presented the baby with many ornaments on the 6th day of its birth.

<small>Birth.</small>

The boy was given the name of Nimai. The biographers differ as to the significance of the name. One of them says that as Sachi's children were generally very short-lived, this humble name was given to ward off all evil influences;

<small>The origin of the name Nimāi.</small>

for death or witches might not take notice of one who was called by such a humble name. According to another the baby got fever and the mother was advised to keep it under a Nim tree for some time, as the air that passed through Nim leaves acted as a cure in fever cases. Being placed under the Nim tree he was called Nimai. On the 20th day of his birth the boy was given a dignified classical name, *viz.*—Bisvambhara or 'the nourisher of the universe.'

Nimai, as he was generally called in his early years, often went to the house of Advaitacharyya to call back his brother Bisvarupa who used to receive his lessons from that veteran scholar. Nimai was only five years old at the time and ran ahead of his elder brother who was then a lad of sixteen and led him homeward by holding the edge of his *dhuti*. This picture of the boy is sketched by Brindaban Das in a charming language.

We find Nimai sometimes carrying out small orders of Srivasa who was then already an old man. But more often do we find him doing all kinds of mischievous things that ever a boy of five did. But how far the descriptions of his boyish pranks are genuine and how far they are a repetition of the stories about Krishna, attributed to him for establishing his identity with that god, cannot be ascertained. For if

The childish pranks.

Krishna followed the footprints of the birds on sand or in his infant freaks stole butter and milk from neighbours' houses, there is no reason why other children before or after him would not do the same thing. But excluding all these little acts which savour of the Bhagavata, we may take many others related of him as unquestionably true. We find Nimai entering temples in the evening and for a mere fun putting out their lights to the extreme irritation of the priests. The pious Brahmins sat on the banks of the Ganges with closed eyes in a prayerful attitude, and Nimai suddenly came, sprinkled water on their faces and disappeared as suddenly as he came. Sometimes a Brahmin stood in the Ganges in knee-deep water and said his prayers; the little boy plunged into the water and carried the man forcibly by one of his legs. Sometimes he threw water into the ear-hole of an urchin of the same age; and at others sprang suddenly on the shoulders of a man and sitting between them declared himself to be the great god Siva. Here did a Brahmin with a copy of the Gita in his hand shut his eyes meditating on the holy text, the boy from behind snatched the book and fled. The little girls who came to bathe in the Ganges had similar treatments from the boy. He put the thorny *okra* seeds on their heads from which it became difficult to extricate their hair and they went in a body to Sachi and complained of her son's wicked acts. One said, "Look here mother, he wants to marry me!" Nimai was only five years old at the time! It was a frequent thing for the young chap to hide himself in a room and give notice of his presence by mimicking the sound of the cuckoo. The plays generally played by Nimai and his comrades were the familiar *geru* play and the monkey play in which the boys showed their expertness by jumping or standing on one leg. The swimming in the Ballala Sagara was one of the favourite sports. Nimai is described at this age as a very handsome lad with a red-coloured *dhuti* on and three braids of hair containing five small gold *jhapas* (pendants) that added grace to his lovely face. One day he placed himself amidst unclean refuses in a drain which a Brahmin would not touch and when reproved by his mother, said "Mother I am an illiterate fool, what do I know of what is clean or unclean? I do not share your prejudices. All places are alike to me." His abundant boyish energies found their expression chiefly in mimicry and jokes, to one of which I have already referred. We have already mentioned how he stood one day behind the veteran scholar Murari and moved his head and hands exactly like the latter, engaged in an animated discussion on some learned subject with another scholar.

NIMAI—AS A STUDENT

Education.

When Jagannatha Misra was persuaded by his neighbours to put Nimai in some school for reforming his conduct, the first tutor appointed for him was Visnu Pandit from whom he learned the alphabet. He read elementary Sanskrit and vernacular with another teacher named Sudarsana and completed his education in the *tol* of Pandit Gangadas, a very learned professor.[1] We learn from a song by Narahari who knew Nimai from his childhood, that in this *tol* he not only obtained a thorough mastery of Sanskrit but acquired a respectable knowledge of Pali.[2]

His devotion to books was great. Says Brindabana Das "he always reads, even when going to bathe or sleep or to dine, one would see a book in his hands. He writes commentaries on grammar himself. What he reads he so thoroughly masters that no one can hold his own when arguing with him. He beats his opponent and establishes a logical proposition with great cleverness, and then, to the wonder of his fellow-students, upsets it himself and establishes the quite opposite theory formerly held by his rival." But though he grew to be such a fine scholar,

In the *tol*.

---

[1] Jayananda's Chaitanya Mangala.
[2] Gaura Pada Tarangini.

his boyish excesses and faults did not cease. What could be more appalling to a veteran professor like Gangadas than the fact that his pupil gave the name of Gangadas to a dog and kept it constantly with him and called it aloud by the name of the professor.[1] The young lad proudly told the old and respectable scholar and physician Murari, that grammar was too complicated a subject for a physician; it would be far better if that scholar would mind his herbs and plants and never trouble himself with Sanskrit grammar.[2] He mimiced and ridiculed the people of Sylhet who resided then at Nadia, without waiting to listen to their just allegation that his own father and mother had been born in Sylhet and that it was extremely ridiculous on his part to be peacocked up as a coqney and to mock at the people of his own native place where the family had lived for generations. Nimai, however, would not wait to argue with them but continue his mimicing so that some of them came forward to assault him with sticks, but the lad took to his heels and could not be overtaken; so some of them ran to the Kazi to lodge a complaint. Old scholars of good repute would shun the path if they saw Nimai coming, for they were afraid of an encounter with him and of the wild pranks

---

[1] Chaitanya Mangala by Jayananda.
[2] Chaitanya Bhagavata, Adi.

and jests which the young scholar was sure to fling at them as a sequel to his triumph after a debate. He had even the audacity of finding fault with a verse of Isvara Puri, the great apostle and saint, and had once said point blank that there were grammatical mistakes in his exposition of the holy texts.

His nature, wild in excessive energy, but transparent and pure as ice, had some restraint. Chaitanya Bhagavata says what is repeated in all biographies,—he did not even do so much as glance at any woman; if he happened to meet one of them in the way he would turn aside and avoid her. He had teased the little girls when only five years old, but when he came of age he scrupulously avoided all contact with women.

While Nimai was still studying in the *tol* of Gangadas, Jagannatha Misra died. It is related in the Chaitanya Mangala by Jayananda that Chaitanya was engaged in copying a text at the house of Gangadas when Haridas reported to him that his father was dying. Shortly after he completed his education and was given the title of 'Vidyasagara'—the ocean of learning. So great was his reputation for scholarship that at that tender age when he had just passed his teens he established a *tol* and began to teach higher subjects to his students.

The founding of a Tol.

This *tol* was founded by the munificence of Mukunda Sanjaya at Vidyanagar, one of the wards of Nadia. Chaitanya Bhagavata says that Nimai Pandit himself took the charge of the education of Mukunda Sanjay's son Basudeva. His nature was still full of boyish frivolities. We find him still matching his lance with Murari Gupta whom he found a quite formidable opponent in learned discussions. None could defeat the other, and this was no small compliment to the young pandit, for Murari was an acknowledged scholar, advanced in years and commanded great respect. Sometimes we find Nimai Pandit trying to draw out Mukunda, another fine scholar and singer, from his study and hold discussions with him. But Mukunda always tried to avoid Nimai for he dreaded the sceptical views of the young scholar. Nimai did not like his conduct at all, and one day told Govinda Ghosh "What does Mukunda find in these Vaishnava scriptures that he so diligently studies them? He does not care to master the science of grammar as I do." Isvara Puri, the great Vaishnava apostle, already mentioned by me, paid a visit to Nadia about this time. He stayed for a few months in the house of Gopinath Acharyya and people

A sneerer of religion.

THE PRANKS 117

assembled in crowds to see the holy man. Mukunda frequently called there and sang songs on Krishna. "As soon as Mukunda's sweet voice, trembling in emotion, was heard Isvara Puri lost all control over himself and passed into a trance" for he was a mystic and had God-vision. Nimai, from whom love for God was yet far away, strayed about Gopinatha's house, unable to leave the spot for some strange fascination, yet in his pride thinking himself to be superior to these men because of his learning. Among those men who had gathered round Isvara Puri and held him in great admiration was Gadadhara, who though a good scholar, cared more for religion than grammar or logic. This young scholar, target-like, frequently bore Nimai's attacks, for the latter often overwhelmed him with many naughty preblems of logic, demanding solutions of them on the spot. With an eye of jealousy did Nimai Pandit see that both Gadadhara and Mukunda had grown to be favourites of Isvara Puri. This was but quite natural, but for some reason or other Nimai did not like the situation. He also called on Isvara Puri now and then but that was more for the purpose of convincing him of his superiority as a scholar than for any other, and when Isvara Puri was one day, reading out to Gadadhara, his enthusiastic listener, a portion of his own Sanskrit work Krishna Lilamrita, Nimai arrogantly interrupted and said "the verb you use, Sir, is not *atmanepadi*."[1]

The people of Nadia delighted in the scholarship of young Nimai who was handsome in appearance and possessed of bright intelligence; but said some " God has given this lad attractive looks about and great scholarship but what is the use of all these as he is irreligious ?" One day we find Mukunda arguing with him in grammar, rhetoric and other subjects and expressing wonder at the all-round scholarship of our young prodigy. Brindavana Das follows the lines of the Bhagavata eulogising Krishna, and says in a glowing language "Scholars see him as a second Brihaspati, the heavenly sage ; women would fain have him for their lover and Yogis see in his person the signs that would mark him out in future as the emancipated one."

It appears that he wrote a commentary on grammar when he was reading in the *tol* of Gangadas. There is a reference to it in many of his biographies. When he had paid a visit to Eastern Bengal he found students reading his commentary, which was called 'Vidyasagara' after his own title. An incident is narrated in the Advaita Prakasa, the truth of which I cannot avow, that as a student he had written a logical

Commentaries on grammar and logic.

---

[1] Chaitanya Bhagabhata, Adi.

treatise and had kept it privately with him. One of his fellow students once said to him that he also had written a book on logic. Both showed their works to each other while crossing the Ganges in a ferry boat. So greatly was that young man struck with the superiority of Nimai's work that he said with a sad look to Nimai. "It was my dream, my friend, that I would shine in this branch of learning, but with such a powerful rival as yourself it seems to be a mere dream which I cannot think of realising." Nimai said "Take heart, my boy, I shall never be your rival in the field of logic." Saying so he threw away his own book into the Ganges. If this account is true, it shows that with all his fondness for display of learning and desire to defeat scholars in polemics, he had a deeper nature inspired by self-sacrifice which lay at that time hidden from people on account of his boyish frivolities.

The defeat of the Scholar Kesava Kasmiri.

An event happened about this time which made young Nimai one of the most prominent men of Nadia. A great scholar named Kesava Kasmiri came to Navadvip knowing that it was one of the principal centres of learning in India. Chaitanya Bhagavata says that this man had vanquished all scholars of the different

The invincible Kesava Kasmiri.

Indian schools of learning, such as, Tibet, Delhi, Benares, Guzrat, Kanchi, Telegu countries and Darbhanga. He had with him a large number of letters in which the pandits of these various centres had acknowledged his superiority as a scholar. He was dressed like a prince and came riding on an elephant with a large number of attendants. The veterans of Nadia pointed out to Nimai as the fit person to discuss learned subjects. For this young lad had achieved a notoriety by challenging every one to a free debate and prided in his talents and power of conducting a controversy.

Nimai received the great scholar with courtesy. The latter, however, held the youth in little regard as he was so young and taken to be a mere smatterer in grammar. Nimai asked the proud scholar to compose some *extempore* verses in praise of the Ganges on the banks of which they had been seated. Says Brindavana Das "As if a hundred clouds roared together, the cadence and grand music of the *extempore* verses filled every one with admiration—nay awe. Even Nimai's students were struck by the superior merit of the verses." The scholar said to Nimai Pandit, " You have only an elementary knowledge of grammar. How can it be expected that you will appreciate my verses in which there are so many excellent examples of figures of Poetics, of which you know so little?" Nimai, however, dissected the poem as a doctor does a corpse and showed that each line of the poem had at least one error from the standpoint of Poetics. In the first line was the word ভবাণীভর্তুঃ spotted with the fault called *Biruddhamati*. The next line furnished an instance of the fault *Kran.abhanga* in the word বিভবতি and in the word শ্রীলক্ষ্মী the fault *Punuruktabadabhasa* and so forth. The great scholar could not hold his own and, having been thoroughly humiliated, fled away.

'Lion of debate.'

The scholars of Nadia all assembled and gave Nimai the title of 'Badisingha' or 'the lion of debate' on this occasion. It is said that people held him with so much regard that even millionaires as they passed by him in palankins, would stop and bow to him and then resume their journey. Some referred to the old prophecy that a Brahmin of Nadia would be the king of Bengal "Who knows, he might be the same man?" Others said very justly, "We never saw a man so brilliant as Nimai Pandit."

CHAPTER V

MARRIAGE—TOUR IN EASTERN BENGAL—VISIT TO GAYA, RETURN TO HOME. TRANCES—CLOSING OF THE *TOL*, SANKIRTAN PARTIES—REFORMATION OF JAGAI AND MADHAI

Marriage.

Just before founding a *tol* of his own Nimai had married Laksmi, the beautiful daughter of Ballavacharyya of Nadia. Curiously Dr. MacNichol in his book on Indian Theism mistakes this man for the leader of the Ballavi sect who bore the same name. No Indian scholar would make such a mistake. Ballavacharya of Nadia—Nimai's father-in-law, and Ballavacharyya of Brindavana—the founder of the line of the Gokul Gosains were altogether two different persons. The marriage of Nimai with Laksmi, according to all accounts, took place by mutual selection. Nimai and Laksmi had often seen each other on the banks of the Ganges and conceived a liking mutually.

<small>Nimai in love with Laksmi.</small> Banamali Acharyya, a matchmaker, was appointed by Ballava to negotiate the marriage. But Sachi Devi rejected

BANAMALI—THE MATCH-MAKER

the proposal at once. She said to Banamali, "He is yet a boy and has not completed his education. He is, besides, fatherless. This is not at all the time for our thinking of his marriage. Help him by all means to complete his education." Dejected at this refusal Banamali was plodding his way homewards in slow steps when Nimai met him and heard the result of his interview with Sachi Devi. Nimai coming home said to her "What have you spoken to the Brahmin Banamali that he is so sad? Why did you not speak to him sweet words that would make him happy?"

The mother took the hint and understood that Nimai was willing to marry. She immediately sent for Banamali Acharyya and assented to the proposal. Ballavacharyya was a poor man and could not offer him a dowry. But the bride was fair and accomplished and the nuptial relation was based on mutual choice So they were happy. Owing to the reputation that Nimai had already established as a scholar at Nadia his earnings were now considerable, and according to all accounts he lived in moderate affluence. Govinda refers to the five beautiful and spacious huts that he had built on the banks of the Ganges. Like the Brahmin youths of well-to-do circumstances, Nimai used to wear the *Krishnakeli* cloth with fine black borders. He

He marries and lives happily at Nadia.

wore golden rings on his ears. His memoirs praise the beauty of his long curling hair scented with oil and washed with *amlaki*. A golden locket tied to a string of the same metal hanged on his breast and it was usual in that age to wear floral wreaths. This is his portrait as a professor of Nadia and the Nadia potters still make clay images of their beloved Nimai Pandit as such. They would never recognise him as a monk and ascetic that afterwards he became, implying his severance of all connections with Nadia.

Tour in Eastern Bengal.

As a Vaishnava he would never touch fish or meat. At his home excellent vegetable and milk-preparations were made by his mother. Govinda Karmakar gives us a menu of the daily food prepared by her, amongst which the *mocharghanta* and *sukta*, besides various preparations of milk, are emphasized as relished most. The *beta sak* often occurs in the description as inviting appetite by its sweet smell.

At the age of 21 Nimai paid a visit to Eastern Bengal. The object of the trip was to earn money, as the villages in those days visited by distinguished Brahmin professors used to contribute lump sums as honorarium to them. Chaitanya Bhagavata says that he visited various *tols* on the banks of the Padma, where he found students reading his commentary on Sanskrit Grammar. Lochan Das errs in the chronology of events and says that Nimai had converted hundreds of men to Vaishnava faith during his tour in Eastern Bengal. As yet he was innocent of all religious zeal, nay, people at that period of his life, regretted his sceptical tendencies. Jayananda in his memoir says that when Nimai visited Eastern Bengal there was a considerable number of Brahma-Kshatriyas there. Who were these Brahma-Ksatriyas? Were they of the caste of the Sen kings of Bengal?

Nimai's tour in Eastern Bengal according to Nityananda extended up to Assam but the last two and a half cantos of that author's metrical history which contain the account, are held as unreliable. The point, however, has not been finally decided. In this book we find Nimai visiting the villages of Nurpur, Subarnagram, Betal and Vitadia. The last named village was, it is said, a great centre of Sanskrit learning; and Nimai met there Loknath Lahiri whose mother, a daughter of Jayarama Chakrabarti hailed from Nadia. Loknatha's step-brother Purusottama took *sanyasa* and was known as Svarup Damodara—a name well-known in Vaishnava history. From Vitadia he came to his ancestral place Dhaka Dakshin in Sylhet, where his uncle and even his grand-father Upendra Misra, according to the account, still lived. It is said that here he made a fair copy of Markandeya Chandi for the use of his grand-father. For further details of these tour I refer my readers to pp. 225-26 of my Chaitanya and His Companions. The tradition current in the district of Faridpur is that Nimai Pandit visited the village of Kotalipar at this time. This village, as every one knows, is even now a seat of large Brahmin population. The authenticity of these pieces of information are called in question on the ground that it should be nobody's care to keep notes of his tour at that time, when Nimai had not achieved distinction as a religious leader. All that has been said with regard to this tour by subsequent writers is based on vague memories and traditions, and it is not improbable that some villages put in their names, without any sufficient ground, simply to heighten their importance; just as we find in the case of the Kirnahar people who have tried to associate their place with certain incidents of Chandi Das's life.

When taking leave of home, Nimai is said to have made over his sacred thread to his wife Laksmi to be preserved as a token. The wife had behaved exceedingly well as we find in Murari's Chaitanya Charitam, and Sachi Devi was well pleased with her. But the young wife was not destined to live long. She was beaten

LAKSMI'S DEATH

on a toe of her right foot by a snake and died within a few hours, though all the *Ojhas* of the locality expert in curing snake bites, had been called to her aid. Before her death, the sacred thread of Nimai was put on her breast at her wish.

<small>Laksmi dies of snake-bite.</small>

Jayananda says that Laksmi, herself a good painter, had drawn a picture of Nimai on a canvas framed with wood. With her eyes fixed on this picture and regretting the absence of her husband -from home to her friend Chitralata she breathed her last. Nimai was just on his way back when this event happened.

Return to home.

He returned with considerable money which was the honorarium he had received, and was in a jovial spirit. He met Gadadhara and others when he was coming home, and mimicked to them the accents of East Bengal men. But at his house he found his mother weeping. He could immediately feel that there had been something wrong with his wife. He showed a remarkable calmness and advised his mother not to regret that which could not be retrieved. But from that time forward none saw him indulging in those frivolities which had been his wont. His deeper nature was roused presaging the advent of the most memorable epoch of his life.

Nimai sought his mother's permission to go to Gaya for visiting the shrine. He said that for the good of the spirit of his father, *pinda* offerings should be made to the lotus feet of Visnu at the place. But his mother before granting the permission got him married again to Bisnupriya, a daughter of the famous Pandit Sanatana of Nadia. Nimai was not at all willing to marry. It appears that without waiting for his assent Sachi Devi with the help of Kasinatha Ghatak, a matchmaker, had already negotiated the marriage and Sanatana was engaged in making preparations for the ceremony on a large scale, aided by his friend Buddhimanta Khan. But when the report of the proposed marriage reached Nimai's ears he said with vexation "what marriage are you speaking of? whose marriage? I do not know anything." The mother was very sorry and sent word to Sanatana that all preparations should be stopped as her son was not willing. But Nimai afterwards repented his conduct, as much pain and worry were not only caused to his mother, but to Sanatana and his family who had already spent much money for preparations. Nimai called Kasinatha Ghatak to him and said, "Go and tell my mother that I cannot go against her wishes. How can I undo what she

Nimai at first rejects the proposal of marriage and yields afterwards.

has already done?" The marriage was thus performed with great *eclat*.

Immediately after marriage Nimai Pandit started for Gaya with some pious pilgrims bound for that shrine. At a place called Mandar he got fever and drank water touched by some Brahmin's feet which, it is said, cured him of his illness. He did not speak much. A turning point had come in his life. One given to prolific speaking and frivolities had become a good quiet boy and his companions were all struck by this change. Entering Gaya he saw Ishwara Puri, that saint and scholar whom he had so often ridiculed. He longed for a sight of him. Never did Ishwara Puri appear in such a light to the young scholar. Chaitanya in great emotion held him close to his breast and said "My visit to Gaya is a great success. I have seen you, Master. You are the holiest of shrines. If offering *pindas* to the spirit of my forefathers would save their souls, a mere sight of you would do so a hundred times more. Gaya and all the shrines put together have not that sanctity which you have." He trembled in great emotion as he said this; for the great scholar, the haughty youth of Nadia, did no longer exist, and in his place, behold a young Brahmin, low and humble, yielding to the emotions which faith brings in.

In the temple he found priests offering flowers and scents to the Lotus feet of Vishnu. They were singing the praises of the Feet in the language of devotion and reverence. Nimai heard it recited that from the divine Feet flowed the Ganges to save humanity from sin;—it was under these Feet that Vali, the king proud of his liberality, was humiliated;—sages and Rishis have contemplated the Lotus Feet of Vishnu from age to age. The recitation of the beautiful Sanskrit *slokas* gave rise to strange emotions in Nimai's mind. He saw, as it were, the whole world bending low before the Lotus Feet, the emblem of divine power and love. He could no longer bear to hear the sweet recitation, but wept and fell senseless under the spell of an overpowering emotion.

Trances.

The companions of Nimai thought that all these were but the after-effects of the fever from which he had recently recovered. He had grown weak and nervous and they tended him with care, but when he recovered his senses, he said, "Oh Krishna, my father, where art Thou? I thought I had found Thee, but Thou art not now with me." Saying this he recited some Sanskrit verses and began to cry vehemently. He told his fellow-pilgrims to return home. "Think of me as one lost. I have no other home than the

Brinda-groves. Thither shall I go to seek my Krishna."

As one delirious in high fever he behaved all the way back, and it was with great difficulty that his companions brought him home. At Kumarhatta he stopped. Ishwara Puri had returned to this place, which was his native village. Nimai partook of the food, cooked by Ishwara Puri, and wept and said that he was blessed. When about to leave Kumarhatta he took a handful of dust from the ground in his hand and tied it with the edge of his *dhuti*. "This dust," he said, "is sacred, because Ishwara Puri, the saint, was born here. This dust is as dear to me as all my wealth, as my life itself." As he said so he wept and fainted again in great emotion.

Nadia had sent the proudest and haughtiest of her young scholars as a pilgrim to Gaya. But he returned as a mad man, whose handsome figure was besmeared with dust and whose eyes stared in a strange manner shedding incessant tears. His companions came one by one and were dismayed to see his condition. To Gadadhara and others he said, "Hear my friends, I have seen a sight at Gaya—the most wonderful thing that human eyes ever beheld. Stop, I shall tell you what I saw." But at this stage he trembled in emotion reclining on the arms of Sriman Pandit and fell senseless, shedding tears which would not stop. He could not tell what he had seen. His attempts to do so brought on a trance.

Poor Sachi Devi was in great fright. People came in crowds to see him and all of them said that it was madness; the physicians prescribed *shivadi ghrita* and some medicated oil. In order to divert his mind Sachi made the beautiful Vishnupriya sit near him, but Nimai did not care to glance at his bride. He recited Sanskrit verses and always wept occasionally bursting into exclamations, such as, "Oh Krishna, where art thou?" Lochana Das describes his condition at this stage, "One always finds him prostrate on the ground, weeping. At noon-day he asks what time of night it is. With joined hands he bows to some one; and then recites the name of Krishna with tears." Jayananda says "He does not wear his usual apparel, nor perfume himself with sandal as was his wont.

<small>Lost to the world.</small>

The curling hair is all uncared for. His golden rings and lockets he has thrown away and he walks in slow careless steps absorbed in something unknown, when Sachi Devi calls him aloud from behind he does not pay any heed to her. The costly couch is there, but he sleeps on the bare ground. The evening and morning prayers and worship with the *tulshi* leaves he has eschewed, acting as one who is lost to this world."

They all discovered symptoms of lunacy in Nimai—the physicians and all, especially the sympathetic women-folk, who said to Sachi "Why do you seem to be yet uncertain about his malady? Know definitely that it is a case of lunacy, bind him hand and foot, and keep him under proper treatment." But the band of Vaishnabs headed by Adwaitacharya, who often met at the house of Sribasa, thought it might be something other than lunacy. No one had yet asked Nimai why he behaved in that way, excepting Sriman Pandit, a Vaishnab, who having put the question to Nimai, received this answer from him " I shall to-morrow pay a visit to the house of Suklambar Brahmachari and fully state my case to you."

Nimai taken for a mad man.

Next morning in the house of Sribasa all Vaishnabs met as usual to pluck flowers for worship; for in that historic courtyard were rows of *kunda* plants which supplied their treasures of beautiful white flowers in all seasons. There the Vaishnabs, as they gathered flowers in small cane-baskets, talked about the condition of Nimai. One said "On the barest reference to Gaya he bursts into tears and faints. What is the reason of this madness, if it be so indeed?"

Sriman Pandit said, "This evening by the wish of Nimai all of us should meet at the house of Suklambara where he has promised to speak out his mind."

Just when this conversation was going on, a man came to Sribasa with a message from Sachi Devi that she was in great distress as her son had gone off his head. Sribasa forthwith went to Nimai's house and Sachi began to weep bitterly. But Sribasa said " I shall privately see Nimai and find out if it is really madness or not." And Sribasa entered the room where Nimai sat all alone.

They had a long talk and when Sribasa came out from the room, his own eyes were full of tears. He said to Sachi that her son was a god ; he had brought such spiritual treasure from Gaya that she should thank God for it.

<small>A close interview; Sribasa's verdict.</small>

He returned to his comrades to say that he had beheld what he had only read of in the sacred Scriptures. Nimai was a second Suka or Prahlad. " He has seen the Unseen. He cannot for a moment forget what he has seen. It is a bliss to behold his great love."

Sachi had great confidence in Sribasa and felt reassured. Medical treatment of her son was given up. Nimai in the course of his conversation with Sribasa had said " You have heard all; say if I am mad " to which Sribasa had replied " If you are mad, we all covet a bit of such madness. It will at once sanctify our lives." And Chaitanya said " If you too, Sribasa, had joined these people and called me mad I would have drowned myself in the Ganges." It is just the same sort of thing that we read of Mahomet. When the prophet related all the miracles he had seen to Khadija, and besides told her that people called him mad, she said " I can disbelieve heaven and earth but not you." And Mahomet took heart at her words, and she became the first of his disciples.

The closing of the tol.

It was in a place called Kanaier Natsala that the first vision of God had first dawned on his soul. " Some one plays on the flute calling me. It is the most wonderful thing I have ever seen "—said he to the Vaishnabs. But he had to attend his *tol*. During the period of his absence from Nadia his pupils would not read with any other professor. In the court-yard attached to the temple of Mukunda Sanjoy, the *tol* sat as usual. The professor came, but when he was teaching grammar, he spoke of *bhakti*. In explaining the derivation of words he said that the universe was derived from God. The students laughed and said that all this was due to something wrong in the head of the *pandit*. They applied to Gangadas Pandit who was Nimai's tutor, and told him that they were

<small>How the professor did his duty of teaching.</small>

in great distress as their professor would not teach them any science but continually discoursed on spiritual devotion. The old teacher called on Nimai and reprimanded him saying " Why should you give up teaching your students ? Your father Jagannatha Misra was a great scholar and your grand-father Nilambar was also reputed for learning. They were both pious men. Both on your father's side and mother's side there is no one who did not attain high reputation as a scholar. Do you want to say, Nimai, that purity of soul and devotion are not compatible with study ? How, then, were your father and grandfather pious and learned at the same time ? You are yourself a great scholar. Why should you behave in this way ? " Nimai told him that from that day he would pay attention to his work and that his old professor would no more have any occasion to find fault with him. The next day he attends *tol* and goes on vigorously with giving notes on grammar till evening. But he suddenly hears Ratnagarbha, a friend of his father, reciting some *slokas* from the Bhagavata and he loses all control over himself, and weeping, passes into a trance. Coming to his senses he runs to meet Ratnagarbha and says " What you have recited, is so sweet, say it again." And then he passes again into a trance and mistakes all objects of senses for his Krishna. Thus his proper professional work as professor was continually interrupted.

"Krishna is my father and mother; and all of you, I pray on my knees, sing his praises." Saying so he fervently speaks on God's love and discourses on spiritual philosophy. But he was a teacher of grammar and rhetoric. However highly the students appreciated his devotional fervour they justly remarked that it was not that which they wanted to hear from their professor at school. "All that you say, Pandit, is very right, but what about our text-books"— they said. Still for 10 days more he continued his lectures. They looked with wonder on his fervent faith; they were charmed by his most engaging trances. It seemed to them as if a Suka or Prahlad, a Narada or Vyas had assumed mortal shape again to redeem fallen humanity by teaching devotion to God. But they were justified in complaining that they had made no progress whatever in their studies all these 10 days. Then came a confession from the professor, which was plain enough. I quote the following from the Chaitanya Bhagavata.

"He was pleased with what the students said and addressed them thus:—

<small>He closes the *tol*.</small> "What you say is true enough. My own sentiments are such that I cannot speak of them everywhere. I am persuaded by a vision from which I cannot escape. All sounds bear a message of Krishna to me. All space to me looks like His abode. My prayer to

you to-day is that I have no further lessons to give to you. I give you permission wholeheartedly; go wherever you like and read with some other professor. For myself I cannot speak of anything which is not connected with Krishna. What I say is true and you may rely on me." Saying so with tearful eyes he closed the book that was in his hand. Then he blessed them saying, "If for even a day I have believed in Krishna and done any act worthy of His servant, I pray to Him that you may prosper."[1]

The Sankirtan parties.

Nimai thus formally closed his school and formed a band of Vaishnabs with Narahari,

---

[1] " যত শুনি শ্রবণে সকলি কৃষ্ণ নাম ।
সকল ভুবন দেঁখো গোবিন্দের ধাম ॥
তোমা সভাস্থানে মোর এই পরিহার ।
আজ হৈতে আর পাঠ নাহিক আমার ॥
তোমা সভাকার যার স্থানে চিত্ত লয় ।
তাঁর ঠাই পড় আমি দিলাম নির্ভয় ॥
কৃষ্ণ বিনু আর বাক্য না স্ফুরে আমার ।
সত্য আমি কহিলাম চিত্ত আপনার ॥
এই বোল মহাপ্রভু সভারে কহিয়া ।
দিলেন পুথিতে ডোর অশ্রু সিক্ত হৈয়া ॥
দিবসেকো যদি আমি হই কৃষ্ণদাস ।
তবে সিদ্ধ হউ তোমা সবার অভিলাষ ॥ "

Ch. Bha.

Gadadhar and Sribasa, who all danced together and sang the following couplet :—

"হরয়ে নমঃ কৃষ্ণযাদবায় নমঃ
যাদবায় মাধবায় কেশবায় নমঃ।"

The couplet is nothing but a repetition of the idea "I bow to thee, Oh Krishna" composed in two lines in which the various names of Krishna are used to heighten the devotional sentiment. They danced in a circle as they sang this. Forty years ago, in my old native village in the district of Dacca, I first heard this couplet sung by a few young men who acted a drama on Chaitanya's life. I remember the impression then made on me by the music and dance, and can well imagine why people gathered by hundreds at Nadia attracted by this *Kirtan*. Nimai was only 22 years old. His great devotional fervour lent a charm to the music; and as the number of his admirers increased, they held their performances in the spacious courtyard of Sribasa every night.

Our young hero was a completely changed man now. Whomsoever he met, he used to address humbly and say "Bless me, my friend, for I am badly in need of your blessings. You have from my early years tried to impress on me the value of faith. I was indeed a poor learner, who did not pay any heed to you then."

To Gadadhara he said "Fortunate are you friend, for from your early youth you have been a devoted servant of God." Then turning to others he said " If I serve you, my friends, I find devotion for Krishna grow in me " ; saying so he carried the basket of some one from the banks of the Ganges to his house inspite of his protest. He sometimes washed the clothes of humble bathers to their intense fear, for it was considered a sin to accept such menial services from a Brahmin. Sometimes Nimai helpe a man by carrying a part of his load, and sometimes he was found to gather *kusha* grass and dig sacred earth from the banks of the Ganges for some Brahmin worshippers. Where they tried to stop him, he said " Forbear, my friends, these little services make my vision of Krishna clearer "[1] Nimai preached a doctrine of love which may be thus put here.

1. To recite the name of God, considering oneself humbler than a straw.

---

[1] " তোমা সভা সেবিলে যে কৃষ্ণ ভক্তি পাই ।
এত বলি কাব্রু পায় ধরে সেই ঠাঁই ॥
নিঙ্গড়ায় বস্ত্র কারো করিয়া যতনে ।
ধুতি বস্ত্র তুলি কারো দেনত আপনে ॥
কুশ গঙ্গা মৃত্তিকা কাহারো দেন করে ।
সাজি বহি কোন দিন চলে কার ঘরে ॥
সাজি বহে ধুতি বহে লজ্জা নাহি করে ।
সম্ভ্রমে বৈষ্ণবগণ হস্তে আসি ধরে ॥ "

Ch. Bha.

ANOTHER YOUNG MAN JOINS

2. Without seeking honour for one's own self to give it freely to others.

3. To bear all ills patiently like a tree.

The tree does not defend itself if one cuts it to pieces. It does not seek a drop of water from any one though it dries up. It gives flowers, fruits and shade even to one who cuts it. This ideal love is of Christ, for did he not give love to those who crucified him and was not his last word a prayer for their forgiveness?

At Sribasa's courtyard the Vaishnabs sang and danced with Nimai in their midst; and songs of exquisite poetic beauty were composed by Narahari, the inspiration coming from Nimai's trances.

At this time another young man, older than Nimai only by eight years, paid a visit to Nadia. He was Nityananda. He resided at the house of Nandanacharya. He wore a blue coloured *dhuti* and a large blue turban. In appearance he bore a resemblance to Bishwarup, Nimai's elder brother, who had gone away as a *sanyasi*. This made Sachi Devi call him her son. His eyes were large and beautiful, and Brindavana Das says poetically "Where are the lotuses that could be compared to them?" Nityananda as a young *sanyasi* had travelled over the whole of India, visiting all her shrines. He had come to Nadia at last in order to meet Nimai. He thus explains the object of his visit.

—Nityananda.

"I saw many shrines—in fact all associated with Krishna. There are many temples, but I did not find Krishna in any of them. I asked saints and holy men 'How is it, revered sirs, that I see His throne empty—the God I seek I do not find anywhere?' One of them advised me to return to Bengal saying 'In Nadia you will find Him. He is there to redeem the fallen.' And I have forthwith come here,—for none is so sinful and fallen as I am."[1]

By this time Haridas, the Mahomedan convert to Vaishnabism, who, as stated already, had suffered all kinds of persecution for his adherence to Vaishnab faith, came and joined this small band of Vaishhabs at Nadia.

---

[1] দেখিতে আয়ত দুই অরুণ নয়াণ ।
আর কি কমল আছে হেন হয় জ্ঞান ॥
নিত্যানন্দ বোলে তীর্থ দেখিল অনেক ।
দেখিল কৃষ্ণের স্থান যতেক যতেক ॥
স্থান মাত্র দেখি কৃষ্ণে দেখিতে না পাই ।
জিজ্ঞাসা করিল তবে ভাল লোক ঠাঁই ॥
সিংহাসন সব কেন দেখি আচ্ছাদিত ।
কহ ভাই সব, কৃষ্ণ গেলা কোন ভিত ।
তারা বলে কৃষ্ণ গিয়াছেন গৌড় দেশে ।
পতিতের স্থান বড় শুনি নদিয়ায় ।
শুনিয়া আইনু মুই পতিত হেথায় ॥ "

Ch. Bha., p. 181.

KRISHNA-CULT IN BENGAL

Bengal is dedicated to Krishna-worship in a sense in which no other country of India is.

Bengal a fit soil for the chosen seed.

All other cults here have been influenced and modified by Vaishnab faith. The air of this province is resonant with the songs of Joydeb, Chandidas and Vidyapati, and becomes charged with the red powder of *fag* during Vaishnab festivities which lends scarlet charm to the blue landscape, forming a favourite theme for the descriptive powers of our Vaisnava poets. Love for Krishna here is not only in the air, but in the gardens and meadows, where the blue-coloured flower that blooms the sweetest, is called the *Krishna pada* or the feet of Krishna, and the big red flower on the top of largest flower-trees is called *Krishna Chura* or the crown of Krishna. The cow dust—'*godhuli*' darkens the pastures reminding every rural Bengali of Krishna's return home with the cows; and Nanda and Jasoda are the typical parents whose names are on the lips of every Bengali woman. The temples in the evening draw men and women of this pastoral country by the sounds of their sweet bells, and then through the scented smoke and five lovely lights waved by the priests, the images of the divine cowherd and his consort, half veiled by incense that burns there, and amidst the chanting of sacred verses, shine forth as visions seen in a dream.

In this land where love for Krishna had entered deep into the hearts of rural villagers inspiring the devotee and the poet—the rich man and the peasant alike—inspiration which Nimai's love-ecstasies imparted to the people was almost overwhelming. Night and day he spoke of nothing else than Krishna; he fasted and wept like a maiden in love and yielded himself constantly to recitation and singing of Krishna's name. His pride was gone, he took no care of his dress or of personal comforts, and his scholarship was considered by him as mere vanity. He had so thoroughly identified himself with all that belonged to Krishna, that it was no wonder that the people soon identified him with Krishna Himself and called him an *avatara*.

The courtyard of Sribasa, where these *Sankirtan* performances were held, was accessible to only a limited number of devotees headed by that old and veteran scholar—Adwaitacharyya. Nityanada was of course there. Gadadhar and Narahari waved *Chamara*, when Nimai danced and sang; Bakreswara was nearly as handsome as Nimai and excelled in dancing; there were his old teacher Gangadas, Govinda Ghosh, Vasudeb, Murari Gupta, Haridas and others who sang in chorus. The Chaitanya Bhagavata gives names of nearly 40 men who formed this blessed party and who met every night in Sribasa's courtyard

The Kirtan party.

THE MANOHARSAI KIRTAN

and occasionally only in that of Chandrasekhar—a Vaidya by caste.

The *Kirtan* music was heard from outside; but the non-believers had no entry. The music was grand. The lays of Jaydev, Chandidas, Vidyapati and of Narahari had hitherto been sung in the different modes of the Hindu musical system. But it appears that Nimai gave a new turn to their singing. He resuscitated the pastoral tune of boatmen's songs adding to it a lovely musical mode which was quite original; it sprang from his intense and fervid emotion. This was the origin of the famous *Manoharshai*. It was invented in a rude form by some people of the *pargana* of the same name in the Burdwan district of Bengal. But its power to create pathos was no doubt accentuated marvellously by Nimai's devotional spirit. The *Manoharshai* became a powerful instrument in the hands of the Vaishnabs and it is now unrivalled in producing an effect so far as tender emotions are concerned; it is for this reason that when Pratap Rudra, the King of Orissa, charmed with *Kirtana* had asked Gopinath Acharyya as to who originated it, remarking that he had never heard a music so sweet, Gopinath said that it was Chaitanya who created by his intense fervour, the pathos of that musical mode. In the temple of Puri the songs of Jaydev were constantly sung in Gurjari and other modes. But since

Chaitanya's time these songs have been sung in the *Manoharshai*, which should not be taken as a gift from the musicians but from the Vaishnab-devotees and which have given a novel interest to the songs of Jaydev, Chandidas and others. If a material comparison is not considered as beyond the mark I may say that in subtlety and fineness of its tunes it resembles the fine weaving of the Dacca *muslin*, and in the spiritual world there is no force comparable to this in its power to appeal to the emotional side of our nature. The *Kirtan* thus introduced by Nimai Pandit, was developed by the Vaishnabas and classified into three different styles,—the Manoharshai, the Garanhati and the Reneti.

The Vaishnabs gradually became a power in Nadia. But howsoever the layman appreciated and enjoyed the emotional felicities afforded by the creed, the scholarly people there became hostile to it. They proudly asked as to where could be the text in the scriptures which justifies such dancing and this play of emotion. One should silently offer his prayers to God. Where was it ever heard that people in the name of religion should create such an uproar and disturb others' sleep ? As no outsider was allowed access, various rumours were spread about the party. One of these was that Sribasa being a wealthy man served these people with rich meals every night, hence

Hostilities.

SRIDHARA—THE FAITHFUL

they attended the meetings so eagerly. Sridhara, the faithful, who was a very poor man had been advised by Nimai Pandit to give up his devotion to Krishna and worship other gods and goddesses that would fetch him money. This of course Nimai had done when *bhakti* had not yet dawned on his soul. But on all such occasions Sridhara's reply was " Well hast thou said, Oh Brahmin lad, yet time passes and at the end makes no difference. The king in his golden hall partakes of rich meals and behold the birds that live on the boughs of trees. When death comes it levels all. Each has his lot apportioned by God." Sridhara now attended these meetings very punctually, and besides sang Krishna's name aloud in the streets. The hostile party reviled him saying " This mean fellow is not worth a *kowri* but wants to figure as a big devotee ; he is half-famished hence he cries aloud in the streets to suppress the pangs of hunger."[1] One of these scholars

---

[1] " কেহ বলে ব্রাহ্মণের নহে নৃত্য ধর্ম্ম ।
পড়িয়াও এগুলা করয়ে হেন কর্ম্ম ॥
কেহ বলে এগুলা দেখিতে না জুয়ায় ।
এগুলার সম্ভাষে সকল কীর্ত্তি যায় ॥
ও নৃত্য কীর্ত্তন যদি ভাল লোকে দেখে ।
সেও এই মত হয় দেখ পরতেখে ॥
পরম সুবুদ্ধি ছিল নিমাই পণ্ডিত ।
এগুলার সঙ্গে তার হেন হৈল চিত ॥ "

says, "Think of the matter seriously, what mischief may not ere long be forthcoming. This uproar and disturbance of sleep and rest of honest people will not long remain unnoticed, and the Emperor of Gour may any moment send an army to stop all these, and the result will be that honest people will share the fate of these wicked men." Another man said "The great scholar Nimai is now a totally ruined man. He had fine talents but he has altogether given up his studies. If one does not read grammar for a month, he forgets its rules, it is a complicated science."[1] One says "At night these people bring five fairies by witchcraft and incantations," to which another

কেহ বলে আজ্ঞা বিনা সাক্ষাৎ করিয়া ।
ডাকিলে কি কার্য্য হয় না জানিল ইয়া ।
আপন শরীর মাঝে আছে নিরঞ্জন ।
ঘরে হারাইয়া ধন চায় গিয়া বন ।
ও কীর্ত্তন না দেখিলে কি হইবে মন্দ ।
জন শত বেড়ি যেন করে মহা দ্বন্দ ॥
যতেক পাষণ্ডী বোলে শ্রীধরের ডাকে ।
রাত্রি নিদ্রা নাই যাই দুই কর্ণ ফাটে ॥
মহা চাষা বেটা ভাতে পেট নাহি ভরে ।
ক্ষুধায় ব্যাকুল হৈয়া রাত্রি জাগি মরে ॥ "

Chaitanya Bhag, p. 224.

[1] " কেহ বলে পাশরিল সব অধ্যায়ণ ।
মাসেক না চাহিলে হয় অবৈয়াকরণ ॥"

Chaitanya Bhag. p. 214

added "They have learned black art from *Madhu-mukhi*—a fairy." Others ascribed the famine that threatened the locality then to the anger of God who, it was alleged, was provoked by the great uproar and dance of these false people.

The hostility of the scholars and other people did not stop here. They applied to the Kazi complaining of the great uproar which caused disturbances of sleep, and asking him to stop it at once in the interest of public peace. The Kazi whose name, I believe, was Gorai, ordered

কেহ বলে কলিযুগে কিসের বৈষ্ণব।
যত দেখ হের পেটপোষাগুলা সব॥
কেহ বলে এগুলারে বাঁধি হাত পায়।
জলে ফেলি জীয়ে যদি তবে ধন্য গায়॥

Chaitanya Bhag., p. 319.

The view they took of the Vaishnab songs was full of acrimonious attack and ill-disguised malice.

" কোন জপ কোন তপ কোন যজ্ঞ দান।
তাহা না দেখিয়ে কবি নিজ কর্ম্ম ধ্যান॥
চালু কলা মুগ দধি একত্র করিয়া।
জাতি নাশ করি থায় একত্র হইয়া॥
পরিহাসে আসি সভে দেখিবার তরে।
দেখি তো পাগলগুলি কোন্ কর্ম্ম করে॥
পাষণ্ডী পাষণ্ডী যেই দুই দেখা হয়।
গলাগলি করি সবে হাসিয়া পড়য়॥
পুনঃ ধরি লয়ে যায় যেবা নাহি দেখে।
কেহ বা নিবর্ত্ত হয় কারো অনুরোধে॥

Ch. Bha.

that no man should be allowed thenceforth to sing the name of God in the public streets. *Kirtana* was thus stopped by the hand of the law.

But when Nimai heard of this order, he showed a bold front; he said that the whole air of Nadia must ring with *kirtana* songs in the evening. Formerly Haridas and Nityananda and some other Vaishnabs used to sing in the public streets in small bands. Their main dance and music had hitherto been confined to the courtyards of the houses of Sribasa and Chandrasekhar. But on that memorable night Nimai ordered that all of them would come out and hold their performance together in the public streets and make their round through the whole city. Great preparations were made, though it had been known to all that in the night previous some police officers had assaulted Sridhara and broken his tabor, while singing in the public street.

Nimai's defiant attitude.

That day the great love in which young Nimai was held by the people was strikingly in evidence. The people had all along been sorry that they had no access into Sribasa's house to see the *kirtana* performance. When it was announced that Nimai with his whole party would come out in the public streets in the evening, every house was illuminated, picturesque

The great love of people for Nimai.

A DEFIANT ATTITUDE

banners were waved aloft from the top of every house, and men and women dressed in fine apparel waited with anxious eyes to see the grand procession coming. It showed that though the hostile party was all along active and inveterately set against Nimai, their number was insignificant. The whole of Nadia was astir with love and curiosity to have a sight of the young Pandit who, it was believed, had brought a message for them from Heaven.

The procession was divided into four groups. The first was led by Adwaita-

The great procession.

charya; the leader of the second party was Haridas; the third was led by Sribasa and the fourth by Nimai himself accompanied by Nityananda. Each party consisted of a large number of Vaishnab musicians and dancers. Some people carried jars full of scented oil to help the lighting of hundreds of torches by which the whole city became ablaze. Nimai had frequent trances often falling senseless on the ground. And when he recovered he asked everyone with a piteous look " Oh where is my Krishna gone ?" He wept and behaved as one separated from his love. The people were moved to tears as they saw his appealing looks and his love-ecstasies. The Chaitanya Bhagavata records that so intense was the effect, that thieves and pilferers who had planned to carry on thefts that night, availing themselves of the general carelessness that prevailed in the city, forgot their object as they saw Nimai crying for God, like a young woman for her lover. Balarama Das, the poet, says that wherever Nimai went dancing in the midst of the procession there hundreds of lights were brought forward by people anxious to catch a glimpse of his face.[1]

This immense crowd that gathered and passed through the streets with torches making the night bright as day,—the deafening sound of tabor and the shrill clang of cymbals and *mandira* could not remain unnoticed by the Kazi. The procession passed through Gadigaccha, Pardanga and other wards of Nadia. The Kazi probably felt that it would be impossible to stop the enthusiastic crowd. He had sent several constables to learn all particulars. One old man amongst them returned with the message that as he had been coming up to prevent the crowd, lightning fell close

The Kazi welcomes Nimai.

---

[1] " নাচিতে নাচিতে গোরা সেই দিকে যায়।
লক্ষে লক্ষে দীপ জ্বলে কেহ হরি গায় ॥
কুলবধূ সকল ছাড়িয়ে হরি বলে।
প্রেম নদী বহে সবার নয়নের জলে ॥
বাচিয়া ঠমকে কিবা প্রভু মোর নাচে।
রমাই সুন্দরানন্দ মুকুন্দ গান পাছে ॥"

Gour Pada Tarangini, p. 249.

JAGAI AND MADHAI

to him and singed his white beard—that was surely a sign of divine wrath. The fact seems to be that the defiant attitude of the crowd overawed the Kazi's constables and they were not prepared to meet the situation. It is further on record that the Kazi's admiration was roused by the enthusiasm of the people. After all they had been singing God's name and were harmless. Nimai with his party passed by his very gate and some of the crowd pelted his house with stones. But he did not take any serious notice of it. The sight of Nimai had filled his mind, as it happened in hundreds of other cases, with admiring love. So young bright and handsome—he had foregone all the pleasures of the world and was so devoted to One for whose interceding love and grace there is need in every heart. The Kazi came down from his house and said to Nimai sweet words apologizing for his order and adding "You do not know how dear you are to me, lad, your father and grand-father were my close friends. Happy am I to see you to-day, so devoted to Allah."

Reformation of Jagai and Madhai.

Jagai and Madhai. Then comes the episode of reformation of Jagai and Madhai, two notorious ruffians of Nadia. They were grandsons of Subhananda Roy. This man had two sons Raghunath and

Janardan. Jagai or Jagannath was a son of Raghunath and Madhai or Madhaba of Janardan. They belonged to an aristocratic Brahmin family of Nadia and were very powerful. Jagai and Madhai were dead drunkards. Though Brahmins they ate beef, burnt houses and took away women by force. Jayananda says that they not only took beef but also ham. These two ruffians resolved to assault Nimai Pandit and his followers for singing *kirtan* songs in the streets. Accordingly when Nityananda was singing Krishna's name one day, Madhai flung a broken bottle at him which cut his forehead and it bled profusely. Nityananda took no offence and blessed him, and when Nimai came and saw the condition of his friend, he simply said " Madhai, if it was in your mind to strike one of us, why did you not strike me?" Saying this he silently took Nityananda with him and the crowd followed them in deep but silent sorrow.

Jagai and Madhai stood wonder-struck. They had reviled and assaulted these pious men and one of them was badly hurt. Yet not a word of anger came from them but they blessed them instead. They could not sleep in the night and in the morning they paid a visit to the saintly men and repented. One of the songs current in the country-side attributed this speech to Jagai " Oh Madhai, go and see what sweet sound is there on the banks of the Ganges! Formerly the sound of *Kirtana* pained my ears, to-day it soothes my soul."

Jagai and Madhai thenceforth became totally changed men. Madhai though assured over again by the saint, whom he had hurt, that his sin was pardoned, could not find any rest for his soul, and one day said " You sir, you have forgiven me, but in a drunken state I assaulted many men and the thought of this weighs heavily on my mind. How can I find rest until I have made adequate atonement?" He was advised to build with his own hands a bathing *ghat* on the banks of the Ganges where men and women could gather to bathe every day. He built the *ghat* himself with a spade in his hand like a hired labourer and he recited the name of God day and night. And when people came to bathe there he approached each new comer with joined hands and said with repentant tears "If, sir, consciously or unconsciously I ever gave you any offence, be pleased to forgive me. I deeply repent my conduct." And many wept to see this humility of one who had been a dreaded man in Nadia. The bathing *ghat* of Madhai, called after his name, has now disappeared. Narahari who wrote the Bhaktiratnakar about 1725 A.D. had seen it ; and Mahamahopadhyay Ajitanath Nayaratna of Nadia tells me that he saw in his childhood some bricks of the old ghat.[1] He is now verging on 75.[1]

---

[1] The old scholar died last year.

Like all events of Nimai's life associated with Nadia, the simple story of the reformation of these two ruffians has become mixed up with marvellous tales. It is stated in the Chaitanya Bhagavata that Nimai, angry at the conduct of Madhai, called for the disc which belonged to Vishnu and on which he, as that god's incarnation, had every claim. And the disc came rolling in the air, and the ruffians were completely overawed by seeing the divine weapon. We shall later on find in more authentic records, stories of many similar reformations; but there Nimai did his work by the simple marvel of his love and faith.

Just about this time Nimai organised a dramatic performance at Nadia. It was of course about Krishna. Krishna according to the legend in the Mahabharata had taken away Rukmini from her father's house by force. The old king her father, had settled her marriage elsewhere. But Rukmini had written a letter to Krishna saying that she had resolved to give herself up to him and none else. So when all the princes had gathered to witness the marriage, Krishna carried away the bride in a chariot—Rukmini herself doing the work of a charioteer. Krishna shot arrows on all sides to disperse the army that pursued them. So it was a very romantic situation.

Nimai, as organiser of a Krishna play.

THE KRISHNA PLAY

The performance was held at the house of Chandrasekhar. Buddhimanta Khan supplied the requisite costumes and jewellery. Adwaitacharya became the stage-manager. As the spiritual love in the play might be mistaken for sexual romance, Nimai had said before the commencing of the performance " Those that have fully controlled their passions should be privileged to witness the play." Upon which Adwaita said that he could not say that he was worthy. Sribasa also in clear language declared that he was not above human passion, upon which Nimai smiled and did not press his point. Adwaita played the fool's part and Sriman that of a sweeper. The performances of the two created much humour and mirth. Haridas, as the head of His Majesty's police force, came on with a pair of peculiarly cut whiskers and a huge turban. Narada with his long flowing white beard and a lyre that hung down from his shoulders had so marvellously changed himself that none but his wife Malini could recognise him to be Sribasa.

But when Nimai came from the green room dressed as Rukmini, the princess, even his mother could not recognise him. The spectators questioned if the figure before them was Sita or Lakshmi or kindness or love that had come there assuming a human shape. Rukmini wrote her love-letter to Krishna. Here her tears were real, for Nimai had forgot that he had been playing the part of the princess and was in his love-ecstasies at the recollection o Krishna. What he wrote playing the part of Rukmini he could not read, for his voice was choked with tears. The romance became real and the audience were taken by surprise at the emotion of the players, especially of Nimai—elevating them to a high spiritual plane. The play continued till dawn exciting a warm interest supplied by the real spiritual emotion of the *bhaktas*, and when the first streaks of the sun's rays entered the stage they thought that the happy night had ended too soon. According to Chaitanya Chandrodaya by Kavikarnapur the drama played by Nimai was about Radha and Krishna, and not about Rukmini—Nimai is represented by that authority to have played the part of Radha. It does not materially alter the situation. For whether Radha or Rukmini, Nimai had played the part of one lost in Krishna's love. That Sribasa played the part of Narada, a common figure in both the plays, is admitted by both accounts. According to one account Nityananda played the part of an old woman who carried Rukmini's love letter to Krishna and according to the other he figured as Yogamaya, who was also an old woman carrying Radha's love messages to Krishna. There are certainly some points of difference between the two plays but I think we should credit the account of Chaitanya Bhagavata, the author having heard everything from Nityananda himself who had taken an active part in the play. Chaitanya Chandrodaya Natak was written in 1572 A.D. and Chaitanya Bhagavata in 1573 A.D. Both the works are no doubt admitted by orthodox Vaishnabs as authoritative on Nimai's life. The Chaitanya Bhagavata was written a year after the Chaitanya Chandrodaya, and no doubt corrected the mis-statement of the latter work on this point.

Thus we find Nimai Pandit's intense love for Krishna expressing itself in hundreds of ways by which he attracted people. Murari Gupta's Chaitanya Charitam says " When left alone at home he wept all night for Krishna's love." Govinda Das says " If any one makes the slightest reference to Krishna his eyes become full of tears." " In his heart," says the latter, " he bears the pain of separation from Krishna which gives him no rest." Bashu Ghosh says that " his looks are constantly towards where the flowers bloom and he suppresses with some effort the tears that come to his eyes at the sight of the lotuses as if they remind him of some One." Lochan describes him as reclining in his trances on the arms of Narahari and Gadadhar, shedding tears from his closed eyes, and Bashudev asks in a song "What is the thought in which he remains absorbed resting his chin on his hand ? Look how he enters his room and comes out again without any cause. Why does he look so sad to-day ? 'Some one will come to me'[1] he says and sheds tears!" This abstraction and ecstacy proved a fascination, and each word that fell from him while in a trance sounded sweet as a note of a lyre, irresistibly attracting people's minds.

The pain caused by love for Krishna became more and more intensified as time passed on, till he entirely lost all touch with his environ-

---

[1] " আজু হাম কি পেখলু নবদ্বীপ চন্দ ।
করতলে করই বয়ান অবলম্ব ॥
পুন: পুন: গতাগতি কর্ ঘরপন্থ ।
ক্ষণে ক্ষণে ফুলবনে চলুহ একান্ত ॥
ছলছল নয়নে কমল স্ববিলাস ।
নব নব ভাবে করত পরকাশ ॥
আজু কেন গোরাচাঁদের বিরস বদন ।
কে আইল কে আইল করি সভয় নয়ন ॥"

Gour., p. 313.

"নাহি জানে দিবানিশি   কারণ বিহনে হাসি
    মনের ভরমে রহুঁ ভোর ।
ক্ষণে উচ্চৈঃস্বরে গায়   কারে পছুঁ কি সুধায়
    কোথায় আমার প্রাণনাথ ।
ক্ষণে আঁখিযুগ মুদে   হা নাথ বলিয়া কাঁদে
    ক্ষণে ক্ষণে করয়ে সন্তাপ—315.
সহচর অঙ্গে গোরা অঙ্গ হেলাইয়া
চলিতে না পারে যেন পড়ে মুরছিয়া

Gour., p. 317.

ment and seemed to live in the poetic plane of his godly vision. And Sachi Devi now felt that the family tie was held in very little regard by her son. She felt greatly depressed in spirit and frightened whenever she saw any *sanyasi* coming to Nimai. Keshab Bharati, the reputed Vaishnab ascetic, had come to Nadia and Nimai was observed to pay more than usual regards to him. Sachi silently approached Nimai and said softly with tearful eyes, "Why have I this weakness that if anybody speaks of *sanyasis*, I feel a chill in my heart? The other day you paid great reverence to Keshab Bharati. Why did you do so? My heart was filled with terror at the sight. Tell me my dear, assure me, that you will not turn *sanyasi*." Nimai said in reply, "Why do you indulge in all these foolish fears? How can I think of cutting my ties with Nadia?" Then said Sachi again, "My eldest son Bishwarup had given me a manuscript and told me that it should be kept for Nimai for his use when he would grow up and become a scholar. I had kept the manuscript with me long, but when Biswarup had turned a *sanyasi* and left me, I thought that it contained a message of *sanyas* for you and I burnt it." Nimai was very sorry at having lost the precious manuscript—a gift from his brother. But when Sachi Devi expressed her remorse and

Presentiment of the coming disaster.

prayed for pardon, he said, "It ill becomes you, good mother, to ask pardon of me, your son. There can be no offence for which you can do so. In all matters it is I who should ask pardon."

Thus a few months before Nimai resolved to turn a *sanyasi*, a presentiment had been already working in the mind of Sachi Devi. In the courtyard of Sribasa where *kirtana* songs and dance went on every night, only a selected party, as I have already said, had access. At the gate of the house, Ganga Das, the old teacher of Nimai, acted as a guard to keep out crowd.

A curse on Nimai.

Once a Brahmin who was an ardent admirer of Nimai wanted to enter but was not allowed. The next day he met Nimai on the banks of the Ganges. In great rage he tore off his sacred thread and uttered a curse, "As you kept me outside and didn't allow me to hear the *kirtan*, may you remain outside your home, the rest of your life." Nimai smiled and said "This is not a curse Brahmin, it is a blessing."

The Sankirtan party now came out in the public streets oftener and there used to be immense gatherings on such occasions. So great was the fascination created by Nimai's presence that, wherever Nimai was found to sing and dance in the midst of the procession, hundreds of torches were lighted to get a sight of his face. In such processions fourteen tabors usually sounded together, and a poet who was an eye-witness describes how old Adwaitacharya looked grand with brows pursed up and charming gestures of hands, as he kept time while singing.[1] Nimai was always in a state of frenzy, communing with Krishna with tearful eyes. Sometimes the sight of blooming flowers or the note of a bird reminded him of the Brinda-groves and, immersed in joy, he gradually lost his senses. People of India had for long been longing for a saintly personality who would show by his life the absolute saving power of the idea of devotion. The six schools of philosophy and all the current theological controversies in which subtle reasonings predominated could not give them any peace of mind. In fact the world had already grown weary of this cold and heartless intellectualism. They saw Nimai in actual touch with God, nay in him they had found a man who loved God more than a wife ever loved her husband or a mother her child. In that dry and sceptical epoch of our history, it was a revelation to all that one unseen and unknown could be so greatly loved. But however highly the popular sentiments might have been in favour of this attitude to God, the scholars of Nadia and the advanced students of her *tols* were too proud, as already stated, to accept it. The emotional religion repelled them, as it rejected reasoning and intellectual subtleties which reigned supreme in the Nadia-colleges.

---

[1] "ভ্রূকুটি করি করতালিকা রচি অদ্বৈত জন মন মোহয়ে।"
G. P. T., p. 339.

CHAPTER VI.

(*a*) Chaitanya's *Sanyas*.
(*b*) His tour—visit to Santipur.
(*c*) The incidents at Puri.
(*d*) His resolve to go to the Deccan.

Nimai now resolved to take the step so dreaded by his mother and friends. In the first week of February, 1509, he disclosed his intention of turning *sanyasi* to Mukunda. He said "The scholars of Nadia are still hostile to me. They have gone so far as to threaten to assault me. I shall see how they do it; for I shall be a beggar at their doors for Krishna's love." So long as he was a house-holder the country would not accept his spiritual services to mankind as absolutely disinterested and prompted by the highest of motives. A tangible proof of renunciation in the shape of the severance of all earthly ties was the instinctive demand of a people that was accustomed to associate religion with the entire self-dedication of an ascetic. It was dire news to the people who were fondly attached to him, and they numbered thousands. They all, however,

The resolve to turn a sanyasi.

THE GENERAL MOURNING 165

knew that his word was inexorable. On the 30th of Magha (mid-February) 1509 A.D. he took leave of Sachi Devi and with a single follower Govinda started early in the morning for Katwa. The mother lay unconscious overwhelmed with grief, for a *sanyasi* would never visit his home again. The morning marked the beginning of a universal mourning throughout Nadia. "The images of god," describes a poet, "in Nadia-temples looked pale." Another account says that all the shops were closed in that city and no one smiled. Vashu Ghosh asks in a song, "What are you doing, Oh people of Nadia, this is not the time for you to sit stupefied by grief, stretch your hands to stop him." Nityananda cries like a child, and Sribasa at his courtyard, where there were music and dancing every night, sobs aloud and is mad with grief. "He spoke of nothing but of Nimai after his desertion of Nadia and dreamt of him in his sleep. Often while gathering flowers for worship he recollected Nimai and the basket of flowers fell from his unconscious hands as he lay lost in reveries.

Sribasa's grief. Sometimes going to the banks of the Ganges he missed his great companion and sat for hours together meditating on him who was dearer to him than everything else in the world, and he forgot that he had come there to bathe. In his own courtyard the Sankirtana party sang the praises of the Lord again with the high sounding cymbals, the tumbrel and dance and he stood there listening to the singers; but often his voice was choked with tears and he fell down on the bare earth in grief crying like a child. Sometimes he felt that the God of his songs and Nimai were the same, so that while offering flowers to Krishna, instead of saying "I bow to thee, Oh Krishna" he said unconsciously "I bow to thee, Oh Nimai." And, as he remembered himself, tears rolled down his cheeks."

When Sribasa met Sachi Devi on the day of Nimai's desertion, she said "Everything that you see in this house belongs to you all. I have nothing to do with these. I have nothing in this world to call mine." Bishnupriya, the young wife, practically gave up eating. She never lifted her face to look at any one, only one or two maids remained with her. On the day previous to that of Nimai's desertion of home "she went" says a poet, "to bathe in the Ganges. She heard something there and when she came back she was in tears. The mother-in-law asked, "What is it that ails thee, child?" But she wept and could not speak. Another poet describes her seeking Nimai in her sleep in the bed, when he had gone away, and then with her mother-in-law running in the streets enquiring of every passer-by if he had seen him going. When Sachi Devi heard that her son had gone to

Kanchannagore to become a *sanyasi*, she exclaimed, "Do not call it Kanchannagore (*lit.* golden city) it is Kantaknagore, the city of thorns." The popular belief is that Katwa which is an abbreviation of Kantaknagore is a name given to that city by Sachi Devi. I have not, however, found this tradition supported by any written record. Sachi is said to have fasted for 12 days, and Bashu Ghosh says that one night towards its close when Malini—Sribasa's wife—came out of her room, she saw some one lying on the bare ground of the courtyard where Nimai had danced and sung a hundred times. Coming nearer she discovered Sachi lying on the dusty ground in that dead hour of night, weeping. She embraced her and they both wept without saying a word. One morning, according to another poet, Sachi described to Malini a dream in which she saw Nimai approach her and say, "Mother, I have travelled to many places as a *sanyasi*, but nowhere could I stay without seeing you" and when, charmed with the familiar voice she came out of her room, her dream had vanished.

His tour and visit to Santipur.

All this grief, and these outbursts of popular feeling could not, however, stop Nimai from his course. He proceeded towards Katwa in all haste, driven by his emotion, "like a flower" says a poet and

<small>Leaves home and reaches Katwa.</small>

biographer, "swept by rushing wind." Sometimes he embraced a tree in the way mistaking it for Krishna, and fell senseless on the ground at the sight of the Ganges mistaking it to be the Jamuna. At Kanchannagore he stopped. Govinda Karmakar's wife came there and solicited Nimai that he might allow her husband to return home. Nimai told her that it was good for his soul to devote himself to spiritual pursuits and to the good of the world. But the importunate cryings of 'Sashi-mukhi' moved him and he ordered Govinda to go back home. But Govinda after a stay of a few hours at Kanchannagore ran in all haste to overtake Nimai who had gone a few miles ahead of him.

Nimai reached Katwa on the evening of the 30th March, Saka 1430 corresponding to 1509, A.D. There hundreds of men and women gathered to see him. From under a *bel* tree he gave instruction to them. They listened to him with great respect and attention, but all people regretted his *sanyas* as he was young, and the women-folk particularly. They said "How would his poor mother and wife live, parted from him for ever?" Keshab Bharati was to be his Guru. They all tried to persuade Keshab to refuse him initiation into *sanyas* at that young age. Keshab acceding to their request told Nimai that his was not the proper age for *sanyas*. But Nimas said, "If I die early, I shall be deprived of the chance of following the best path for men." His great love for God and eloquent appeal could not be resisted, and the Bharati consented. A barber named Deva[1] was called to shave his head. The women of the town said "Deva, do not do such a cruel thing. Do not cut off such fine curling hair." This shaving of the head implied the cutting off of all family ties, so when the barber applied the razor to his hair the women stood there like silent pictures and shed tears.

He had his head shaven, and when wearing an ochre coloured cloth, the young *sanyasi* stood up "he looked" as a poet says " like mount Sumeru clad in clouds of deep purple." This was the ideal life towards which the enlightened in India have always moved—the severance of the family-ties and adoption of a cosmopolitan life for the good of the world. Nimai as a *sanyasi* was given the name of Krishna Chaitanya or one having God-consciousness. Though not literally, the name Chaitanya has nearly the same significance as the Buddha or the enlightened one. We find in an old record that the name Krishna Chaitanya

---

[1] The popular belief is that the name of the barber was Madhu. But in Govinda Das's *karcha* we find the name Deva distinctly mentoned and therefore cannot disbelieve the word of an eye-witness. " Madhu " seems to be a general name for the barber who shaves a man before his *sanyas*. In the Mainamati songs, we find " Madhu " shaving Raja Gopichandra on the eve of his *sanyas*. If Madhu is a traditional name given on such occasions, the popular belief and the evidence of the eye-witness may both be accepted in this case.

in the place of Nimai, sounded strange to the ears of the Nadia people. Henceforth, however, we shall call him Chaitanya the name by which he is popularly known everywhere.

The news of his *sanyas* had by this time spread all over the country, and at Nadia it was received with great sorrow.

His tour.

Even the non-believers who had reviled Nimai repented of their conduct and joined the general mourning. After *sanyas* Chaitanya came to Kulia, where a large crowd from Nadia and neighbouring places assembled to see the new *sanyasi*. "So great was the excitement" says Brindaban Das "that hundreds of men tried to cross the Ganges to go to Kulia and though all the ferry-boats were engaged and filled to their utmost capacity they were not equal to the demand. Many swam across the river, others seated in earthen jars plied them across the Ganges. Some cut banana-plants and made rafts. Many boats sank in mid-Ganges owing to the excessive crowd and these people had to swim across the river." They were all eager to have a sight of their God-man who was never to visit Nadia again, and Bashu Ghosh the poet regrets his *sanyas* in these words "Those days of music and dance and God-intoxication are over at Nadia, we shall not have them again—the thought pierces the heart like a dagger."

Govinda Karmakar along with other biographers have mentioned the names of the noteworthy men who went to meet Chaitanya at Katwa. Other books mention only the names of the orthodox Vaishnabs. But Govinda gives also the names of the distinguished visitors outside the Vaishnab community, who had joined the assembly. We find these names not recorded elsewhere :—Chanda Chandeswar, Kasiswar Nayaratna, Panchanan Vedantik. They are spoken of as princes amongst Pandits.

After *sanyas* Chaitanya felt himself free from all worldly bonds and his heightened emotions and ecstasies became marked. He had, on the eve of his *sanyas*, proclaimed to all his object : " I shall wander from house to house giving the holy name of God to all. The Chandals—the lowest caste—women and children all will stand with wonder and love to hear His name. Even boys and girls will sing His praise. The Aghore Panthis and other vicious *tantriks* will be attracted by His sweet name. The banner of His name will wave high in the air. Princes and poor men alike will sing His glory. If I do not turn a *sanyasi* how will the sinners and those that are stung with the world's sorrows be saved ? My heart weeps to see the misery of the people around."

The great saviour may not have a high recognition from the aristocracy. But look at the rural villages of Bengal and see how the poor people—the artizans, the labouring classes, the beggars and the diseased ones throughout this great province—have placed in their heart a throne for Chaitanya whose heart wept for their sorrows. This throne is far more glorious than that of an Emperor who has ever laid claim to recognition and immortal fame. In the evenings go to the huts of rustics in any village of Bengal however insignificant, and you will find the artisans and peasants gathered in a room at the close of their day's work and singing the name of Chaitanya "the friend of the fallen." The merry sound of the cymbals and *mandira* accompanied by the deep-mouthed voice of the *khola*, giving a sweet and solemn grace to the songs sung in chorus. In the mornings the Vaisnava ascetic visits every house and sings the praise of Chaitanya in this strain :—" Name him, my good man, and I shall hold you dear as my life." What prince at the dawn of the day and towards its close receives such a universal tribute of sincere affection and esteem ?

As he proceeded on his way to the south, his emotion gave him no rest and he so totally lost himself in his felicitous communion with God that he cared not for food or the needs of his physical body. Once for three days he fasted, and wherever he saw a river, the memory of the Jamuna in whose stream Krishna had sported came so vehemently into his mind that he ran to jump into it weeping and crying. Nityananda took advantage of this, and when Chaitanya told him that he was going to the Brindagroves, he said " I will lead you thither." The Ganges was shown him and falsely called the Jamuna, and Chaitanya in great love followed his guide along her banks till they reached Santipur. He brought Chaitanya by this trick to Adwaita's house. And Chaitanya, when he knew that he was duped, was not sorry, for he was glad to see Adwaitacharya again. Adwaita was 76 years old at the time, but his devotion to God and Chaitanya was wonderful. He was a rich man and lived in a great mansion called the ' *Upakarika* ' or the ' beneficient home.' He had longed to meet the young *sanyasi* and made great preparations for his reception. He, besides, sent a message to Nadia asking Sachi Devi to come and see her dear son at his own. The message was received by Sachi Devi with tears and she said " How shall I bear the sight of his shaven head? I shall not go to Santipur to see that sight,—rather I will go to the Ganges and drown myself."

<small>At the house of Adwait.</small>

Though she said so in grief, she left Nadia for Santipur in great haste. The interview between the mother and the son was full of pathos. Chaitanya found his mother reduced to a skeleton owing to grief and fasts, and she saw him, in the words of the poet, "shaven of his beautiful curling hair, and greatly reduced he wore a *kaupin* as the *sanyasis* do, with an outer cloth hanging from his shoulders. His body was besmeared with dust and he looked like a mad man abstractly gazing at the sky and shedding tears." Then the mother said "You are going to preach religion to the world. Is desertion of a poor mother and wife a part of that religion? Behaving in this way, how can you be fit for teaching religion to others? Don't you know that I have none else in this world besides you? Return home and go on singing God's name with Sribasa and others as you used to do. I shall engage Brahmins to invest you with the sacred thread again though you have left them." Nimai seemed to be greatly moved but said "For the cause of universal good, mother, this renunciation must be made. Think of Kausalya who gave permission to Ram to go to the forest,—of Devahuti, who permitted Kapila to turn an ascetic. You and Bishnupriya will surely find me ever near you; for in spirit, good mother, I can never be far away. In your kitchen where you prepare food, you will feel my presence; for there is nothing so

---

[1] For a Brahmin who gives up his sacred thread, a penance is necessary to resume them involving the observance of some sacred rites.

delicious, mother, as your preparations." Then Sachi, whose tears flowed as did her son's, slowly said again "Bishwarup turned a *sanyasi* and never saw me again, do not be so cruel." To which her son sweetly replied, "Mother, this body of mine has sprung from you—it is yours. How can I requite the immense debt of your affection. Wherever you will order me to stay I shall stay there." And saying so he bowed to his mother again and again. But when Adwaita asked him to stay there for some time, he said "It is not proper for a *sanyasi* to live anywhere accompanied by his relations." Adwaita had made vast preparations for his reception. Looking at the rich food served before him, prepared by Sita—Adwaita's wife, Chaitanya said,—"This food is not proper for a *sanyasi*. How can an ascetic learn abstinence so necessary for self control, if you tempt him in this way."

The *Kirtana* sounded its high music for ten days, and the God-intoxicated youth was in the height of his emotional felicities and passed into trances often and fell down on the bare earth in an unconscious state. Sachi's anxious solicititude for her son was full of pathos on such occasions. She made entreaties to Adwaita and to every one present, to hold her son fast so that he might not be hurt by his fall. Twenty-four years after this time Chaitanya passed away from this world having an inflammatory fever caused by a hurt on his foot from such a fall at Puri.

Then he left Santipur, as already stated, after a stay of ten days. Adwaita was disconsolate and went some distance with him; while bidding him farewell the old man cried like a child; upon which Chaitanya mildly admonished him saying "If a veteran scholar and aged man like you behave in this way, how can I trust my poor mother to your care?"

(c) *The incidents at Puri.*

On leaving Santipur Chaitanya came to Kanchannagore in the district of Burdwan and then crossing the Damodar came to the house of a rich man named Kashi Misra who had made great preparations for his reception. A very fine rice was served him and he asked "What do you call this rice?" They said "Its name is Gopalbhoga (Lit., meal of Krishna)". On hearing this, at the mention of Krishna's name, tears rolled down his cheeks, and he passed into a trance. Then for sometime he was in a state of unconsciousness, running after and pursuing his vision like a mad man with tears which never ceased. Nityananda followed him like a shadow. One day he stopped and staring at Nityananda said "Who

<small>On the way to Puri.</small>

are you?" Nityananda was grieved to see him in this state of frenzy. From Kashi Misra's house he went to Hazipur where a rich young man named Keshab Samanta called on him and offered him money saying, " Here accept this gift from me and satisfy your desires. Leave this profession which is wicked, for you want to deceive people,—surely one so young cannot be an ascetic." Chaitanya gave him many instructions in course of which he remarked "Just as a man drowned in a river cannot see what takes place on her banks, even so does a man fail to realise his real condition, being lost in world's desires." It appears, however, that Keshab Samanta was not convinced. Chaitanya said to Govinda, his companion, " Let us go to Narayanpur. There is no good staying at Hazipur." At the latter place two very respectable and wealthy men came riding elephants, gaudily caparisoned. They were Bireswar Sen and Bhawanisankar who were wonder-struck by seeing Chaitanya's fervour of devotion. From Hazipur he went to Jaleshwar and here he crossed the Subarnarekha and then visited Balasore. He crossed the Baitarani and the Mahanadi and visited Amarda and Ramchandrapur. Here a high official named Ram Chandra Khan helped him to cross the river. The tridents of the contending chiefs were planted in the place marking boundaries, and no one was allowed to go from one country to another on pain of death. This refers to the animosity carried on with great force between Raja Pratap Rudra of Orissa and Hussain Shah, the Gour-Emperor. The boatmen employed by Ram Chandra Khan advised Chaitanya and those that followed him not to speak aloud as the spies of the Mahomedans were everywhere. But Chaitanya, quite fearless, sang aloud God's name saying that the recitation of the holy name would drive away all danger. He next visited Jajpur on the banks of the Papahara, and Jayananda states that he stayed there at the house of one Kamalalochan, who was a member of the family of which Chaitanya was a scion. It should be remembered that the ancestors of Chaitanya were originally inhabitants of Jajpur. From Jajpur he marched to the shrines of Shiveswar, Jameswar and then came up to see the famous temples of Kanarak and Bhubaneswar. Reaching Alalnath he saw from far the great flag of the Puri temple, sparkling with its gold-embroidered decorations in the morning sun. The sight filled him with strange ecstasy. He wept for joy and cried aloud,—" I have found Him at last."

Accounts differ about this tour to Puri. Chaitanya Charitamrita says that after having visited Puri, Chaitanya started for Brindaban but going up to the village of Ramkeli near Gour he came back to Puri *via* Santipur. But

VISIT TO THE TEMPLE

Brindaban Das and Govindadas speak of the visit to Santipur as having taken place during his tour from Katwa to Puri. In matters of chronology of events we can hardly rely much upon the accounts of Chaitanya Charitamrita, written many years after Chaitanya had paid his first visit to Puri. Krishna Das Kaviraj, the author, himself admits that in points of chronology of events, he cannot always vouch for the accuracy of his statements. Visiting the Puri-temple Chaitanya is said to have been so overpowered by emotion that he forcibly made his way through all obstructions of the priests and came up to the very pedestal of the sacred images. There he fell senseless and was whipped by the priests who had taken him for a mad man. Basudev Sarbabhauma, the great scholar, had by chance come to the temple about this time and was struck by the sight of the unconscious young man who looked bright as a god, and who though senseless had been shedding tears of joy, heedless of the strokes of whip that fell on his back. He learned that the young man belonged to Nadia, his own native place, and his interest in him was further roused on hearing that he was a grandson of Nilambar Chakrabarti—a great friend of Sarbabhauma's father Bisarad. By his order, Chaitanya, still unconscious, was carried to his house. But the Chaitanya Chandrodaya

<small>Different accounts regarding his first visit to the temple.</small>

gives a different account. It says that Chaitanya as a young ascetic had attracted Sarbabhaum's attention from the very first, and before going to visit the Puri temple, he had accepted the hospitality of Basudev, and staying at night with him, early in the morning of the day after he had reached Puri, paid his visit to the temple. The description given by Kavikarnapur is very poetic. The doors of the temple are opened and a sweet music bursts forth announcing the time for public entry. From the doors rushes forth the fragrance of a thousand lilies and other flowers. Chaitanya enters the temple delighted and entranced by the sweet smell and by the sight of a hundred blue gems in the temple that reflect the rays of the morning sun. However poetic this description may be, we prefer to believe in the accounts of Chaitanya Bhagavata, the Chaitanya Charitamrita and other biographies on this point. For it seems by no means creditable, that Chaitanya, reaching Puri, would brook the delay of a moment in visiting the temple. In regard to the account of subsequent events at Puri, all biographers are, however, unanimous. It is certain that Basudev Sarbabhaum, the great champion of non-dualistic creed, had little regard for the *bhakti* cult. He took Chaitanya for a young man led astray and seized by a mania. He said to one of his people, " Having

<small>The conversion of Vasu Deva.</small>

left home he feels a great sorrow and recollecting his wife, he weeps which they take as a sign of his devotion to Krishna. He is barely 24. This is not the age for *sanyas*. Let him return home subjecting himself to proper penance [1] and acquire a knowledge of the Upanishads which will teach him his duties. Dancing and singing do not become an ascetic. And how is it that every time meal is served to Jagannath in the temple he partakes of it. A *sanyasi* must not eat at all times." Mukunda, Gopinath and other followers of Chaitanya were sorry at this remark but they said nothing. Basudev called Chaitanya to his presence and said " Young man, you know that Ishwar Puri and others took *sanyas* when two-thirds of their life had passed. What right have you to become a *sanyasi* at this tender age?" Chaitanya replied meekly " Yes, Sir, it is even so. But why do you mistake me for a *sanyasi* ? I have lost all control over myself, parted from Krishna. It is for this that I have shaven my head and torn off the sacred thread. Do not, Sir, think me to be so exalted a person as a *sanyasi*. I am a very humble person. Bless me that my soul may find rest in Krishna's love." As he said this he wept, and Basudev was impressed with the meekness and sincerity

---

[1] Penance is to be undergone by one who having once adopted *sanyas*, would like to return to home-life.

of the lad. He advised him to listen to his discourses on Vedanta Philosophy that he delivered every evening; and Chaitanya meekly sat amongst the audience every day and said not a word. On the day when Basudev finished his lectures, he said "Many of those who attended my discourses raised points to be cleared by me, and I tried my best to solve the questions. But you, who are reported to be a scholar, never spoke a word, but sat plunged in your own emotions, apparently not heeding my lectures. Will you tell me what you have learnt from my discourse?" Chaitanya replied very humbly "Sir your learning is vast. Your eloquence is great and you have the power of creating a wonderful impression by your speech, but your views have not always appealed to me." And Basudev, the veteran scholar, wonderingly asked "What could your views be, child, that do not agree with mine?" Then a regular discussion took place in which the dualistic views were put forth with so much force by Chaitanya that Basudev waivered in his argumentation to uphold the pantheistic theory. The God without quality, without form, inactive, and inert, manifesting himself in every object of the universe and identical with it, could not hold His own against the God, kind, loving and merciful and even willing to save people from their sins. And when Basudev interpreted the text of the Bhagavata

(Sk. 1, canto 7, verse 11) in nine different ways striking the audience with his scholarship and intellectual subtleties, Chaitanya gave 18 different interpretations to it, in which none of the points raised by Basudev was touched, but which at once carried his audience to a far higher spiritual plane than Basudev could ever do. The great emotion, verging on a state of poetic frenzy, mingled with eloquence and great learning, displayed by Chaitanya had a hypnotic effect on Basudev who for sometime had merely admired the young ascetic as a brilliant scholar, but was now struck to find in him sparks of Divinity that he had seen in no one else. He at once accepted him as his God and saviour, and from that time became one of his staunchest followers. The news of Basudev's defeat and acceptance of Chaitanya spread all over the country, and great scholars came to Puri to pay their respects to Chaitanya. But how far the details of the points of discussion given in the Chaitanya Charitamrita are reliable I cannot say, for it is found that in course of the debate, one party quoted the Bhaktirasamritasindhu written in the year 1541 A.D. whereas the debate took place in 1509 A. D. The great scholar Krishnadas Kaviraj, the author of Chaitanya Charitamrita, had identified himself so much with the theological views of his school that he missed no opportunity of introducing them, though in some cases his scholarly ardour clouded his historical sense. The Chaitanya Chandrodaya does not speak anything regarding the debate. We have rejected the statement made in the Chaitanya Charitamrita that Chaitanya went to Ramkeli shortly after he had arrived at Puri. He must have done so after returning from the Deccan about the year 1512 A.D.

Sometime before Chaitanya came to Puri, Raja Pratap Rudra of Orissa had gone to Bijaynagar in the Deccan to fight with the king of that place. On his return to the city Pratap Rudra heard of the great impression on his people that Chaitanya's visit to Puri had produced. At first he had his doubts. We read in Sterling's History of Orissa that this king was at first a Buddhist. He often cut pleasant jokes at Ram Rai, his minister, for his fervent faith in Vaishnabism. It is therefore quite natural that the sight of a *sanyasi*, who displayed so much emotion and lay besmeared with dust, weeping like a woman, should produce an unfavourable impression. The Chaitanya Bhagavata tells that this was really the case. Chaitanya Charitamrita says that the king once said to Sarbabhauma " How is it that the ascetic takes meal without bathing or shaving himself? The rules of the shrine do not allow it." But though at first he had his doubts, he

<small>Chaitanya and Raja Pratap Rudra.</small>

soon felt a great admiration verging on love for Chaitanya, as he saw him singing the name of God in the midst of his followers. The emotion and the poetry of the situation, a young man loving God with all his heart, had an effect which irresistibly appealed; and the Raja is said to have exclaimed as he saw Chaitanya passing by the streets from the roof of his palace: "I never saw such a sight, I never heard such music, I never saw such dance." The king wanted to be allowed to see Chaitanya. But the young ascetic told Basudev Sarbabhauma, who communicated the king's wish, that as a *sanyasi* he should keep himself aloof from the fountain of power and wealth. It is stated in the Chaitanya Chandrodaya and Chaitanya Charitamrita that Pratap Rudra felt very sorry at this refusal, and asked Basudev and others to intercede for him again, regretting that the humblest of his subjects had a privilege which was denied him because he was a king. But though a king he was poor in spirit and claimed admittance to the Master's presence on that ground. I think there is an exaggeration in the account given by some of these biographies that so grieved was the Raja at not getting the permission that he fasted for ten days. The interview, however, took place shortly after. Chaitanya was lying in an unconscious state in the house of Gopinath Acharya, when the Raja stole into the room and held

fast the Master's feet with imploring looks. A picture drawn half a century later showing Chaitanya and Pratap Rudra in this situation, will be found reproduced in my work "Chaitanya and his Companions." When Chaitanya recovered from his trance, he drew his feet off and said "Ah! I have touched a man given to worldly power!" But when the Raja bore the remark humbly, and said that he was ready to give up his power and wealth for the sake of the Master, Chaitanya, convinced of his sincerity, embraced him in deep love. And Ram Ray, the minister and poet, in his celebrated work the Jagannath Ballav, wonders as to how such a great warrior as the Raja was, whom all Indian wrestlers dreaded and who was the most formidable enemy of the Pathans, could be so overpowered by emotions as to melt like a soft thing at the Master's touch. Govindadas writes:—
"When the *kirtana* party passed by the public street with Chaitanya in the centre, the king Pratap Rudra walked behind them all like the very humblest of his subjects."

Chaitanya's fame had by this time spread all over India, and pilgrims came to Puri to visit him as they did to visit Jagannath in the Great Temple. We read in the accounts, that presents of rich food came to him in large quantities from his Nadia-friends and admirers, and the young scholar Jagadananda was the custodian of these and Govinda was entrusted to serve them. The request in each case to Govinda was "Pray, Govinda, see that Chaitanya tastes a little of these." Some presented *pedo*—the famous milk-preparation of Gaya, some very nice cakes and *sarbat*. Adwaita Acharya used to send the excellent *sarpuria*, the thickened layer of milk, prepared with sugar and spice, for which the locality he lived in, is still famous. The *amrita batika* or the nectar balls also formed one of the delicious presents. Sribas sent his sweet cakes and *karpur kupi*—a preparation scented by camphor. Various other things were presented by Basudev Datta, Murari Gupta, Buddhimanta Khan and others. Young Jagadananda attended Chaitanya at the time he took his food and insisted on his taking a portion from each of these. But Chaitanya stuck to his ascetic-vows and would not touch any rich food. Jagadananda became angry at such refusals, and silently retired into his room with the resolve of not eating anything himself. On one occasion a jar of perfumed oil was presented to Chaitanya by an admirer. The scent was very pleasant and it was the ardent wish of Jagadananda that Chaitanya would use a little of it at the time of bathing. But he did nothing of the kind, and ordered that the jar of oil should be sent to the Jagannath

The present of rich food.

Jagadananda.

temple where the lamps would burn with that oil at the time of Evening-Service. Jagadananda fasted for three days in anger, and when Chaitanya would not still use the oil, he ran to the store-room and brought the jar and broke it to pieces, and its contents flew down in the compound. Chaitanya slept on the bare floor and the stone on which he rested his head was hard. Jagadananda one day brought a pillow for him upon which Chaitanya said "Jagadananda should bring a couch for me from the palace. This man wants that I should enjoy life as worldly men do."

Damodara one of Chaitanya's constant associates, and an ascetic who followed the rules of his Order to the letter, often reprimanded him for not observing too closely the *shastric* ordinances for *sanyasis*. He even went further and occasionally gave advice to Chaitanya as regards his morals. A Brahmin boy at Puri, greatly devoted to Chaitanya, came frequently to pay him respects. The mother of the boy was a young widow and very handsome. One day Damodara said to Chaitanya :—"You are a god in human shape and privileged to do as you wish. But how can you stop the mouth of the people. Can't you judge your situation ? The mother of this boy is very beautiful though of course she has the reputation of good character. You are a

Damodara.

youth and have adopted stern asceticism. Why do you allow this boy to come to you so often and thereby give opportunity to scandal-mongers?" And Chaitanya said "I admire you for your sound advice. You should go to Nadia; my poor mother and wife will certainly need the help of such a disciplinarian and guardian."

(d) *His resolve to go to the Deccan.*

Day and night visitors came and allowed no rest to Chaitanya. One day he addressed Nityananda and others and said "Permit me, brethren, to leave Puri and go on a tour to Southern India." He referred to Nityananda's having broken his ascetic's staff on his way to Puri. His intention was that by doing so he would be able to make Chaitanya return to his home and live there as a house-holder. Turning to Nityananda he said again " I do as you wish me to do. I have no option to act independently. I was going to Brindaban after my *sanyas* and you brought me to Santipur. You deceived me by shewing me the Ganges and calling the river Jamuna. The affection of you all for me is unbounded. But this is a great hindrance to me. Jagadananda wants me to taste life's pleasure as a worldly man. Whatever he wishes I do for fear. For if I do not do so he will not talk with me for three days. My friend Mukunda is grieved to see me observe the austerities of an ascetic's life that

I bathe in winter three times every night and sleep on the bare ground. I am an ascetic but Damodar acts as the guardian of my morals and admonishes me for breaking the rules of asceticism. He cares for his religion only, but I cannot forget that I am a human being and have some duties to do to my fellow-men. For all these reasons, you, my friends, should remain here and I must go abroad visiting shrines for a while."[1] Nityananda said that he knew all the shrines of India and would act as his guide, and hundreds of others offered to accompany him. Basudev Sarbabhauma is said to have exclaimed thus at the news of Chaitanya's resolve to leave Puri :—" If a thunder-bolt falls on my head and even if my son dies I can perhaps bear that, but not separation from Chaitanya !" But all these were of no avail. Chaitanya had perceived that a new family had been created at Puri in the place of the old one that he had left at Nadia, and that he must extricate himself once more from the ties of affection to be able to impart to millions of people his message of love for God. Then probably recollecting that the news of his departure from Puri from which his mother could always have tidings of him, would cause great pain to her, he said that one of the missions of his tour in Southern India would be to seek out his elder brother Biswarup.

---

[1] The Typical Selections from Old Bengali Literature, Vol. II, p. 1207.

CHAPTER VII.

(*i*) Govinda Das's account of Chaitanya's travel.
(*ii*) Reformation of sinners.
(*iii*) Naroji, Bhilpantha, Muraris and Baramukhi.

(*a*) *Govinda Das's account of Chaitanya's travel.*

Inexorable in his resolve, Chaitanya with a solitary companion left Puri on the 7th day of Baisakh, Saka 1432 (1510 A.D.). He had stayed at Puri for a little above two months from April 1509 A.D.

<small>He starts for the Deccan.</small>

We are glad to say that for an account of Chaitanya for a period of two years and ten months from the 7th Baisakh, 1432 Saka, during his tour in the Deccan, we have a clear and reliable record in the *karcha* by Govinda Karmakar who took notes daily of what he saw and heard. Though the *karcha* begins with an earlier account, *viz.*, that of the period immediately before *sanyas*, yet I believe the notes were actually taken from the time when Chaitanya left Puri. The

<small>The *Karcha* or notes by Govinda.</small>

notice of the period of five or six months previous to *sanyas*, is somewhat imperfect and seems evidently to have been written from memory, whereas the notes relating to the latter period are full and exhaustive, abounding with graphic sketches of all that had taken place. It is natural for us to surmise that the idea of jotting down notes originated in Govinda's mind in connection with Chaitanya's tour in the Deccan. For at Nadia and in Puri there were many scholars who were Chaitanya's companions, who, like Sarup, Damodar and Murari, were ever ready to record the incidents of his life; and an unassuming man like Govinda could not possibly have conceived the idea of writing a sketch of the Master in the presence of these scholars, as his education was of a very humble kind. It was when no one else could be near to record the events of his life, that Govinda felt tempted to do so; and this surmise of ours is substantiated, as already stated, by the very nature of the narration of facts, the earlier events being written off-hand, as if from recollection, and the notes of later ones possessing all the freshness and living interest of a chronicle written on the spot.

The picture of the Master in this narrative is divested from all manner of glorification by ascribing supernatural powers to him. Such exaggeration in reality in most instances mars true glory. The *karcha* shows how the young ascetic wandered from village to village intoxicated with God's love and passed into trances as often as he saw a river, a flower or a newly-risen cloud. The sight of this trance was so attractive that everywhere it drew large crowds. We also read in the *karcha* that in the midst of his maddening love for God, he every now and then displayed a great eloquence inspired by spiritual fervour, and defeated the scholarly argumentations of the great pantheist leaders of Southern India, such as Ishwar Puri of Chandipur, Bhargadev of Tripatra and others. Ramgiri, the famous Buddhist leader, had a tough fight with Chaitanya on spiritual questions. The Raja of Trimanda acted as judge. Ramgiri was completely defeated and became a follower of Chaitanya adopting the Vaishnab name of Haridas. On many occasions the extraordinary learning of the young ascetic made a great impression; but when establishing the cause of devotion and faith by his scholarship, he recited the name of Krishna fervently with tears in his eyes and followed his vision through woods and marshes, heedless of physical pain, they all beheld in him something more than human and accepted him as God.

He defeats scholars and they accept his views.

At a place called Tripatra we find him followed by children who cried out "There goes the ascetic mad after God." Some threw dust at him; his outer robes were all torn and his body was covered with mud. Says Govinda "He looks like a mad man." The name of Krishna raised him to a state of poetic frenzy and completely distracted him. At Munna we find him giving instructions listened to by hundreds of men and women with rapt attention, the women shedding tears over pathos created by God's name.

(b) *Reformation of Sinners.*

Govinda Das gives several instances where Chaitanya reformed sinners. The accounts are so simple that we can quite understand how great faith is capable of sanctifying the lives of the fallen. We have seen how a story of simple faith, the parallel of which is so often furnished by Govinda, was magnified by the Nadia-people into a tale of legendary character in which Chaitanya is said to have assumed all the power and dignity of Vishnu and called on the *chakra* (the divine disc) to punish Jagai and Madhai. But punishment is not the adequate means in such cases. Even the majesty of Vishnu with his mortal disc can terrify the sinner but cannot turn him into a saint. Near Bateswar the rich young man Tirtharam, given to frivolous pleasures, thought that Chaitanya as a young man would easily be captivated by the charms of young women, and with that purpose brought two very lovely harlots, Satyabai and Lakhibai, to try the ascetic's spiritual force.

"Instructed by Tirtharam they sat near Chaitanya and began to smile, partially uncovering themselves to display their charms.[1] But

---

[1] " ধনীর শিক্ষায় সেই বেশ্যা দুইজন ।
প্রভুরে বুঝিতে বহু করে আয়োজন ॥
সত্যবাই লক্ষ্মীবাই নামে বেশ্যাদ্বয় ।
প্রভুর নিকটে বসি কত কথা কয় ॥
কাঁচুলী খুলিয়া সত্য দেখাইল স্তন ।
সত্যেরে করিলা প্রভু মাতৃ সম্বোধন ॥
থর থর কাঁপে সত্য প্রভুর বচনে ।
তাহা দেখি লক্ষ্মী বড় ভয় পায় মনে ॥
কিছুই বিকার নাই প্রভুর মনেতে ।
ধেয়ে গিয়া সত্যবালা পড়ে চরণেতে ॥
কেন অপরাধী কর আমায় জননী ।
এইমাত্র বলি প্রভু পড়িলা ধরণী ॥
খসিল জটার ভার ধুলায় ধুসর ।
অনুরাগে থর থর কাঁপে কলেবর ॥
নাচিতে লাগিল প্রভু বলি হরি হরি ।
রোমাঞ্চিত কলেবর অশ্রু দরদরি ॥
গিয়াছে কৌপীন খসি কোথা বহির্ব্বাস ।
উলঙ্গ হইয়া নাচে ঘন বহে শ্বাস ॥
আছাড়িয়া পড়ে নাহি মানে কাদা খেঁাচা ।
ছিঁড়ে গেল কণ্ঠ হৈতে মালিকার গোছা ॥
* * * *
ইহা দেখি সেই ধনী মনে চমকিল ।
চরণ তলেতে পড়ি আশ্রয় লইল ॥
চরণে দলেন তারে নাহি বাহ্য জ্ঞান ।
হরি বলি বাহু তুলে হৈলা আশুগ্মান ॥
* * * *
'বড়ই পাপিষ্ঠ মুই' বলে তীর্থ রাম ।
দয়া করি দেহ মোরে প্রভু হরি নাম ॥'
তীর্থরাম পাষণ্ডেরে করি আলিঙ্গন ।
প্রভু কহে তীর্থরাম তুমি মহাজন ॥
পবিত্র হইনু আমি পরশে তোমার ।
তুমি ত প্রধান ভক্ত কহে বার বার ॥"

Govinda Das's Karcha. pp. 56-58.

Chaitanya sat quiet singing the name of Krishna—unmoved. Lakhi felt that he was too far saintly to be led astray by temptations. She bowed to him in all humility and Chaitanya remarked " Why do you bow to me, mother, humility of others towards me begets sin, for I am the humblest of men." Saying so he sang the name of Krishna, shedding incessant tears ; he sometimes fell down on the thorny ground which hurt him and sometimes danced in ecstacy of joy. He lost all consciousness of the physical world and his outer mantle flew away. The wreath of flowers that some admirers had put on his neck was torn to pieces. He pushed away Tirtharam with his feet, quite unconscious of the latter's presence. So great was his emotion that it moved to tears some of the Buddhists who were there. Tirtharam wept, falling at his feet and said, " I am a great sinner, save me O Lord." Chaitanya for a while could not speak but recovering from his trance embraced Tirtharam and said in a tone of deep love " Brother, you are a pious man." This made the repentant young man weep and cry for mercy. Tirtharam made a gift of his vast property to his wife Kamalkumari and taking the beggar's bowls in his hands turned a Vaishnab mendicant. His friends all said " Look there, this fellow is lost." Kabikarnapur had said of

Tirtharam.

Chaitanya; "The effect of a sight of him is wonderful. Whoever beholds him feels God's love." Other apostles, saints and prophets, of whom we read, communicated their messages to the world by instructions and sermons. But Chaitanya worked wonders in spiritual and moral fields, often without any sermon or speech. The very sight of him raised people to a higher plane of existence, so Kavikarnapur was right in saying that the effect of a sight of him was wonderful.

(c) *Naoroji, Bhilpantha, Muraris and Barmukhi.*

In the woods of Choranandi there lived a gang of formidable bandits in those days headed by Naoroji. Chaitanya marched from Munna to the forest of Bogula of which Choranandi formed a part.

Naoroji.

Ramgiri, a *sanyasi*, said "Choranandi is no shrine.[1] What attractions are there for a Sadhu? The woods are infested with wicked men." Chaitanya replied "What have I with me that these people may rob me of?" Chaitanya entered deep into the forest and sat under a tree. There were many bad men there who lived by robbery. One fellow spoke a language that was jargon to me. Chaitanya talked to him in that language. The man stood silent for a while and casting

---

[1] Govinda Das's Karcha, pp. 146-148.

a searching look around, entered the jungle. Then came to that spot Naoroji himself, their chief,—a strong-built man he came well armed with weapons.

Three or four men came with Naoroji and they all bowed to Chaitanya (as he was an ascetic). Naoroji said "Come with me, Sir, you will spend the night in my place." Chaitanya said "I shall spend the night under this tree."

"Hearing this he ordered some of his people to bring some alms for the *sanyasi*. They went away and Chaitanya sat there singing the name of Krishna. Some brought fuel, some sugar, milk and butter and others brought rice, fruits and sweet roots. They brought heaps of these. A keen appetite grew in me at the sight of these things. I had travelled with Chaitanya in many countries but nowhere did I find such palatable things and in such quantities. Placing all this food in proper place Naoroji's men stood surrounding us. At this moment Chaitanya had passed into a trance and lost all consciousness. And as he danced in joy, his nimble feet threw away the heaps of food stored before him for he was unaware of everything. The milk flowed in the ground and fruits were crushed under his feet. One or two men among them said 'What sort of *sanyasi* is this? He is wilfully spoiling the articles.' Naoroji said 'I never saw a sight like this. Why does my

NAROJI REFORMED

heart weep at the sight of this young *sanyasi* to-day? My heart bursts in grief and remorse. What is this snare that the *sanyasi* has laid before me? The food is spoiled, no matter I will give again.'

"Naoroji stood on one side, and looked at Chaitanya with eyes full of wondering love. Large drops of tears were flowing from Chaitanya's eyes, and the people there stood as pictures silently beholding the sight. The news had spread, and all the robbers assembled there one by one. In the evening Chaitanya fell on the ground senseless. His body was trembling in great love and tears were incessantly falling from his eyes.

"Naoroji wept aloud and said 'Tell me, young *sanyasi*, what magic you know. From seeing you I feel that I should not live the sort of life that I have hitherto done. I am sixty years old and a very wicked man, though I am a Brahmin by caste. Give me a little dust from your feet; to-day a new chapter in my life will open. I shall no more be the leader of robbers.' Saying so he looked at his companions and threw away the weapons that he had with him.

"Chaitanya said 'Naoroji listen to me. Wear a bark-dress; that will be enough to cover your shame; go and live the life of a mendicant by begging. If a handful of rice is enough for preserving life what is the use of hoarding money by evil ways? The hollow of your palm may serve you as cup, why should you care for securing the latter? The fountain will give you excellent water. The millionaires, I say, shall have one day to go to the realms of Death. By the same path the Emperor and the meanest of his subjects will go.'

"Naoroji expressed his wish to accompany us. He said 'I know all the jungly paths and shall be able to act as your guide while visiting the various shrines of this country. From to-day no more shall I have to do anything with these weapons. Oh how many murders have I not committed with these hands and what vile language have I not spoken with this mouth! No more do I care to be the leader of the robbers. You are my saviour and have shown me the real path.' Saying so the robber-chief left all that he had and accompanied us wearing a bark dress. Other robbers went away to their place, but Naoroji followed us."

Naoroji accompanied Chaitanya through Khandal on the river Mula, Nasik, Panchabati, Daman, Varouch near the Tapti up to Baroda. After having crossed the Narmada they reached Baroda 'Where,' writes Govinda Das, 'a calamity befell us after three days' stay. Naoroji died of fever. At the moment of his death Chaitanya sat near him and tended him with his own lotus-hands. When his eyes closed for ever, Chaitanya sang Krishna's name to his ears. Chaitanya begged alms from people and gave Naoroji a burial there."

In the Bogula-woods there was another
Bhilapanthi. robber named Bhilapantha, and Chaitanya reformed him in the same way. But I think it is not right to say that he employed any means consciously for reformation. Just as a flower smiles, no matter if anybody sees it or not,—its attraction being a part of its nature—as a gift from the All-Beautiful One, Chaitanya attracted people by the, Charm and poetry of his devotion and trances. There was no propagandism, the very sight of him revealed to them the wonderful beauty of spiritual life and the reformation came as a matter of course without any conscious effort on the part of the reformer. His life was a concentrated spiritual force which proved irresistible in most cases and produced a wonderful effect. Says Govinda of Chaitanya " Reduced greatly by fasting, so weak that he can scarcely walk, he gives the name of Krishna to all from door to door. The people of the country (near Bankot) speak jargon, yet he imparts love of God to them. One who sees Chaitanya has not the power to leave the spot." At Bankot he lay three days in a trance under a tree. During these three days he did not touch any

food. "From Bankot he went to Girishwar where he met a *sanyasi* who had taken the vow of silence. This *sanyasi* was maddened by emotions as he saw the trances of Chaitanya. Next he went to Panna Narasingha and there crossed the Bhadra. He next visited Kalatirtha and thence went to Sandhitirtha, ten miles off from the former place, on the confluence of the rivers Nanda and Bhadra. He met Sadananda Puri there and held a discussion in which Puri was beaten and he acknowledged Chaitanya's superiority. Thence Chaitanya proceeded towards Chaipalli (Trichinopoly) where he met a female anchorite hundred years old, looking grand and beautiful inspite of her age. Thence he went to Nagar "covered with mud, with hair bound into a knot, speaking of nothing else but of Krishna all the way."

<small>A mute *sanyasi* at Girishwar.</small>

<small>Sadananda Puri.</small>

We find him paying a visit to the Muraris, those bad women who professing themselves to be the wives of Khandova, the deity worshipped in the temple at Jizuri near Poona, led vicious lives. Their leader was Indira Devi, an aged woman, who struck with emotion and spiritual fervour of Chaitanya became thoroughly reformed. The Muraris are still to be seen near Poona. About 450 years have not improved the state of things.

<small>The Muraris.</small>

Scholars approached from different localities to hold controversies with him and make him adopt pantheism, but went away after debate, as convinced Vaishnabs reciting the name of Krishna. The women-folk flocked in large numbers to have a sight of him everywhere he went, for his name and fame had already spread up to the farthest interior of Southern India, and Govinda says " The women wonderingly asked ' Is this the famous Chaitanya ? Ah ! how young he is ! Why does he in this tender age wear the knotted hair of ascetics ? Look how reduced he looks by fasting ! ' but often their compassion turned to admiration when Chaitanya spoke of God and wept in great love. At Gurjari he defeated a great scholar named Arjuna after a long discussion and then stood up and cried aloud ' Oh my Krishna ! '

Arjuna, the proud scholar.

" The place at once turned as if into Baikuntha —the heaven of Vishnu. The air blew gently, the villagers came in large numbers. Hundreds of men stood surrounding him to listen to Krishna's name recited by him. It appeared as if the very gods of heaven stood overhead to hear the name. A smell of lotus came flowing in the air. Chaitanya absorbed in poetic frenzy spoke of Krishna. All eyes were fixed on him and all eyes shed tears. The big Mahrattas came there and all heard the recitation of the name. Behind them all I saw hundreds of women of noble families assembled, listening to him with devotional sentiments. The women were weeping and wiping away their tears by the edge of their *sari*. Many Vaishnabs and Shaiva ascetics stood on the spot listening to Chaitanya with closed eyes. By his religious instructions Chaitanya maddened the people of this country. I never saw such a wonderful sight. Sometimes Chaitanya spoke in Tamil and at others in Sanskrit."

The story of the reformation of Chaitanya does not end here. In the Bhakta-Mal by Navaji, a Hindi writer, we find mention of Baramukhi a beautiful harlot. It is stated there that a Sadhu reformed her and she turned a Vaishnab saint. Navaji gathered his information about Baramukhi from the Deccan after Chaitanya's name had been forgotten there. So that the Bhakta-Mal does not give a full account. It is in the pages of Govinda Das's *karcha* that we find a graphic description of this reformation. I shall quote the account here.

<small>Baramukhi, the harlot.</small>

At a village named Ghoga near Dwaraka Chaitanya arrived, accompanied, of course, by Govinda Karmakar and also by two other Bengalis who had met him in the way—Ramananda Basu and Govinda Charan Basu. To their great surprise and delight they had discovered

Chaitanya in the shrine of Dwaraka which they had come to visit.

"At Ghoga lived a harlot named Baramukhi. She was immensely rich. She had acquired this wealth by her bad livelihood. Her apparels and ornaments were like those of a princess and she lived in a large palatial house. She used to wander about her house and the adjoining garden with a view to tempt rich people. Her dress was like those of the women of Peshwar and she had many male and female servants. Attached to her residential building was the garden called *Peyari-kanan*. Chaitanya came and sat near that garden and became totally lost in God's love. I had travelled with him in different countries so long but never did I see so much emotion in him. Ramananda and Govinda Charan stood on two sides and clapped their hands to keep time, as they sang the name of Krishna. There was a large pit near the road and Chaitanya fell into it in an unconscious state. A wicked man came there and began to abuse Chaitanya. He addressed him and said 'Why have you come to deceive the simple villagers here? You want to take money from them by feigning devotion to Krishna. I shall presently see what sort of *sanyasi* you are. I have seen many impostors like you.' When the wicked man spoke in this way, the villagers became excited and were about to give him a sound thrashing, but Chaitanya who had recovered himself, interceded on his behalf and said : ' Whom are you going to beat, brethren ? Here is one whose heart is dry, give him a bit of God's love. His mind has grown sterile without devotion. It is like a desert. Put in him that which may restore it to its natural fertility.' Turning to the man he said : ' Now, my pious brother,' will you come to me, I shall recite to you the name of Krishna and all your sorrows will be removed.' Saying so he went to him and began to sing the name of Krishna.

"Baramukhi, the harlot, saw and heard all that happened from her window and said aloud ' What a cursed life I have been leading ! this young *sanyasi* appears to me like a god. I shall leave everything and go to him. He has no money with him yet my heart throbs with delight at the sight of him. How long shall I be in this house which is now a hell to me ? Will not this god be gracious unto me ? He has saved wicked Balaji from a sinful life, by what charm he knows best. I shall go to him and fall at his feet and will not leave him until he saves me.'

"From the window of her mansion she uttered her reflections and people who heard her were pleased. They began to speak on this topic in an excited manner and laughed and set up a great uproar. A few moments after the harlot came down and Mira, her maid-servant, walked behind her. Baramukhi at this time said to Mira: 'I give you all the wealth that I have. You know I have immense riches but I long to-day to be a street-beggar.' Saying so, she opened her long tresses which fell down like clouds behind her figure, beautiful like a flash of lightning. The tresses fell a long way behind her back and Chaitanya closed his eyes. Her beauty was of a dazzling nature, and people stared at her face. She stood with joint hands before Chaitanya and said again and again: 'Save me, Sir, from the bonds of the world. I am a great sinner. If you do not show me mercy, what is the good of my bearing this cursed life?'

"And saying so she did not wait but cut off her long hair with her own hands. She put on a very humble dress and again came near Chaitanya and stood with joint hands before him. He said 'Make a garden, Baramukhi, of the sacred Tulsi plants here, and live devoting yourself to Krishna.'

"'You are my Krishna, you are my God,' said Baramukhi and fell at his feet. But Chaitanya moved a few steps as if to avoid a touch. People there admired the harlot and Mira, her maid-servant, began to cry aloud. She however with a smile addressed Mira and said, 'Listen to me, Mira, I give you all my wealth. If any guest comes to the house show hospitality as becomes a house-holder. Recite the name of Krishna day and night and do not live a sinful life. It is good to love, but not a deceitful man. Try to love Krishna.' Saying so she took a string of sacred beads in her hands and gave herself up to Krishna."[1]

The account of the Bhaktamal details how Baramukhi made a garden of Tulsi plants and lived a pious life, giving all her property to her maid servant.

---

[1] Govinda Das's Karcha pp.

CHAPTER VIII.

(*i*) Visit to Travancore and other places.
(*ii*) Reception at Puri; meeting with Raghunath Das.

(*i*) *Visit to Travancore and other places.*

From Ghoga Chaitanya started for Somnath. The details of the tour are given in my work 'Chaitanya and His Companions.' The *karcha* gives a topography of the shrines of Southern India, graphic and full of vivid interest. We find how Chaitanya tried to avoid the big Rajas of the Deccan. Rudrapati, the King of Travancore, sent a man asking Chaitanya to pay a visit to him at his palace. On Chaitanya's refusal to do so the messenger threatened him with punishment. But when the Raja heard that the *sanyasi* would not come to him, he went himself on bare foot and in humble dress, and Chaitanya received him kindly. Another Raja came to see him and offered many presents which Chaitanya declined to accept. Upon which the Raja entreated him to accept from him some alms as he did from ordinary people.

<small>Rudrapati, King of Travancore.</small>

Chaitanya in compliance with the request sent Govinda to his palace who took only a handful of rice from the servants of the Raja. The stern attitude of the *sanyasi* is in perfect accord with the account of his conduct towards Pratap Rudra, the Raja of Orissa as described in the Chaitanya Charitamrita and other works. This also proves why the Brahmins of olden times were respected by the aristocracy of India. They were contented with poverty but were proud of their pure life and culture and never showed any sign of humiliation before those that had power and wealth.

We have seen that Chaitanya held frequent learned debates with many of the reputed scholars of Southern India. But Govinda Das being himself a man of very humble education could not follow them. So he was naturally very brief in his description of these. For instance, when Chaitanya meets Ram Ray, the minister of the king Pratap Rudra, on the banks of Godavari, Govinda Das gives only a very inadequate gist of the learned conversation between him and Chaitanya. He plainly tells us that not even a hundredth part of the conversation is reproduced in his book. But Chaitanya Charitamrita gives us details of the discussion. Krishna Das Kaviraj, the author of the latter work, owed the details to the notes left by Sarup Damodara.

Chaitanya started from Puri, as already stated, on the 7th of Baisakh 1432 Saka (1510 A.D.) we find it mentioned that he reached Dwaraka on the Aswin of the next year. Here he stayed 15 days. He arrived at Alalnath in December, 1511 A.D.

The impression that Chaitanya had made in the Deccan lasted a long time. I stated in the course of my previous course of lectures that

The impression made in Southern India. the statue of Haribola in the temple of Rameswaram is in all probability that of Chaitanya. Professor D. R. Bhandarkar tells me that he has got two *avangas* of Tukaram in which that saintly poet says that Chaitanya appeared to him in a dream. The *avangas* have not yet been translated. But no research has been yet made in the fields of old Tamil and Maharatta literatures to ascertain if the mention of Chaitanya's tour occurs in any of them.

Chaitanya avoided self-glorification of all sorts so that even Govinda took the notes "very privately" as he tells us. It is not probable that the people of Southern India kept any information about Chaitanya beyond the fact that he was a great Sadhu. For it is not the courtesy in India to enquire about anything relating to the life of a Sadhu, previous to his *sanyas*. But still if proper research be made, some traditions about him may be found in the vernacular literatures, of the different countries that he had visited; for there is no doubt that he had made a very great impression.

(ii) *Return to Puri and the reception.*

When from Rissa Culla, the weary wayfarers came to Alalnath after their long journey, the news spread all over the country in a few hours. The companions of Chaitanya, not permitted to go with him as attendants, were awaiting his return with great eagerness. They all hastened to meet him. We find the party that marched from Puri to give him a reception headed by the lame scholar Khanjanacharya. Says Govinda Das "though lame he ran ahead of others." The veteran scholar Vasudev carried a drum himself and beat it with his own hands to indicate his joy. Murari Gupta came up in great haste and when Chaitanya embraced him, the old man overpowered with his emotion, knelt down. Ram Das, the famous musician, sounded the horn. Narahari, the saintly poet of Srikhanda, appeared with a flag in his hand. The famous singer Lakhan's voice was heard above all voices, for he sang sweet songs of reception. Haridas, the Mahomedan convert, and Krishna Das, whose big belly was a noteworthy sight, came up in breathless haste, and hundreds of others followed. Some danced for joy and

THE RECEPTION

others sang. Says Govinda "The joy of this union cannot be expressed in words." They all began to sing the praises of Krishna, and in their midst was seen Chaitanya with tearful eyes, beautifully moving his head in emotion, joining the singers. On the 3rd of Magh 1433 Saka (1511 A.D.) Chaitanya reached Puri with these men. Thousands of men gathered to have a sight of him; and Raja Pratap Rudra, throwing aside his royal pomp, joined the procession, and behind Chaitanya and behind every one, like the humblest of his subjects, went on bare foot. Chaitanya visited the temple of Puri and as he saw it he was absorbed in his love-ecstacy. Basudev Sarbabhauma says "There is the image of Vishnu in wood, lifeless, but you are living Vishnu" and Chaitanya when he heard this admonished Vasudev saying "That is blasphemy, I am a common mortal, do not speak in that way." The account of Chaitanya's return to Puri as we find in the *karcha* and that given in Chaitanya Charitamrita are very much alike. Many people had certainly witnessed it in Orissa, so that Krishna Das could easily gather correct historical information from direct sources.

On his return to Puri Raghunath Das, that princely youth who had given up his vast landed properties and turned an ascetic, met him. His income from landed estates was 12 lakhs of rupees a

<small>Raghunath Das.</small>

year, and he enjoyed besides a further large income from taxes levied upon sea-going vessels and other sources. It should be remembered that the value of money at that time was much higher than now. When barely 16, he had, ere this, once come to give himself up to Chaitanya. But the latter had then said "Do not feign asceticism, it is not easy in your age to turn an ascetic. You are a young boy. First go and do the duties of the world. But be not too much addicted to it. And when by discharging worldly duties you will be fit for renunciation, then Krishna himself will show you the way." And Raghunath spoke not a word but returned home to the great joy of his father Gobardhan Das and uncle Hiranya Das,—as he was the only heir to their joint estates at Saptagram. Raghunath was dearer to them than all their riches. When the lost one was found, the joy of this return sounded through the streets of their city by loud Nahabat Orchestra. Raghunath had married one of the handsomest girls in that part of the country. A quarrel ensued soon after between his uncle and father on one side and Hussain Shah the Emperor on the other, and the result was that the latter's troops attacked their palace at Saptagram. They had however absconded. Young Raghunath was fearless and came forward and was forthwith arrested. Though he was so highly religious he knew business tactics well.

RAGHUNATH DAS

When brought before the Emperor he cleverly managed affairs and an amicable settlement was the result. After doing his duties to the letter, even as the Master had advised, for five or six years, Raghunath again longed for joining Chaitanya. It was his course of preparations for the great renunciation which his parents had mistaken for worldliness. They were therefore alarmed to find Raghunath's growing tendencies towards ascetic's life again. He was kept continually under watch and several Brahmin scholars were appointed to teach him that there existed no higher duties than taking care of old parents and doing duties of the world by helping people in distress and the like. But Chaitanya's frenzied love for God and poetic life had a fascination which could not be overcome by such advice. And one day it was discovered that availing himself of a little relaxation on the part of the guards, young Raghunath had made his escape.

Chaitanya had just returned to Puri. Raghunath had walked on bare foot through jungles and woods to avoid detection; for ten horsemen were behind him trying to trace him out. He fasted many a day. In the way he hardly found shelter to sleep in nights. After 12 days of great hardship he reached Puri. Chaitanya was then in the house of Kashi Misra, and Mukunda Datta recognised the youth from a distance and cried aloud "Look there Raghu, our beloved Raghu comes. How pale and imatiated does he look!" And Raghu touched the feet of the Master with tears and said "Do not leave me this time." Chaitanya appointed Sarupa Damodara to teach him Vaishnab scriptures. For a fuller account of Raghunath Das the reader is referred to my works 'Chaitanya and his Companions.'

CHAPTER IX.

(*i*) Proposed visit to Brindaban.
(*ii*) Interview with Rupa and Sanatan—their *sanyas*.
(*iii*) Private tour; Baladev's account.
(*iv*) Stay at Brindaban; on the way back, meeting with Bijali Khan.

(i) *Proposed visit to Brindaban.*

After a short stay at Puri Chaitanya expressed his wish to go to visit the Brinda groves, and Nrishinghananda, one of his admirers, became ready to devote his whole fortune towards making a road from Puri to Brindaban on this occasion. He built the road up to Kanai's Natsala near Gour, and Chaitanya Charitamrita gives a description of the magnificence of the plan. The road was well metalled and was paved with coloured stones and on both sides tanks were dug and rows of flower-trees were planted. When Chaitanya marched out flowers were spread on the way, so that the *sanyasi* could walk pleasantly on bare foot. Arrangements were made by Raja Pratap Rudra to keep record

The road made by Narsinghananda.

of this trip. He sent three of his chief ministers, Mongoraj, Harichandan and Ram Ray with orders that every place where Chaitanya would bathe might be turned into a shrine. A monument should mark such spots. Owing to Raja Pratap Rudra's continued animosity with Hussain Shah the places beyond Pichilda, the limits of the jurisdiction of Uriya Raja, were very unsafe for the pilgrims who intended to travel beyond the boundary-line. The Mahomedan Governor appointed near Pichilda was, however, a great admirer of Chaitanya and he made friends with the ministers of Pratap Rudra and arranged every facility for the pilgrims. The road made by Nrishighananda was called Nrishinghananda's "Jangal" and may probably be still traced near Kanai's Natsala. A crowd of thousands of men followed Chaitanya, but he, overjoyed at the thought of visiting the groves sacred by associations with Krishna, heeded not these magnificent arrangements but went absorbed in his own thoughts. When he had come up to Ramkeli, Hussain Shah heard the report of the great crowd that attended the *Sanyasi* and sent one Keshab Basu to make enquiries as to what sort of *sanyasi* he was. The Emperor was evidently struck with the impression that Chaitanya had created in the country and wondered how a poor Brahmin lad could command such a widespread influence as to be followed by thousands.

(ii) *Interview with Sanatan and Rupa—their Sanyas.*

It is stated in the Chaitanya Charitamrita that the Emperor felt a genuine respect for Chaitanya, after what he had heard from Keshab Basu. But when Sanatan, the Prime Minister, interviewed Chaitanya at Ramkeli, he told the Master that it was not safe for him to stay there long. "This Mahomedan ruler," he said, "has broken numberless images of gods throughout the provinces of Bengal and Orissa and greatly oppressed the Hindus. It is true that at the present moment he seems to be favourably disposed towards you, but who knows when his good disposition will pass away yielding to despotism which is his element." And Sanatan further remarked that it was not becoming for a *sanyasi* as he was to go to visit a shrine with such a large number of men. Chaitanya who had not so long minded the external things around him was roused to a sense of his duty as an ascetic by this remark and expressed his desire to return to Puri. He came back to Puri but not without leaving an impression in Gour which bore great fruits later on in the cause of Vaishnavism. Sanatan and Rupa, one the Prime Minister and the other an assistant in the court of Hussain Shah, were formerly called by the Mahomedan names of Sakarmallik and Dabirkhas respectively, for they had practically given up their Hindu ways though they had been originally Brahmins, and adopted Mahomedan habits. The names of Sanatan and Rupa were given to the brothers by Chaitanya. Sanatan was a great Sanskrit and Persian scholar and Rupa afterwards became the foremost Sanskrit poet of Bengal of those days.

Their visits to Chaitanya produced the usual effect and the brothers saw in him what others had seen before. This *sanyasi* had actually fallen in love with God, hitherto believed to be too high for human comprehension. They beheld with wondering love the beauty of his mystic trances and this fascination did not cease but grow with lapse of time. Rupa left the court, turned *sanyasi* and joined Chaitanya at Puri about the year 1516 A.D. leaving a note for Sanatan his elder brother. This was in the form of a Sanskrit verse which may be thus rendered into English " Where is, alas, now Ayodhya, the the kingdom of Rama ? Its glories have vanished and where is the reputed Mathura of Krishna ?

<small>Rupa and Sanatan.</small> It is also devoid of its former splendour. Think of the fleeting nature of things and settle your course." The Prime Minister, however, could not so easily leave the capital as the Emperor kept him under watch after his brother had fled. He asked him to accompany him in his expedition

against a Hindu kingdom. But Sanatan plainly told the Emperor that he could not be a party to help iconoclasm, upon which the Emperor threw him into prison. But his relations bribed Mir Habul, the jailor, with Rupees 7,000 and helped his escape. He joined the Master at Puri. Chaitanya sent both the brothers to Brindaban with the mission to identify places associated with Krishna and write books about Vaishnavism. There might have been a political reason for Chaitanya's sending the brothers away. If they lived at Puri, the hostilities between Prataprudra and Husain Shah might be renewed on this plea, as both the brothers had fled from Husain Shah's court and one had actually made his escape from prison after having bribed the Jailor. The manner in which Sanatan met Chaitanya, his great spiritual humility and the pathos of the situation have been vividly recorded in the pages of the Chaitanya Charitamrita. He would not allow Chaitanya to touch his body afflicted with eczema. But Chaitanya embraced it saying that there was nothing so dear to him as that body in which a self-sacrificing spirit and love for God dwelt. Sanatan left the ordinary path leading to the temple and walked through the sun-burnt sands which scorched his feet. He had avoided the public road owing to the fact that the Pandas might object, as he had once adopted Mahomedan ways. When Chaitanya pointed to the burns on his toe, Sanatan said "I did not know or feel these, so overjoyed was I that Master had called me." And Chaitanya said "Even the very gods of heaven would be sanctified by a touch of yours. You are the holiest of the Brahmins that I have ever met, yet you did not despise the ordinary rules of the temple. This only shows your superior breeding and noble character." Chaitanya gave Sanatan instructions on Vaishnab religion and its tenets for a period of three months and these were elaborated and compiled by Sanatan in his *magnas opus*—the Haribhakti-Bilas, the highest authoritative work of jurisprudence with the Bengali Vaishnabs. Both the brothers, Sanatan and Rupa, went to Brindaban and settled there by the Master's command, and it is they who eventually raised the old shrine to such a great eminence. Formerly it was a pastoral village dotted here and there with cottages, but it now claims some of the most magnificent temples of India, and is one of the most splendid of her ancient cities. The resuscitation of the old shrine is due to the efforts of a few ascetics led by Sanatan and Rupa, who had no house to live in, who slept under trees— and lived upon the scantiest of meals by begging, and wore rags. This noble renunciation which has marked them out as recurring types of the Buddha and Mahabir in Indian History, attracted millionaires who built temples to commemorate the shrine. We thus find that the inspiration of Chaitanya had a far-reaching effect in moulding the fortunes of the cities far remote from Bengal.

(c) *Private tour—Baladev's account.*

After a short stay at Puri Chaitanya again planned a tour in Upper India mainly with the object of visiting Brindaban. He expressed his intention to a companion in these words " Last time I had intended to go to the Brinda groves, but there was such an immense crowd that it was impossible for me to proceed after having gone some distance. .Wherever I stayed, people ascended the roofs of houses and tops of walls and it looked as if all the buildings would fall with a crash ; wherever I happened to glance I saw only the heads of men and women; deserted paths were filled with teeming population, and this did not stop, but increased from day to day. It had been my object to visit the shrine alone but I looked like a Marshal or a Captain followed by a large army who beat drums to announce the visit. "

Tour in Upper India.

This time he was resolved not to allow any such thing. The arrangement proposed by him was that when people would come, after he had left, as usual in the morning to see him, they should not be given any report of his departure from Puri for some time ; so that they might not hasten to overtake him on the way. He would allow no one to accompany him; the entreaties of friends and followers were all in vain. One Baladev Bhattacharyya was already proceeding to Brindaban and the friends of Chaitanya insisted on his taking him as companion. Chaitanya after a protest acceded to this request. The matter was kept private for some time, according to his desire, so that the whole Puri was taken by surprise at the news of his departure of which they heard many days after Chaitanya had left the city. A popular song thus describes him as a pilgrim to the famous shrine of the Vaishnabs :

"Look how Chaitanya goes to the Brinda groves! Look at his shaven head, the rag on his back and the beggar's bowl at his hand."

Baladev's account is very inadequate. He did not evidently take any note but tried to take his audience by surprise by narrating miracles about him. He also seizes every opportunity to emphasize the point that Chaitanya was greatly pleased by the manner in which he offered his services to him. It pleased his vanity to say all these and this no doubt heightened his importance in the eyes of the Vaishnabs. He said that the plants and trees of the Brinda groves came near Chaitanya to offer him their tributes of flowers and fruits and that even the tigers on the way recited the name of Krishna, when Chaitanya had bidden them to do so. Krishnadas Kaviraj, a devout Vaishnab and scholar, recorded these in spirit of implicit faith, nay, threatened the non-believers with imprecations. The contrast between Baladev's account recorded in the Charitamrita and what we find in the *karcha* of Govindadas is striking. One is mostly a fairy-tale and gibberish and the other a simple and unassuming piece of history. But on this we need not dwell any more.

One of the important facts in regard to Chaitanya's tour in Upper India relates to incidents that happened at Benares. While in that city he put up with one Tapan Misra and later on stayed for some time at the house of Chandrasekhar, a Vaidya. The leader of the sanyasis at this time in that city was the far-famed scholar and saint Prakasananda. He was a son of Benkat Bhatta of Southern India and brother of Gopal Bhatta who latterly rose to eminence as one of the six Goswamis among the Gauriya Vaishnabs. Like all Indian scholars of that age Prakasananda was a pantheist. One account says that he had suffered from leprosy for a time. It is recorded that one of his Mahratta disciples paid a visit to Chaitanya and found the

<small>At Benares.</small>

Nadia-ascetic merged in the love of Krishna. Prakasananda's scholarship was equal to his pride and he did not like when his Mahratta pupil came to him and spoke eulogistically of the Nadia-sanyasi. His love for God was reported to be so great that it sanctified every man who beheld it, that his tears created pathos which were irresistible and taught men a love for God without a sermon. The disciple declared that he believed Chaitanya to be an Avatar of God. Prakasananda only sneeringly replied " He is an impostor; I too have heard of him. I do not know what black art he knows, but he has certainly a power to hypnotise people as he seems to have done you. Benares, however, is a city of the learned ; here all these emotional nonsense will not do. Do not go to him again. Read the Upanishads carefully and leave the mad man alone." The Brahmin was sorry to hear Chaitanya abused in this way and reported all these to him. He, feeling how deeply the young scholar's feelings were wounded, said "I came to sell a little of the emotional sweetness with which my soul is charged, to the people of this city. But there is no purchaser here. The burden of my emotion oppresses me and fain would I sell it to you at whatever small price you would offer."

VISITING THE SHRINES 227

(*iv*) *Stay at Brindaban,—on his way back— meeting with Bijli Khan.*

Chaitanya felt immensely delighted with the forest-path through which he went. At Jharikhanda he passed through a regular amphitheatre of woodland scenes and was beside himself with joy. He danced in emotion and cried aloud 'Krishna' 'Krishna,' while tears flowed down his cheeks that knew no bounds. He came to Allahabad and stayed there for a few days. On arrival at Mathura he stopped near Bisranti Ghat. Here he met a Sonoria Brahmin whose status in society was low but who was a disciple of Madhabendra Puri and had been initiated into the Bhakti cult by that famous apostle. Chaitanya paid him great respects. He visited the twenty-four landing ghats of the Jamuna, each of which was a great shrine of the Vaishnabs. He came next to the village of Arit and thence went to Annakut. He proceeded to a village named Gathuli and lived in Brindaban for some time. His religious ecstasies in this favoured place of the Vaishnabs knew no bounds. At the sight of the neck of a peacock, the bluish dark colour of which reminded him of Krishna, he fell senseless to the ground and for days together remained absolutely without any food whatever. For several days he did not talk with anybody. The rush of visitors

At Jharikhanda.

became so great that it became almost uncontrollable. Baladev Bhattacharya one day told the Master "These people who cannot have an interview with you, as you often remain in your trances, disturb me in such a manner that it is not possible for me to stay here any longer. Every one comes to invite you and how can a thousand invitations be accepted every day? The great Mela of the *Sanyasis* will take place at Allahabad on the 30th of Magh and let us go to visit it." It was probably the Kumbha Mela of the year 1517. Chaitanya made no objection and being accompanied by Baladev Bhattacharya, a Rajput Chief named Krishna Das and three Brahmin admirers of Brindaban, started for that city. In the way a milkman was playing on his flute; at the sound, Chaitanya began to tremble; the memory of Krishna's flute became vivid and he swooned away. Ten horsemen headed by Bijli Khan, the son of a Pathan Nawab, came up there at this moment and suspecting that the five men had drugged the ascetic in order to rob him of his money, arrested them. Krishna Das, the Rajput, was a valorous man and was not to be cowed down. He threatened the Mahomedans saying that he had an army behind him who would soon come up to teach proper lessons to them. When a hot discussion was going on,

Leaves Brindaban.

Krishna Das's encounter with Bijli Khan.

BIJLI KHAN

Chaitanya recovered his senses and said "Brethren, your suspicion is ungrounded. I am an ascetic and have no money to be robbed of. I am suffering from epilepsy and these friends have kindly attended me during my illness. Kindly release them." Attracted by the sweet courtesy and his exceedingly attractive manners, one of them who was a great scholar in Mahomedan theology entered into a discussion with Chaitanya who at once convinced him of the superiority of the *bhakti* cult. The eloquence and devotion with which all was said made a great impression, and Bijli Khan with his Mahomedan followers became converted into Vaishnab faith.

CHAPTER X.

(*a*) Chaitanya at Benares, discussion with Prakasananda.
(*b*) Tour in Bengal.
(*c*) At Puri.

(*a*) *Chaitanya at Benares ; discusion with Prakasananda.*

At Allahabad, the confluence of the Ganges and the Jamuna, Chaitanya produced such a wonderful impression that Krishnadas Kaviraj remarks "The joint streams of the Ganges and the Jamuna could not plunge Allahabad, but the flood of Krishna's love brought by Chaitanya did it." At Allahabad Sanatan met Chaitanya and both stayed there for ten days. He returned to Benares and was received there by his two old friends Tapan Misra and Chandrasekhar. The Mahratta Brahmin, the pupil of Prakasananda, also came up to meet him. He stayed this time at the house of Chandrasekhar where Sanatan also called on to pay his respects. Chaitanya gave him further instructions about the *bhakti*-cult. These teachings occupy a long space of the Chaitanya Charitamrita. Then took place the much expected controversial discussion which had been reserved during Chaitanya's last visit, between him and the great leader of the *sanyasis* of Benares, Prakasananda. This was of course relating to the respective merits of the pantheist school and that form of dualism in which *bhakti* is emphasized. The details of this discussion, it is said, were embodied in a work called the Panchatattyakhyan (Chaitanya Charitamritra, verse 8, p. 25) written by Krishnadas Kaviraj. This book seems to be lost. The author of the Chaitanya Charitamrita says that having once given particulars of this discussion in his Panchatattyakhyan he did not think it worth while to repeat the same in the Charitamrita; but that he would only briefly refer to it in that book. So the particulars are not yet known; but from what has been written in the Charitamrita we see that Chaitanya did not try to demolish pantheism as he had done in other places, as much as he tried here to establish the religion of Bhakti. Thus by elucidating and elaborating the texts of the Bhagbat Sk. 10, Ch. 14, verse 4, Sk. 10, 2, 26, Sk. 3, 10, 3 and 4, Sk. 1, 5, 12, Sk. 6, 14, 4, Sk. 8, 1, 8, Sk. 2, 9, 30, 31, 32, 33, 34, 35, Sk. 11, 2, 53, Sk. 11, 2, 43, Sk. 10, 30, 4, Sk. 1, 2, 11, Sk. 3, 5, 23, and Sk. 11, 3, and 28 and those of other scriptures, he clearly established the superiority

(a) Discussion with Prakasananda.

of the *bhakti* cult; and Prakasananda who had so long scaled great intellectual heights and in his arrogance considered God and man to be identical, felt that a new fountain of soul was discovered from which sprang sweetness, resignation and love, capable of thoroughly spiritualising and sanctifying his life. And when at the end of his discourses Chaitanya wept for love of God, Prakasananda discovered in him a new man with a far deeper spiritual force and wider moral outlook than he could ever conceive it to be possible in a human being. The element of pedantry which had characterised young Chaitanya as a scholar of Nadia, though now thoroughly overcome by his spiritual humanity, showed itself, it is said on this occasion, in his startling interpretations of the verse 10, canto 7, of the first *skanda* of the Bhagavata, which he is said to have explained in 61 different ways. The difference in the present case became apparent in the fact that his speech was not only divested from all arrogant manners of a young pedant, but was also sweetly chastened by emotion and was full of spiritual felicities that made the deepest impression. So great was the effect of Prakasananda's acceptance of Chaitanya as his Guru that all Benares and its neighbouring localities gathered to have a sight of the divine man. "When Chaitanya went to visit the temple of

Bishwanath," says Charitamrita, " immense crowds gathered on both sides of the road to have a glimpse of his face." When Chaitanya sobbed for Krishna and called Him aloud in a voice choked with tears, the people shouted 'Krishna' 'Krishna,' with tearful eyes, so that the whole atmosphere, as it were, rang with Krishna's name.

(b) *Tour in Bengal.*

On his return to Puri Chaitanya is said to have again made a trip to Bengal.
<small>Conflicting accounts of this tour.</small> Jayananda says that during this tour he visited Kulia, staying at Barokona *ghat* near Nadia, where his mother Sachi Devi had again an opportunity of seeing him. He paid a flying visit to Kumarhatta and stayed for a short while at the residence of Sribas. He also met there Bashudev Datta, son of Mukunda Sanjay, at whose house, it should be remembered, Chaitanya used to hold his *tol* at Nadia. From Kumarhatta he came to Panihati where he was a guest of Raghab Pandit. He next visited Baranagar near Calcutta, where his sandals are still preserved in the temple erected by Bhagavatacharya. I am not, however, quite sure of chronological accuracy in regard to these trips. Most of the biographers seem to suggest that Chaitanya had paid a visit to the above villages on his way back from

Ramkeli, before he had started for Brindaban a second time. But Govinda Das, who was with him, says nothing about his visit to these villages. This makes it doubtful if Chaitanya had ever visited them before he returned from Southern India. But I have already stated that Govinda Das's account of the brief period before Chaitanya started for the Deccan is neither perfect nor given in detail. Hence with some hesitancy we are inclined to credit the account of the other biographers on this point.

(c) *At Puri.*

His tour in the Deccan and in the Upper India altogether took six years and he spent the remaining 18 years of his life at Puri. He became a *sanyasi* on the completion of the 24th year and passed away from this world in his 48th year—in 1533 A.D.

<small>Eighteen years in Orissa.</small>

It appears that King Pratap Rudra used to appoint reporters wherever Chaitanya travelled. Kavikarnapur says that one Mallabhatta, the court Pandit of Raja of Karnat, had reported to Pratap Rudra the details of Chaitanya's tour in the Deccan. The reporters are also observed to give the Raja details in regard to the doings of Chaitanya and some of his

<small>Reporters appointed by Pratap Rudra.</small>

followers at Puri. We find several Brahmin reporters bringing to the Raja information about Chaitanya's interview with Ram Rai on the banks of Godavari. From incidental references of this nature I have firm conviction that Chaitanya's life, especially that of the long 18 years that he had spent at Puri, was preserved in State papers in the Uriya language by the order of Pratap Rudra. For that monarch and his chief queen Chandrakala, daughter of Shekhara, were the staunchest followers of Chaitanya and interested themselves profoundly in every act of the Master. After Chaitanya had passed away, we have it on the authority of Kavikarnapur, that on an occasion of the great Cart festival of Jagannath (sometime after 1533 A.D.) the Raja saw the immense gathering at Puri from the terrace of his palace and sadly reflected that everything looked void and unmeaning to him, when the great personality of Chaitanya—the living fountain of faith that had so long inspired such gatherings—was no longer there to gladden his eyes. Kavikarnapur was commanded to write a drama on Chaitanya to give some consolation to the Raja in his great grief. Once every year the Puri Raja, with a golden broom in his hand cleansed the temple of Jagannath according to an old custom, and one of the biographers says that after Chaitanya's passing away, the Raja, while discharging this function, could not suppress his tears in recollection of Chaitanya. From all these evidences of his great love for the Master and the incidental references to his appointing reporters to record the incidents about him, I am almost certain that if the old papers and documents of the palace are searched, important biographical sketch of the Master may still be recovered. Babu Suprakash Ganguli, a grandson of Maharsi Debendranath Tagore, tells me that he had purchased a large Uriya MS. in six volumes, containing Chaitanya's life, for Rs. 125 from a Panda of the Puri temple and sold it almost immediately after to an American tourist for Rs. 1,200. We have Rajas and Maharajas whose munificence in the cause of Vaishnab religion is well known in this province. Surrounded by Uriya scholars and Uriya king's chief officers, Chaitanya had lived 18 years of his life in the Uriya country where admiration for him is still so great that his images are worshipped in almost every important village. But though popular regard for Chaitanya is great everywhere, no one has ever thought it fit to ransack the store of old Uriya MSS. and find out what facts about the life of the Master might be found from that very probable source. The poet-laureate of Pratap Rudra's court was Banipati. Surely if his verses are still extant, some of them may be found to contain hymns and adulatory lyrics in honour of Chaitanya. We call upon the aristocracy of Bengal to found research scolarships for initiating historical investigations in this very important field. Not only Banipati, but other contemporary poets and writers might have, it is presumed, something to say about the inspiring personality of the Master. Rupa and Sanatan saw Chaitanya occasionally as they had made Vrindaban their permanent home. The Bengali admirers and friends of Chaitanya came to visit him at Puri for some short months of the rainy season, so the sources availed of by Krishnadas are not at all of an exhaustive nature. It is in the Uriya books and records that we may naturally expect to find far larger materials about the epoch of Master's life spent at Puri.

On his return to Puri we find Chaitanya literally merged in love-ecstasies. When he went to see the sacred images in the Puri temple, he became so overpowered with emotion that he could not control himself. Sometimes he ran to the very pedestal, to embrace the images. Coming to his senses—he regretted his conduct and made it a point not to enter the temple. He stood resting his elbow on the Garur pillar at the gate of the Temple and saw through eyes overflowing with tears the images from afar, lost to all other sights or things of the world.

The Gadura-Pillar.

The mark caused by his elbow, which touched the pillar every day, for a period extending over 18 years, is still to be seen. Many incidents of this period of Chaitanya's life are related in the Chaitanya Charitamrita and in these we find exhaustive notes on some of his followers such as Rupa, Sanatan and Raghunath Das. These I have detailed in my work called "Chaitanya and his Companions" and I need not repeat them here. We find Chaitanya greatly admiring Bidagdha Madhava and Lalit Madhava, two Sanskrit dramas written by Rupa, the inspiration of which had come from Chaitanya himself,—the famous *sloka* in one of these works beginning with " *Tunde tandabini,*" etc., being specially appreciated. These dramas were held in great admiration by all Vaishnabs specially by Ram Ray, the author of Jagannath Ballava in Sanskrit, who was himself a great dramatist. About this time we find a poet of Eastern Bengal who had written a Sanskrit drama on Chaitanya, paying a visit to Puri and getting himself introduced to the Master by one of his followers Bhagaban Acharya. The young poet was very willing that the Master would listen to a recitation of his work. But Chaitanya declined to do so on the plea that he was not the proper critic, evidently avoiding to hear his own eulogies. On the

Margin note: Lalit Madhava and Bidagdha Madhava.

BALLAVA BHATTA

persistent entreaties of the poet, Chaitanya's companion Swarupa Damodara heard the verses of the drama but found many rhetorical flaws in the work. Another man Ballava Bhatta, the renowned leader of the sect that goes by his name, came to pay respects to Chaitanya. Though holding him in high admiration Ballava had little regard for his companions. But Chaitanya said in reply to the eulogies with which Ballava had accosted him, "Sir, your praises are misplaced, for I am an ascetic devoid of any love for God. My esteemed friend Adwaitacharya, learned in all the branches of human knowledge, has fertilized my heart by infusing into it a bit of his great love. There is Nityananda whose mind is an ocean of spiritual felicities, and Bashudev Sarbabhauma who knows the six schools of philosophy as few know them in India. These truly saintly men have taught me the little devotion to Krishna that people find in me. Ramananda Ray knows the niceties of spiritual emotion to an extent which is my constant joy to hear, and Damodara Swarupa is a living fountain from whom spiritual sweetness ever flows. Besides these men, there are Jagadananda Bakreshwar, Kasishwar, Mukunda, Bashudev, Murari and others whose saintly company has helped me to acquire a little faith which has attracted you.

Some distinguished visitors fail in the objects of their visits.

to visit me." Ballava had thought that there was none at Puri with him he could discourse on religion except Chaitanya for whom he had of course a high regard. He however, did not much relish the words of Chaitanya, but for the sake of courtesy asked where these worthies could be interviewed. Chaitanya said " They are all here now to see the Car festivities." Ballava invited them all to his house and was struck by their great devotion and scholarship. During *Rathajatra* seven great parties marched to hold *Kirtana* in the public streets. Sribas, Mukunda, Govinda Ghosh and three others led six of them, Chaitanya himself, accompanied by Nityananda, leading the main party. The joy of the procession was great, and the more did Ballava see of Chaitanya the more was he convinced of his divinity. Ballava had written a commentary on the Bhagavata and had an ardent desire that the Master would see it. But Chaitanya said that he was not fit to listen to a discourse on the Bhagavata, as that scripture was too high for his comprehension ; the two letters कृष he says were a fascination to him and beyond this he needed no expansion of the religious idea. Then Ballava said that he had elaborately interpreted the two letters explaining the religious import they carried. But Chaitanya told him that to him the word was enough and it meant a simple thing and further interpretations would only cloud his faith. The truth is that Ballava had found fault with the established commentary on the Bhagavata by Sridhar Swami, and Chaitanya had already heard of this. He did not like to hear any one blaspheming the saintly commentator, and hence he tried to avoid Ballava Bhatta. But when one day Ballava vaunted before him that he had rejected the Swami (lit. husband) Chaitanya is said to have made a pun on the word and said "How can one be called true who has rejected the Swami?" Ballava was very sorry at being treated with indifference by the Master and wondered why Chaitanya had changed his attitude towards him; for thought he " When I had first seen him at Allahabad he had received me very kindly." Coming home he reflected on this again till suddenly he felt that it had been very wrong on his part to discard Sridhar's commentary. Sridhar Swami was the prince of Bhagavata commentators and a saintly man; whereas he proceeded to establish his points being guided by pride alone. "This pride," he thought, "must be given up," and the next day when he met Chaitanya again, the Master received him with more than usual kindness, for he had marked in his remorseful looks that true spiritual humility had dawned on him in the place of the haughtiness and pride of mere scholarship. "Ballava Bhatta," says Charitamrita, "was a worshipper of Bala Gopal—child-Krishna. He practically changed his views in respect of Vaishnavism by the teachings of Jagadananda, a young scholar and admirer of Chaitanya." This account of Ballava Bhatta is to be found in the Charitamrita and must be substantially correct, but as Ballava is the reputed leader of another sect of Vaishnavas, and though a contemporary of Chaitanya had not accepted the latter's form of faith but founded a new school, we must await a scrutinising enquiry into the literature of his school before accepting *in toto* the account of the Charitamrita.

We find in the old Assamese literature frequent references to the Vaisnava apostle Sankara interviewing Chaitanya. There are clear evidences of the great influence which Chaitanya exerted on the great Vaishnav saint of Assam of the 16th century.

At Puri occurred that melancholy incident causing junior Haridas to leave the city and drown himself at the confluence of the sacred rivers near Allahabad.

<small>The tragic end of junior Haridas.</small>

Chaitanya had heard that this young ascetic had begged alms from Madhabi, an accomplished woman and a sister of Sikhi Mahiti, who was a copyist in the king's court. The Master said, "Being a *sanyasi* he interviews a woman, I cannot bear to see his face" and he never allowed him to come near him. Ram Ray the great friend of Chaitanya, used to have his dramas played by women and directed their rehearsal himself. Nityananda had two wives. But Chaitanya had never objected to this. He was, however, cruelly hard upon junior Haridas. The reason seems to be that this young ascetic who had a sweet musical voice had not yet extinguished his sexual desires, though he had taken the vows of asceticism, and this Chaitanya knew well; whereas in regard to the worthies mentioned above, he knew them to be men of approved character and saintliness, about whom he had not the least shadow of doubt. This accounts for the difference in treatment referred to here. Junior Haridas tried in vain to soften the attitude of Chaitanya, but failing, drowned himself in the Jamuna near Allahabad where he had gone for penance. The supernatural tale about this man, full of pathetic interest, related in the Charitamrita, has been reproduced by me in my work "Chaitanya and his Companions."

The people of Nadia and the neighbouring localities had the Master's permission for coming to Puri and staying there for four months of the rainy season, —all except Chaitanya's poor mother, wife and Nityananda. But Nityananda paid little heed to the order of Chaitanya and came often to Puri to see him. The leader of the party

Shibananda Sen.

from Nadia was that veteran Vaishnava Sibananda Sen, who knew all the paths and was rich enough to bear expenses of those who had not the means. Sibananda was an inhabitant of Kanchrapara near Naihati, and his son Paramananda Sen who is generally known by his title of Kavikarnapur, is the author of the celebrated drama Chaitanya Chandrodaya and other works in Sanskrit.

It appears that about the year 1520 A.D. sometime after Chaitanya's return to Puri after his tour in Upper India, a few pilgrims from Bengal reported to him that Adwaita had eschewed the *bhakti* cult and reverted to that of *jnan* and was busy explaining the five-fold paths of emancipation from desires (*Mukti*) according to pantheistic views propounded by Sankara and other leaders of that school. Chaitanya did not put much faith in the reports of the people which he took for mere story. Then came a letter from Nityananda himself, saying "Adwaitacharya has given up the *bhakti* cult and is explaining the tenets of non-dualistic belief." A great discussion took place at Puri amongst Ram Ray, Gopinath Acharya and Bashudev Sarbabhauma as to the course to be adopted for preventing the veteran leader of Vaishnava from the mischievous course he had been following. They all expressed themselves against him in

<small>Adwaita's change of views.</small>

SUSPICION ABOUT ADWAITA

a somewhat free language. But Chaitanya, when he heard their speeches, made light of the whole thing and said with a smile " I am afraid it is a mere trick on the part of Adwaitacharya to pursuade me to visit Bengal once more. For somehow or other he has conceived the notion that when the interests of the *bhakti* religion will be at stake, I shall not be able to sit quiet at Puri like a mere looker-on. Adwaita who is mine in every respect regrets my *sanyas* and desertion of home more than any one else." The scholars of Puri, however, headed by Ram Ray, sought divine grace in the Puri temple for safeguarding the interests of Vaishnava religion and the High Priest came up with reassuring looks, saying that the cause of Vaishnavism would flourish for ever ; as a sign of divine blessings he presented a garland of flowers, 21 feet long, from the Temple, and in the meantime a reply came from Adwaitacharya himself to whom Chaitanya had written a letter. It said in a sort of enigmatic language like the *Sandhya bhasa*—in which conversations were sometimes carried on amongst Chaitanya, Nityananda and Adwaita, that everything was right and that even Nityananda had misunderstood him. The letter further assured that it was impossible for Adwaitacharya to swerve an inch from his loyalty to Chaitanya. That a sort of quarrel on some minor points of religion had arisen between Adwaita and Nityananda, is hinted by Brindaban Das himself in many places of his work, substantiating the statement of the Prembilas from which we have taken the above account.

<small>Adulatory verses written by Sarvabhauma.</small> Kavikarnapur says, what is reproduced by some of the later biographers, that Sarvabhauma had written two verses in honour of Chaitanya Dev and entrusted them to Mukunda Datta to be shown to the Master. But the latter tore off the verses. Only a portion of the torn paper could be recovered by Mukunda, and the Charitamrita quotes the portion and remarks in a language of flourish that the high quality of the verse was like the trumpet-sound of victory announcing Bashudev's unparalleled poetic talents.

<small>Gopinath's trouble.</small> Ramananda Ray, the poet and dramatist, and a great friend of Chaitanya, had four brothers. One of them was Gopinath Ray—a feudatory chief under Pratap Rudra. Their father Baninath was still living. Gopinath Ray was in arrears of rent to the Uriya king to the extent of Rs. 200,000. But as he was financially embarassed he made an application to the king stating that he had a large number of horses in his stable and that His Majesty might be pleased to take some of the best horses in lieu of money, after having settled their price by an expert. The king

requested a friend of his, a prince of a neighbouring country, who had expert knowledge in respect of the price of horses, to go and settle the matter on his behalf. This young man had a peculiar mannerism; he used to turn his neck and stare at the sky in the midst of his speech every time that he spoke. This prince under-valued the horses in his zeal to serve the interest of his friend, the Uriya king. Gopinath was greatly offended with him for having thus under-valued his horses and said in a rude manner "My horses do not turn their necks and stare at the sky, why should they be priced so low?" The prince naturally took umbrage at this insulting reference to himself and spoke against Gopinath to Pratap Rudra and convinced him that the object of that chief was to defraud the Raja of his just revenue. Pratap Rudra, highly incensed at this report, ordered an arrest of the whole family, and even old Baninath was not spared. Gopinath was ordered to be punished with death by a process called the "*Change Charāna.*" The exact nature of this capital punishment is not known, but from the account of Charitamrita and other books we have a rough idea of it. The offender was raised to a high place prepared with bamboo sticks and thrown down upon a spot where unsheathed swords were kept ready to receive him.

At this crisis all the friends of Ram Ray who were also Chaitanya's followers, headed by Swarupa, applied to Chaitanya requesting him to speak to the king in their behalf. They justly pleaded that the family of Baninath were all deeply attached to the Master, and that they should be saved by all means from the great danger. One man came at this stage to inform Chaitanya that Gopinath was about to be carried away by king's men to be put on the *Chang*.

Chaitanya regretted the incident, but sorrowfully remarked " It is for this reason that I did not like to come in touch with the king. As an ascetic I can beg only five *gandas* of *kowri* (a little above one pie) and not more. How can I ask the Raja to remit Rs. 200,000 ? It is not for me to meddle in matters of State. I am very sorry for Baninath, ask him to seek the aid of God. For me I should not henceforth be near the Raja and must at once start for Alalnath, for these sorrows of worldly men pain me, though I find no means of remedy." He made himself ready for leaving Puri. The king had already withdrawn the order of capital punishment that was on Gopinath by the intercession of his minister Hari Chandan, and when he heard that Chaitanya was leaving Puri, he sent word that should the Master take such a step he would give up his royal throne and follow him. He said that he had no knowledge of the punishment; it was passed by his officers. He not only cancelled the order of capital punishment on Gopinath but remitted him the outstanding dues of Rs. 200,000 and moreover made him a grant of a Jaigir. Chaitanya had never asked for these, nay, he had declined to beg any favour of any one. But the Raja did all these to please him.

It was about the year 1530 that Haridas, the Mahomedan convert to Vaishnavism, breathed his last. Chaitanya had the highest respect for him, and he held Chaitanya to be his God. Chaitanya had once told him "I have marked that you bless those who assault you and pray for them. Your thoughts have ever been as holy as the Ganges. All your acts have in themselves a sanctity as if they were the rites of a great religion. Your ideas have the grandeur of Vedic hymns. What Sadhu or Brahmin is there who may be compared with you?" To which Sanatan had added "There are people who preach religious truths but do not live them; others there are who lead pure life without caring for the good of others; but you have preached the truths and practised them in life." When Haridas's last moment came, he looked at Chaitanya and said that all his spiritual inspiration, whatever their worth might be, had come from the Master, and that it was his greatest joy to pass away from the world in sight of the Master. Chaitanya

The death of Haridas.

made all present there touch the feet of the great saint; and good Brahmins and ascetics did so at his bidding. Though Haridas had originally been a Mahomedan, Chaitanya and his men carried his body to the sea-shore where Chaitanya himself was the first to help in digging a grave for his burial.

CHAPTER XI.

(*a*) Reveries and ecstacies gradually increasing.
(*b*) His passing away.

The last part of the Chaitanya Charitamrita bristles with incidents like these, and not infrequently are the theological discourses full of learned quotations and references introduced. In these accounts we surely catch occasional glimpses of Chaitanya's spiritual nature which appears to us like a full-blown flower, but towards the close of this book specially, the theological element and scholarship generally speaking preponderate in the pages of Krishnadas. As I have already stated this great work on Chaitanya belongs to a school of Vaishnava philosophy with complicated theological ideas which sometimes fail to interest us,—lay men that we are. But however much Chaitanya might have been appreciated by learned men, he had a side in his character which created a storm of popular admiration wherever he went and

The last chapters of the Charitamrita.

this side of his character we find more vividly portrayed by Govinda Das than any other biographer, though judging as a whole, the Charitamrita must always be considered as one of the world's greatest books of theology.

The incidents described above, relate however to points of minor interest :—the real man Chaitanya was absorbed in God's love night and day. In the nights particularly "the pain of God" distressed him greatly. He sometimes saw Krishna come to his embrace and at others missed him, and in that stage he cried and wept like a bereaved soul. He spent the whole night hearing the songs of Chandidas, Bidyapati, Jaydev and Billamangal, sung to him by Swarupa. At every stage he interpreted the songs in a charming manner, elaborating the sweet appeals and messages that they bore to a man's soul of a love of the infinite. He read the 10th *skanda* of the Bhagavata and those passages of it particularly where the milkmaids, distracted by Krishna's love, prayed to *kunda*, *juthi* and other flower-plants to give them tidings of Him. Chaitanya's tears fell incessantly on the pages of the Bhagavata spoiling its letters, and this copy was for a long time with Bhagavat Acharya who showed it, according to Premabilas, to Srinibas about the year 1600 A.D. Sometimes Swarupa sang and the Master danced

Fine frenzy of the lover.

JAIDEV'S SONGS

and wept, unmindful of his physical exhaustion, for famished with fast and vigil, he had become very weak. For hours together he danced and wept in this way, and Swarupa would sing no more, feeling that the excitement would prove too severe a strain on the nerves of Chaitanya ; but with solicitous eyes full of tears, Chaitanya would beg him to go on. One day Swarupa sang the famous song of Jaydev beginning with

"রাসে হরিমিহ বিহিত-বিলাসং
স্মরতি মনোমম কৃত-পরিহাসং।"

and Chaitanya fell unconscious on the ground as he heard it.

During the last two years these love-estacies came upon him so often that the emaciated body could bear them no more. One day a female musician attached to the Puri temple—a Seva Dasi—was singing a song of Jaydev in that sweet musical mode called the *Gurjari Rag*. At this time Chaitanya heard it from a distance and knew not whether a man or a woman sang the song. He ran with open arms to embrace the singer through briers and thorns that pierced his feet. Govinda overtook and caught him in the midway, and he was roused from his dream by the attendant's voice saying aloud "It is a woman that is singing." And Chaitanya thanked him for saving him from touching a woman.

The fits of unconsciousness came often and sometimes he was taken as dead; but constant recitation of the name of Krishna by his friends brought him back to his senses; and he said on one occasion on thus coming back to himself "Ah friends, I was with Krishna, why have you disturbed the sweet union?" His body became so reduced that the hard floor whereon he slept pained him and Jagadananda brought a pillow for his head. The stern element of asceticism, however, never forsook him, and he reprimanded Jagadananda for having brought the pillow which he called a luxury, not to be enjoyed by an ascetic. And Jagadananda was so sorry at seeing his condition that he considered it prudent to leave Puri; for thought he, it would pain him very much to see the end of Chaitanya which every one felt was imminent. He accordingly left Puri with the permission of the Master and stayed at Brindaban for some time. There he met Sanatan, Rupa and others, but was unable inspite of himself to stay long without seeing Chaitanya. He came back to Puri after a short sojourn. Meantime Chaitanya had grown even more restless; the verses of the Bhagavata continually supplied inspiration to him and stole away sleep from his eyes, night and day. The clouds brought on trances by their dark blue colour which reminded him of Krishna. He fainted at the sight of the lightning which he mistook for the bright purple robe of the Lord. The chirp of birds was continually mistaken for the sound of flute, and he thought that Some one called him to His embrace by the sweet music. The cranes flew in the dark-blue sky in flocks looking small from a distance, and Chaitanya thought them to be a string of pearls decorating the breast of his dark blue god. At the sight of every hillock he fell into a trance, reminded of the Gobardhan hills where Krishna had sported, and every river showed him the ripples of the Jamuna on the banks of which the pastoral god had played with his fellow cowherds. The flowers reminded him of the beauties of Krishna's eyes and he wept when he touched them, reminded of the divine touch, soft and sweet. Sometimes the smell of flowers emanating from the Puri temple kept him fixed to the spot like a picture; he thought that his Krishna was approaching and the scent of a thousand flowers announced his approach, and he trembled in deep emotion with tearful eyes and passed into a trance.

The rush of people to drink his *padodak* (water touched by his feet) became so great that he had to hide himself whenever he went to visit the Puri temple. The place he had selected was a corner of the temple to the north of the Lion-Gate behind one of the doors. The place was over-shadowed by a large Nim tree and called

Baid Pashara. The idea of being deified and allowing people to drink water touched by his feet was repugnant to him and he had given strict order to Govinda not to allow any body to go where he bathed. We find one Brahmin stealing into that nook and drinking the *padodak* without his knowledge. Chaitanya was much annoyed with him when he discovered the trick. At night his reveries and trances grew more and more till he lost all control over himself. He left his bed and sought for Krishna in the flower-garden during his trances; and one night his followers found him out lying in an unconscious state near the Lion-Gate. Another night towards its end he was discovered in the cow-shed attached to the Temple. On recovering his senses he wondered as to how he had come there. We find from the records that he spent nine days in the flower-garden called the Jagannath Ballava, and frequently bathed in the tanks called the Narendra Sarobara and the Indradyumna Sarobara. He lived for sometime in the Gundicha.

Towards the close of his earthly career we find him maddened by the passages of the Bhagavata describing the sorrows of the milkmaids parted from Krishna, and to this a reference has already been made. He passed into trances as he interpreted the verses to Swarupa and Ramananda Ray who were his constant attendants at this stage. A Brahmin named Sankara was appointed to keep watch over him at nights so that he might not leave his room in an unconscious state. But one night he stole away from his chamber and came to the sea-shore, and delighted with the colour of the dark blue waters jumped into the sea, thinking that he ran into the embrace of Krishna or into the waters of the Jamuna, the favourite resort of his dark blue God. One fisherman who used to catch fish towards the close of every night by net, caught him up and brought him to the shore. Meantime Swarup Damodar, Ram Ray and hundreds of his followers were seeking him everywhere in the streets of Puri, and Raja Pratap Rudra was himself in a state of great anxiety. When the fisherman brought him back, the loud recitation of Krishna's name restored him to his senses, and he looked so pale, exhausted and weak, that they all apprehended that his end might be near. But he gradually survived, and the last act on his part described by the Charitamrita was to give Ram Ray some practical advice in spiritual matters.

<small>Advice to Ram Ray.</small> "Become good and consider yourself humbler than a straw" he said and then, "Be patient as a tree. It does not complain if any one cuts it. It does not beg a drop of water from anybody though it dries up. It gives freely its treasure of flowers and fruits to any one that seeks them. It exposes itself

to rain and sun but gives all its treasure to others. A Vaishnab should be absolutely without pride. He should consider that Krishna dwells in every soul and therefore give respects to others, without seeking any for himself. One who becomes like this and then recites Krishna's name, is rewarded with a love for Him." As he spoke in this way, a feeling of great humility came into his soul, and he prayed to Krishna "Oh Krishna, make me humble and give devotion unto my soul." And then referring to a verse of Padmavali he said "Neither do I want followers, nor wealth nor learning, nor poetical powers, give unto my soul a bit of devotion for thee." He prayed again and again in the spirit of a true servant "Here accept my most humble services but give me as my wages—a bit of devotion for thee." Then he again referred to a verse composed by himself to be found in the Padmavali "As eagerness to taste God's love grows in the soul, tears come to the eyes like drops in the rainy season." He said next "The world looks void without Krishna. Even if he gives me pain that would be my joy; for whatever he gives me, like a loyal wife accepting any gift from her husband,—be it ill or be it good in the world's eyes,—should be always accepted as bliss. I do not covet anything for myself. Whatever he gives is my joy, be it pain or be it pleasure in the world's eyes."

THE UNSOLVED PROBLEM

As he spoke this, his eyes glistened with tears, till trembling with emotion he fell senseless on the spot.

(b) *His passing away.*

Here Charitamrita ends, and Chaitanya Bhagavata also does not illuminate us as to how Chaitanya passed away. Murari's Chaitanya Charita and Kavikarnapur's standard biography of Chaitanya say nothing on the point. In the earlier chapters each one of these works had referred to Saka 1455 (1533 A.D.) as the year of his passing away. But how and when he did so is not mentioned. A general conspiracy of silence is observed by all. In the printed edition of Chaitanya Mangal by Lochan Das, published by Battala Press, there is no reference as to how the end, long expected, at last came about. In one of the recent editions of the work, the reading of which was settled on consulting several very old manuscripts, published by the Bangabasi Press, there is a passage with a bare hint, and this is not found in the main body of the book but the editor appends it to the foot-note.

The conspiracy of silence.

The general belief amongst the educated Bengalis so long was that as Chaitanya fell in an unconscious state into the sea, that was clear enough and that the story of his rescue by a fisherman was afterwards fabricated, the sea must have buried the great apostle under its deep waters.

<small>Drowned in the sea.</small>

The popular superstition is that Chaitanya whose physical frame had nothing material in it, passed into the image of Jagannath at Puri. The priests of the Gopinath's temple relate a similar story in respect of Chaitanya's passing into the image of that temple, and as an evidence to substantiate their statement, point out a sign near the knee of Gopinath which they say, indicates the spot through which Chaitanya was incorporated with the image. The latter tradition seems to be upheld and indicated by a line in one of the biographies, which, however, says in not a very clear language, "We lost Chaitanya in the temple of Gopinath."

<small>The reason of their general silence.</small>

There is no doubt that the Vaishnab biographers do not speak of the end of Chaitanya because they feel a great pain in relating it. Their grief was quite overwhelming; moreover their belief is that it is a sin to hear of the end of one who is for all times and can never die. For fifty years after the *tirodhan* of the great teacher, the Vaishnab community lay enervated by the great shock. Their *Kirtana* music which had taken the whole country by surprise stopped for a time after that melancholy event and was not heard

WHY WERE THE DOORS SHUT   261

for nearly half a century in the great provinces of Bengal and Orissa. We do not get authentic records of the progress of the Vaishnab community for this long period from after 1533,—the year when Chaitanya disappeared from the world.

So we have quite a reasonable ground as to why no mention of the passing away of Chaitanya is found in his standard biographies. But we cannot agree with those who believe that he was drowned. The Charitamrita says distinctly that he was rescued from the sea by a fisherman, and when we find mention of events subsequent to his rescue in the pages of that book, and when no other authority contradicts the statement nor says that Chaitanya was drowned in the sea, what justification is there for attaching so much importance to a mere conjecture that he was lost in the deep waters of the Bay of Bengal. What happened seems to be this; some of our modern scholars having only a superficial knowledge of the Vaishnab literature, perplexed at not finding any clear mention of the end of Chaitanya's career, made a surmise like this, in order to give an easy solution to a difficult historical problem. They might have been excused if they had spoken of it in a language of doubt stating that it was a mere conjecture on their part. But they showed a lack of ordinary historical sense by declaring as absolutely certain what was at best a mere surmise on their part.

We have, however, definite information on this obscure point from Chaitanya Mangal by Jayananda, brought to light some years ago, by Prachyavidya-maharnava Nagendranath Basu and edited by him and published by the Sahitya Parishat of Calcutta. It should be remembered that this work is not recognised by the Vaishnavas; hence the author, who was outside the pale of the school of Brindaban from which sprang all canons and censorship in literary matters, could exercise his own discretion in using his materials and was not handicapped while writing things, such freedom not being allowed in strictly orthodox literature. This book says that during the Car-festival of Jagannath in Ashar 1455 Saka, Chaitanya got a hurt in his left foot from a small brick in the coarse of his dancings. Then on the sixth *tithi* the pain increased and he could not rise from his bed. On the seventh *tithi* at ten *dandas* of night (about 11 p.m.) he passed away from the world having suffered from a sympathetic fever. Now this account seems to be quite true, as several very old Mss. of Jayananda's Chaitanya Mangal have been recovered which proves beyond doubt the genuineness of the printed edition. There seems to be something like an

<small>A true account of how he passed away.</small>

indirect corroboration of this statement by another account given in Lochan Das's Chaitanya Mangal. The text appended to the Bangabasi edition of that book says that on the seventh *tithi* of Ashar on Sunday at *tritiya prahar* (between 3 and 4 p.m.) Chaitanya passed into the image of Jagannath, and at the time the priests shut the gate of the temple against all enquirers. The Chaitanya Mangal further adds that none of the followers of Chaitanya had been allowed to see the Master for a long time before he disappeared. Amongst the crowd that had pressed in vain for entrance into the Temple we find Sribas, Mukunda Datta, Gauridas and others. But the priests could by no means be persuaded to open the gates.

Thus from two independent accounts we find that it was on the seventh *tithi* of Ashar Saka 1455 that Chaitanya left this world. There are two *pakkhas* in a month, the one white and the other dark. Whether the seventh *tithi* belonged to the white or the dark *pakkha* is not stated, but this may be easily found out from the fact that the Car-festival takes place in the white *pakkha*. So it was the seventh *tithi* of the white *pakkha*, and in both the accounts we find Sunday to be the date of Chaitanya's *tirodhan*. The year of course is well known, for not only these two works but all accounts agree in saying that Chaitanya passed in Saka 1455, corresponding to the year 1533 A.D. The only point that remains to be settled is that according to Jayananda the time of *tirodhan* is 11 p.m. and according to Lochan Das 4 p.m. We may, however, make a reasonable guess as to the fact of the case. Chaitanya was in the Jaganath temple when he suffered from high fever. When the priests apprehended his end to be near they shut the Gate against all visitors. This they did to take time for burying him within the temple. If he left the world at about 4 p.m. the doors, we know, were kept closed till 11 p.m. —this time was taken for burying him and reparing the floor after burial. The priests at 11 p.m., opened the gates and gave out that Chaitanya was incorporated with the image of Jagannath. So according to one account he passed away at 11 p.m. But the better informed people knew that he had passed away at 4 p.m., when the doors were closed.

In all our almanacs the *tithis* of births and deaths of all distinguished Vaishnavas are given; but Chaitanya's birth *tithi* is only mentioned there. The compilers of almanacs seem also to have joined the general conspiracy on this point. The Vaishnavas believe in the birth of Chaitanya but would not believe in his death.

I have clearly put my doubt in some of my previous lectures; the question may be asked, if Lochan Das's account is true, why did not the

THE MARK IN THE KNEE

priests open the gates? The answer is a simple one, the priests would not like to shew him dying as an ordinary man. They declared that they had witnessed with their own eyes that Chaitanya passed into the image of Jagannath. This report would certainly prove his divinity and make it absolutely beyond doubt. They buried him somewhere under the floor of the temple and would not allow any outsider to enter it until the place was thoroughly repaired and no trace left after his burial as I have already stated. This is the only rational explanation that may be advanced for explaining their conduct in shutting the temple gate. Probably they did so with the permission of Raja Pratap Rudra. But I think I go too far in suggesting that monarch's conniving at their conduct.

When a report like this got into the air, it is not unnatural that the priests of the Gopinath temple were tempted to give out a similar story associating the event with their own temple. The golden mark on the left knee is still shown to the pious pilgrims, as marking the spot through which the spirit of Chaitanya passed into the Gopinath image, and the priests certainly charge fees for shewing it.

CHAPTER XII.

Chaitanya as a Teacher.

(*a*) Love—its various phases in the spiritual plane.

(*b*) Service to fellow-men and compassion for the depressed castes.

(*c*) Social reformation,—Vaisnava Jurisprudence.

(*d*) His commanding personality, many-sidedness of character and scholarship.

(*e*) Spiritual emotions, love for mother, his influence on the Vaisnava poets.

A European scholar writes "When all possible allowances have been made, it is difficult to acquit Chaitanya of the charge of being lacking in sanity and poise."[1] Another writer of distinction Dr. MacNichol speaks sneeringly of the sensuousness and lack of moral sense in Chandidas's poems and even does not spare Chaitanya. He says "We are told that in his last days he would spend whole nights singing the songs of Chandidas and Vidyapati, and we may be sure that they were the inspirations as well of his earlier years."

Some hostile opinions.

[1] Underwood's article on Chaitanya and Vaishnavism in Bengal, the Calcutta Review, No. 295, p. 50.

Mr. Beveridge, the historian, writes in the Royal Asiatic Society Journal "Chaitanya was a dreamer and more akin to George Fox than to Luther. He abandoned his household duties and his head was always in the clouds. If he did not actually commit suicide, he certainly tried to drown himself. I am not sure if he really helped the world."

It must be said for the sake of truth that inspite of the harsh comment that we have just quoted, both Mr. Underwood and Dr. MacNichol admitted Chaitanya to be a great saint. Says the former "Chaitanya came at a time when Buddhism was a spent force in Bengal and the spiritual life of the people at a very low ebb. But loving God as undoubtedly he did with all the ardour of a passionate and imaginative soul, he was able to fill with blessedness and joy the lives of many in whom the springs of the soul's devotion were well nigh dried up and to whom God seemed far away" and MacNichol follows the strain and writes, "So fervent was his rapture and so intense his desire to be to Krishna as Radha was to her divine lover that we can well believe that he was sometimes heard to murmur "I am He."

Many European writers like Dr. Anderson and Dr. Carpenter (the latter calls him an Indian St. Francis) and others have given just tribute of honour to the great Vaisnava apostle, but we need not refer to their remarks in the present treatise. Chaitanya loved God as no man before or after him has ever loved. The Western idea of love for God is generally embodied in the spirit of obedience that a servant owes to the master. In Christ we see the resigned affection of a child towards father. In the lives of European mystics in a few isolated cases we find human soul longing for Him as a bride does for the bridegroom. Some of the mystics as St. Juan of the Cross, St. Teresa and Angela of Foligno loved Christ as the bridegroom of their soul. In the old Jewish conception of the Church as the bridegroom, no doubt conceived after the idea of the Buddhist Sangha—in the song of songs which is Solomon's, the spiritual desire of the soul with all its sexual demands is expressed in a poetical way. But Underwood tells us that in Europe such things have always been more or less of an isolated nature; and they are no longer held allegorical by the vast majority of Christians but read as literature. Hallam tells us that Buddhist ideas from the tenth to the fourteenth centuries had spread themselves in the religious atmosphere of the Christians.

When love for God assumes the form of a servant's duty to the Master, which is now the generally accepted conception of man's relation to God in Europe, we know that the whole fabric of religion would stand on the fulfilment of a man's moral duty. This is emphasized in Europe's religious literature of the present day which advocates the theory of work to be man's chief if not the only object. I do not believe that Christ's childlike dependence on God forms any real part of the religious views of modern Christendom. Had such an idea developed in Europe, the idea of God as mother would not have been inconceivable to European Christians as it is now. Once granted that man is a child of God, the idea of dependence creates a place for motherhood. Sex in respect of the Supreme power barring our acceptance of the deity in the aspect of a mother is untenable. In India God has been accepted both as father and mother from the Vedic age, and a large literature has developed in respect of the Mother-cult along with that illucidating the fatherhood of the deity.

This paternal relation of the deity is superior in quality to that existing between a servant and a master and emphasizes the moral aspects of religious philosophy in a far less forcible manner. The child resigns and depends on the word of *father* which raises him far above moral obligations. But it should be presumed that the moral sense is perfected in one before one would aspire to accept God as a parent. If there is any flaw in one's moral nature one cannot raise himself from the position of servant to that of a child.

I should here refer to *Batsalya* which presents a unique aspect in the religion of emotion, it is not *filial* but *paternal* feeling. The Vaisnavas have made a departure in their conception of *Batsalya* from the ordinary significance of this *rasa* in the spiritual word.

In ordinary sense God is the recognised Father of the world and we, as children of God, have filial duty to perform to Him. But it should be understood that the Vaisnavas recognise no element in the conception of their spiritual experiences which is not associated with emotions of joy.

<small>The Batsalya rasa.</small>

A son's feeling to his parents is more or less connected with a sense of duty and reverence. The parents delight in the child, but in the first stage the child's position is one of unconscious resignation and latterly that of one who has certain duties to perform. Neither of these positions give him any opportunity to enjoy *rasa* or bliss as conceived by the Vaisnavas.

The Vaisnavas, in the higher stages of their emotional felicities, altogether dispense with every form of sentiment associated with duty or extraneous compulsion. The greatest sacrifices are to be made but the spirit should be such as to proceed in the path of joy, not impelled by a sense of duty.

This sort of sacrifice is made by parents, especially by mother who suffers all, but the spirit

GOD REVEALED IN THE BABY 271

that actuates her is far from one of duty. She suffers for affection, which is her sole inspiring force. The mother, says the Vaisnava, finds a manifestation of God in the child. For the child, whatever may be its external form, reveals to the mother, perfect beauty and perfect bliss. She conceives the blessedness of this feeling to such an extent that she becomes ready for every kind of martyrdom,—but not at all from a sense of duty.

According to the Vaisnavas, God reveals *Himself* to the old, wrinkle-faced, care-worn world in the *child*, as the never-ending promise of the new, the gay and the beautiful. The old, —the rotten and the faded world passes away from view, but the new, the fresh and the surprisingly beautiful takes its place. The Vaisnavas salute this ever *New* and call it God, recognising the holiness and the eternal felicities inspired by the Deity in the small form of the new comer.

The angle of vision is thus changed. The Vaisnavas do not call God Father, or if they have called Him so any time, they have done so as a mere matter of form ; they do not reserve a place of father in their conception of the Diety. They call and know the child—to be God. For this beautiful thing, absolutely pure, fresh and new fills the minds of the parents with infinite delight : God comes as a child to every home, as the loveliest symbol of the preservation of the world, of life in the midst of death, of hope in the midst of decaying forms, and as one for whom the greatest sacrifices are made without a consciousness of duty on the part of those who undergo them and one who typefies in the eyes of the parents, ideal beauty and ideal love. Is it not really wonderful that the tigress, the lioness and the softest of the woman-kind in the human world look upon the new-born with equally tender eyes of affection—eyes full of never to be allayed thirst and unceasing wonder? The most beautiful, the most attractive has come to the home, giving promise of the continuance of this fair world. The dry leaves and the withered flowers here gladly make room for the new which blossoms to-day in the full glory of the present and giving hope and promise of the future. Recognition of Godhead in the child is one of the most attractive features of the Vaisnava theology and this is their *Batsalya rasa*. The child-Christ of the European mystics makes an approach to this conception of the Vaisnava mind, though not in its perfectly flowering aspect.

I need not enter into and discuss the nice five-fold classifications of a man's relation to God as detailed by Ram Ray in his discourses with Chaitanya, when the latter met him on the banks of

The Madurya

Godavari in 1510 A.D. But I must say that beyond this sphere of man's duty to God as of a servant to the Master and even beyond that of resignation and absolute dependence of a child on his parent is the sphere of love between man and woman denominated the *Madhurya rasa* by the Vaisnavas, and it must be said that each of the lower stages comprehends and pre-supposes perfection of moral duty, and without this, ascent to any higher stage is impossible.

This sexual love—the beauty of which has ever attracted the human mind,—which has made Valmiki and Homer write the grandest and most charming epics, and Dante suffer as few have suffered,—which sounds the sweetest on musician's lyre and the shepherd's flute,—the sexual love which forms the quintessence of every lyric and song and on which human energies are ever at work, in hundreds of stories, romances and fables,—this love which forms the chief attraction of some of the greatest dramas, making all other human action subservient to it, of which the whole paraphernalia of natural scenery serves as the background, this love, it must be admitted, is the most significant and the most powerful element in human life, nay it is mystic in its infinite strangeness and maddening force. Every one of us has felt this love more or less in life, and who can say, that howsoever intellectual and sober a man may be, he has preserved the poise and equilibrium of his head when under love. Shakespeare says that the lover, the poet and the lunatic have kindred elements. In fact love is not calm but a storm of nature. The sea when tranquil presents a beautiful sight, but it rises to sublime beauty in a tempest, and what painter will say that he did not get the highest inspiration from the sight of a storm in which beauty and sublimity are mixed together? Equilibrium and poise are not the criterions in the region of poetry and emotion.

Now if storm is the nature of love, if its romance consists in the excess of poetic imagination, we cannot dictate boundaries to its sphere,—much less so when it tries to bring the Infinite to the realisation of and in the nearness of the finite. It must be admitted that Chaitanya was the one man who loved God with an ardou which calls forth the whole poetry of the human mind. He is a poor observer of human nature who says that Chaitanya showed a lack of moral sense. Moral side must be perfect in a man who thinks of scaling the height of loving the Highest. He loved God as a child loves his parents. He served Him as a servant serves his master. But more, he loved God as his bridegroom who had entirely captivated his soul. That he was ever keen to his great moral obligations will be observed from many instances. Let us discuss the reason that led to his *sanyas*. He did not turn a recluse or a pessimist by becoming a *sanyasi*. He had told Govinda and others that because he was a house-holder, the educated people of the country did not accept his teachings. So a great renunciation was necessary. He said he was sorry to see the miseries of the people; he must go from door to door singing the name of Krishna. "The vicious Tantricks, the Aghore Panthies, the Chandals and low-born men, the king and the poorest of his subjects will all feel the irresistible charm of Krishna's name. I cannot be at rest when the world is so unhappy around me. He that threatens to assault me to-day will see me a beggar to-morrow singing Krishna's name at his door." He fulfilled to the letter what he had said; for sinners of all classes, scholars who revelled in intellectual heights, the unbelievers, the robbers and harlots gathered round him and were reformed by the power of Krishna's name, and if Mr. Beveridge says that he neglected his household duties, it was as the Charitamrita says "for the good of all, this sacrifice should not be called a breach of duty." People in hundreds left home and went to kill others and be killed themselves for the sake of what they called nationality in the great war and we praise them though their deaths have created gaps in their families that can never be filled up. But the sacrifice of home-life in the interest of humanity which the Buddha and Chaitanya made without bloodshed and inspired by a real and genuine love for fellow men, cannot be appreciated by Mr. Beveridge!

(b) *Service to fellow-men and compassion for the depressed castes.*

How far are we away from Chaitanya to judge him properly! We love our wives and children and at best our nation, but he alone loved God, which means loving the whole universe—the creation of its Maker. It was not an attempt on his part to reach a high stage of spiritual life by extinguishing his desires. It was the one great factor of his life, the one great inspiration and the one great poetry that moved his whole existence. He was certainly not one like us, and if Mr. Beveridge has any doubt as to what help he did to the world, let him come and observe the villages of Bengal. In almost every house of the rustic peasant and artisan his name is chanted with loving regards. This has sweetened their lives and made them the most well-behaved and virtuous of world's peasantry; and love of God is meaningless, if it does not imply the same ardour in loving humanity. We have seen him at the earliest stage of spiritual life carrying the baskets of worshippers, wringing out waters from the clothes of old men whose hands shook in their efforts to do so owing to infirmity, and carrying the clothes of others on the banks of the Ganges. This service to men, he says, was holy as it helped to bring to his soul devotion for God. The Maddhyakhanda, Ch. 14, Verse 20 of the Charitamrita gives an account of how Chaitanya delighted in feeding the poor. At Munna in the Madras Presidency he begged clothes and food from people in order to provide a half-starved old woman who stood in need of help. At a place named Amjhora in the Central Provinces, we find it described in Govinda's *Karcha*, Chaitanya had once absolutely no food for two days and on the third day he got a present of 2 seers of flour with which he prepared 16 breads. There were four men to be served with these,—Ramananda, Govindacharan, Govinda Karmakar and Chaitanya himself. At this stage one old man came there with a boy and asked for something to eat and Chaitanya gave him his share though he had fasted for two days. These little acts of charity are almost negligible facts in a man who had renounced the world with all its pleasures for God's love. And I would not have mentioned them here but for the reason that these little things seem to carry an exaggerated importance now-a-days, especially with those who having materialistic views of life can understand the value of moral duties but cannot realise the mystic delight of the true and beautiful oriental mind enjoying communion with the Deity. The moral world is one of mere pebbles and stones of the foundations upon which that Diamond Harbour of the soul is built, full of ecstasies and sweet emotions. The great thing that Chaitanya gave to the people was a bit of his love for God which sanctified the lives of sinners and of the fallen and soothed souls that were weary and heavy-laden—not by sermons or speeches, but by what Fraser calls about him, "the mesmeric influence of his presence."[1]

Those that would say that he was lacking in poise should be reminded of his many-sided intellectual activities and his heroic attitude in the reorganisation of the Hindu society. He selected men from amongst his followers to work in different spheres of life for the propagation of faith and social reformation. We find it mentioned in many places of his different biographies that he held secret discourses with Nityananda regarding social matters and so privately was the conversation conducted that none was allowed to enter the room. Nityananda was appointed by him to stay in Bengal with the sole charge of social reformation. Chaitanya had found the caste-system eating

---

[1] Literary History of India by R. W. Fraser, p. 350.

into the vitals of our social fabric, and he and his followers were determined to root out this evil from the land. For, the moment that you say that you love God, all human beings will be your brethren; there will be no Brahmin, no Sudra. Chaitanya proclaimed this in an unqualified language. He said "He that eats a meal cooked by a Dom becomes pre-eminently entitled to the grace of God." The Dom is certainly the lowest caste in Bengal. The motto of the Vaishnavas was "Even a Chandal should be held higher than Brahmin if he has devotion for God" and this is a well-known text of the Naradiya Puran. "If a Muchi (cobbler) prays to God with devotion I bow a hundred times to his feet" said Chaitanya.[1] I am afraid my European readers will hardly be able to realise the position of a *Muchi* in our society. His touch is held to be more hateful than that of a dog. Chaitanya not only preached the equality of men but sometimes advocated a somewhat forward step in the practice of this doctrine. We find in the last chapter of Charitamrita that one Kalidas, an uncle of the celebrated apostle Raghunath Das of Saptagram, used to eat the refuse from the plates of low-caste men. Kalidas was born of a Kayastha family of high status and was himself a great

---

[1] Chaitanya Bhagbat, Antya Khanda.

scholar. This habit that he had acquired from his youth might be construed into a sort of foolish mania, the whims of an unbalanced mind. But he was in reality inspired by propagandism. He had resolved to eat the refuse simply to give a rude shock to the popular prejudice that the man of an unclean caste was not worthy of touch —the food touched by him was unclean. One could eat from the plate from which a dog or cat had eaten, but not even touch the plate used by one of the unclean castes. When the caste-rules were so stringent Kalidas's conduct was certainly held heroic by the reformers. Once at Puri there lived a man named Kanai, who belonged to the sweeper caste, one of the lowest castes in Bengal, but a cleanlier man than Kanai did not exist in the country in respect of morals and devotion to God. Kalidas called on Kanai one day and bowed to him, at which that very humble soul mildly protested saying that as a Kayastha he should not have bowed to a sweeper. Kalidas offered him a mango, and when Kanai had partaken of a part and thrown away the remnant, Kalidas picked it up and began to taste it. This was a horror to all, a Kayastha eating the refuse of a sweeper. But when Chaitanya heard of this he praised and blessed him saying that God's grace would be on him, since he honoured merit and not caste. In his own life his treatment of Haridas, Rupa,

Sanatan and Ram Ray showed that he was no respecter of caste. At a feast held at Puri he ordered that Haridas, the Mahomedan convert, should be first served. In the Vaishnava community the highest respect, generally shown to the most exalted Brahmins, used to be shown to Haridas even at religious functions. Chaitanya often touched Haridas saying "I feel myself purified by your touch." And when Haridas died he made all the good Brahmins drink water touched by his foot. His conduct towards Sanatan also showed the same catholicity and affection. Sanatan, though originally a Brahmin, had adopted the ways of a Mahomedan and had consequently been outcasted by the Hindu society. In the early years of acquaintance when Chaitanya was about to touch him, he would shrink back saying "No Master, I am unclean." But Chaitanya would forcibly embrace him and say, "You have dedicated yourself to me saying 'I am yours from to-day'; that body of yours is mine in every respect; an all-sacrificing and all-loving spirit dwells in it, it is holy as a temple. Why should you consider yourself unclean?" Thus in vain did Haridas protest against Chaitanya touching him. When Chaitanya first met Ram Roy he ran into his arms and wept for joy. The Brahmins who were there on the banks of the Godavari all wondered and said "Look at this

Brahmin ascetic ! He looks brilliant as the sun. Why does he touch a Sudra and weep ?" It should be borne in mind that there was no relaxation of caste-rules in favour of these men, though they were distinguished as saints. It is true that Haridas, the Mahomedan, had accepted the Vaishnava faith and turned a *sannyasi*. But the Brahmins of Santipur headed by Jadunandan Acharya had at first treated him with contempt and offered him great resistance. We have it on the authority of several standard biographies of Chaitanya that the people of Santipur had taken great objection to Haridas interpreting the scriptures of the Hindus. A tank dug by Sanatan in Jessore still exists, the water of which is held unclean up to this day by the Hindus, because it is associated with the name of one who had once adopted Mahomedan ways. His subsequent conversion to Vaishnavism was not regarded as a sufficient atonement. In the country-side the character of Chaitanya, as the redeemer of the fallen and a reformer of the society, is held in high appreciation. In the humble huts of the peasants and other low-caste people, praises and tributes of worship are offered to him every night and the song " Praise unto Chaitanya the god-man of Nadia, the freiend of the fallen and one who does not believe in caste" is often sung in chorus. The popular songs from the time of Govinda Das and Balaram Das who flourished in the sixteenth century down to the present times have all this one burden. Krishna Das, a poet of that period, writing about the evils that were driven out from the country by the advent of Chaitanya, says " Our chief complaint is now removed, there is no distinction of caste." Govinda Das sings in his rhythmical and impressive style, ill preserved in my translation, "Chaitanya never cares for caste ; he is a sea of compassion and embraces Chandals and other low castes with tears in his eyes." Sivananda, the esteemed friend of Chaitanya, says in a song "The high and low in the social scale are brought to the same level by Chaitanya" and Balaram Das repeats the same idea " He weeps embracing the fallen, the destitute and the low."[1]

(c) *Social reformation—Vaishnava jurisprudence.*

Chaitanya entrusted the charge of reformation of society, as already stated, to Nityananda. This saintly man, though a Brahmin, ate the food cooked by Uddharan Datta of the Subarnabanik caste (one of the unclean castes) and he spent his time chiefly in the houses of low-class men. Khardaha, the residence of Nityananda, became the chief centre and resort of the Vaishnavas, from which emanated laws that governed the

---

[1] See *Gaurapada Tarangini.*

Vaishnava community. The Goswamis of Khardaha and Santipur, the descendants of Nityananda and Adwaita respectively, opened their portals of brotherhood to all men irrespective of castes. The fallen Buddhists, mainly represented by the mercantile classes of Bengal with a few exceptions, had lived as out-castes. They were accepted in the Temple of Brotherhood raised by the Vaishnavas. No Brahmin would formerly do any religious function in their houses. But the Vaishnava Goswamis accepted them as disciples, ate at their houses and agreed to do priestly offices in their temples. Had not Chaitanya accepted these men in his Order, in all probability they would have embraced the Islam, as a large number of Bengal Buddhists had already done. Nityananda and his son Birabhadra admitted into the Vaishnava Order 1,200 *Neras* (Buddhist monks) and 1,300 *Neris* (Buddhist nuns). This acceptance of the fallen was a great act of mercy, to commemorate which these *Nera-Neris* held an annual fair at Kharda for about 400 years. The historic fair was discontinued about ten years ago owing to financial difficulties. It does not, however, reflect any credit on the descendants of Nityananda that they have given up this memorable institution. They could raise funds for it by appealing to the public. The spot where this fair used to sit was about six years ago visited by a European scholar who designated it as the place of the death of Buddhism in Bengal.

Many were the complaints that were made against Nityananda for breaking the caste-rules, and Sribasa was called *jati-nasha*, a destroyer of caste, because he had allowed Nityananda to live with him. But the Vaishnavas repudiated caste in an uncompromising way. One of their poets sings, " He that seeks castes among the Vaishnavas is a sinner." In later times Narottam, a Kayastha, was raised to the status of a Brahmin by the unanimous voice of the Vaishnavas gathered at a meeting held at Kheturi in the district of Rajshahi. The leaders proclaimed that one who had realised God in his heart was a true Brahmin and one who merely wears the sacred thread was so in name. We find Narahari Sarkar of Srikhanda, the famous poet and friend of Chaitanya, and Narottam Das of Kheturi who lived in the sixteenth century,—one a Vaidya and the other a Kayastha,—receiving Brahmin disciples. Narahari Sarkar was not an ascetic but a householder. The exalted position of a Guru in our society is well-known. The disciple has to eat refuse from the plate of his Guru and drink the water touched by his foot. The revolution, brought about in the world of caste by these acts, raised a tempest of opposition amongst the orthodox

Brahmins, the extent of which might be conceived from the fact that these Brahmins hissed and clapped their hands when the dead body of Narottam was being carried for cremation. Narasingha, the Raja of Pakkapalli was incited by the orthodox Brahmins to undertake a regular expedition against Narottam and his followers. All these have been elaborately treated by me in my 'Medieval Vaisnava Literature of Bengal.' The lay Vaishnavas would not now excuse any man if he would ask as to what caste they had belonged before adopting Vaishnavism. One of their writers says "if a Mahomedan or a low Sudra turns a Vaishnava he is better than an ordinary Brahmin."

The inspiration of this great revolution came of course from Chaitanya himself under whose instructions Nityananda organised the Vaishnava community in Bengal. It is on these topics that Chaitanya frequently talked in private with Nityananda, and it is for the object of leaving the latter undisturbed in the course of his reconstruction of society that Chaitanya gave him no permission to leave Bengal and pay him a visit at Puri. Owing, however, to his great love for Chaitanya he frequently violated this order and came to interview him. Chaitanya knew perfectly well that Nityananda had not the least vanity of caste or learning and, devoted entirely to God as he was, he was pre-eminently fit to hold the torch of brotherhood and social reformation. Hence if any one came from Bengal and complained to him against Nityananda's conduct in mixing with low-class men and receiving presents from them, Chaitanya spoke with firmness in the following way " Even if I were to hear that Nityananda was a drunkard and had great moral vices, I should not lose faith in him. I know the metal he is made of."

Thus we see that he was behind the great machinery of social reformation set on foot, guided and controlled by him at every stage of the advancement of the cause of Vaishnavism in this great province. Do these acts look like those of one lacking in sanity and poise and could such results be ever achieved by one of such description?

According to the unanimous opinion of Vaishnava scholars Sanatan was the most learned amongst them in Hindu Jurisprudence. Chaitanya had once told Ram Ray about Sanatan, " Where will you find another scholar in the whole world as learned as Sanatan ?[1] " This man who had renounced his high status in life and vast fortune and turned a Vaishnava ascetic was appointed by Chaitanya to write an elaborate work of jurisprudence by which the new Vaishnava community, founded by him, was to be

---

[1] Chaitanya Charitamrita, Antya I, verse 114.

governed. It was not a mere command, but Chaitanya himself supplied the synopsis of this monumental work. Chaitanya in an elaborate discourse impressed on Sanatan his views on religion and drew an outline of the work which Sanatan was required to compile for elucidating the rituals of the *bhakti*-cult. Sanatan said "You have ordered me, Sir, to compile a work of jurisprudence for the Vaishnavas. But how can such a work be undertaken by me? I belong to a low caste and have hitherto led a life, contrary to scriptures. It is only possible for me to venture to take up the work in hand if you inspire me." Chaitanya replied, "When you will be seriously after it, it is God who will inspire and help you. But still I will give you briefly a synopsis of what your work should contain. You should dwell on the following points in an elaborate manner. (1) The necessity of Guru in religious life. (2) The respective duties of Guru and his disciple. (3) The rites of worship and ordinary daily duties of a Vaishnava for keeping his body and mind clean. (4) The signs of a true Vaishnava. (5) The marks to be worn on his person to distinguish him from the people of other sects. (6) The sacred plant Tulasi and the sacred dust Gopichandana. (7) 130 kinds of rituals. (8) The five-fold services of *Arati*. (9) Particulars about images. (10) The power of the holy name. (11) Penances, Japa or recitation of the

Mantras, sacred hymns, perambulation, prostration, partaking of the sacramental meal. (12) Giving up of the habit of scandalizing, of evil company. (13) To hear the recitation of the Bhagavata. (14) Fasting on particular days. (15) The observances of the festivities of Janmasthami (birth of Krishna). (16) Ramnabami (birth of Ram). (17) Nrishingha Chaturdashi. (18) How Vaishnava temples and images should be made.

This synopsis embodies all the details of Vaishnava religion. But it gives a mere outline of what was detailed by Chaitanya himself later on in an elaborate manner. Chaitanya himself did not care to observe rules and used to say that Damodara and Swarupa knew them much better than he did. But when he elaborated the synopsis for Sanatan he showed a wonderful mastery of details. These rituals and outward forms comprised restriction of conduct directing what a Vaishnava should do and should not do. Though Chaitanya described these rituals in minute details, he did not recommend them for those advanced in spiritual life (Chaitanya Charitamrita, Maddhya, 19). He declared that these rituals oftentimes received greater attention than they deserved and instead of helping rather impeded the growth of real spirituality in those men who were above the average run. So at a certain stage the rituals should be given up altogether. The great Hari Bhakti Bilas compiled by Sanatan on the lines directed by Chaitanya is now the one undisputed guide for the Vaishnava community in the performance of their daily duties and religious functions, and the Master inspired every detail of this monumental work. When the work was finished, Sanatan thought that as he had at one time adopted Mahomedan ways, objection might be raised to its acceptance by the orthodox people. So it was published in the name of Gopal Bhatta. But we know both from the account of Charitamrita, the author of which was a disciple of Sanatan, and from the elaborate and scholarly commentary on the work by Jiva Goswami, nephew of Sanatan, that the work was written by the latter under directions of Chaitanya Dev.

So we see that the organisation of the reformed society on the solid basis of scriptural rules satisfying the needs of the *bhakti* cult owed its existence to Chaitanya though the immediate labours of the work were done by Sanatan.

(d) His commanding personality, many-sidedness of character and scholarship.

Though when Chaitanya passed into trances and mystic visions, he remained unconscious of the physical world, yet we mark frequently a dignity in him which commanded respect. In the Narendra Sarobar where Adwaitacharya,

Nityananda and others in the excess of their glee had been once playing boyish pranks, the admonishment of the Master was heard cautioning them against behaving in a light-brained way. He was below thirty at this time and Adwaitacharya, one of the veteran scholars of the day, was over eighty years old. We find him often stopping in the midst of his emotional dance and music at the approach of strangers not initiated in the *bhakti* cult. We find him assume a dignified air at the approach of the pantheists of Benares, though he had been then in one of his heartiest emotional felicities. His motto was " With only men of our own circle, indulgence in emotion and ecstacies of spirit were allowed. But before lay men one should restrict himself to the recitation of God's name only."

In all spheres of religious and spiritual life, his activities were found in the most pronounced form. Many of the great men of the provinces of Orissa and Bengal had joined his Order and in the 15th and 16th centuries these places presented quite a galaxy of them. Some of them, such as Kavikarnapur, Rupa and Ramananda Ray, produced best dramas in Sanskrit. Others shone in the field of vernacular poetry as Narahari, Basu Ghosh and Govinda Ghosh. There were also others great in all-round scholarship, such as Sarbabhoum, Adwaitacharya and Sanatan. There were besides men who showed great renunciation by eschewing temporal glories in preference to ascetic life, such as Raghunath Das, Uddharan Datta and Sanatan. But all of them had been inspired in their great works that distinguished them by Chaitanya Dev. The Bhakti Ratnakar is right in declaring on the lines of what had been originally written by the author of Charitamrita, that Chaitanya manifested his manifold glories firstly through Ramananda Ray whose life was a conquest over passions of the flesh, secondly, through Damodara who showed in his life absolute resignation and unsparing judgment on others' conduct, thirdly, through Haridas who showed an unparalleled power of suffering and patience, fourthly, through Sanatan and Rupa great spiritual humility. "But if we are to name one man who combined in him the four-fold qualities of conquest of the flesh, absolute resignation, patience and spirituality, let us name Chaitanya and none other."

We need not refer here to Chaitanya's trances or emotional dance which are too subtle spiritual phenomena in this materialistic age to be rightly appreciated outside India, and which have perhaps raised the complaint of "lack of sanity" in him. But these social revolutions to which we have referred and of which he was at the helm are indisputable facts of history which showed his remarkable powers as a leader of men; and a leader he was, as it has been the

HIS SCHOLARSHIP

lot of few amongst his contemporaries to be. For the purpose of merely catching a sight of him, whenever he went in big towns, the crowds pressed so thickly around him that they filled all imaginable space, ascending the roofs of mansions and tops of towers; and old buildings often crumbled down under the weight of their feet. Wherever he passed by, people gathered sacred dust trodden by him, so that the paths were shorn of a layer of earth.[1]

His scholarship was great. In fact many of the distinguished professors of pantheism who, so to speak, had monopolised all mediæval Indian learning, such as Prakashananda, Sarbabhoum and Ishwar Bharati were defeated by him in public debates. And even when scarcely above his teens he had obtained the title of " Lion of debate " (Badi Singha) by defeating such a haughty scholar as Keshab Kashmiri of the Punjab. Chaitanya was also a master of many languages, the parallel of whom in that period is difficult to be found in the annals of India. We learn on the authority of Narahari Sarkar, his friend and contemporary, that he had acquired Pali and a thorough knowledge of Pingal's Prakrit Grammar in the tol of Gangadas Pandit at Nadia.[2] He had obtained

---

[1] Chaitanya Bhagbata.
[2] Goura Pada Tarangini.

the title of 'Vidyasagar' for his proficiency in Sanskrit.[1] He wrote a commentary on Sanskrit Grammar which was taught in the tols of Eastern Bengal. That he excelled in Poetics is proved by his successful encounter with Keshab Kashmiri. According to Ishan Nagar, he had written an excellent treatise on logic. Some of the verses he wrote in Sanskrit are still extant and amongst these eight stanzas are to be found in the Kavyaprakasha compiled by Rupa. His great proficiency in Vedanta philosophy was always in evidence in his public discussions with the leaders of the pantheistic schools all over India. His knowledge in the scriptures elucidating the *bhakti* cult was of course without a parallel. He lived in Orissa for 18 years during which he acquired a thorough knowledge of the language of that province and that he actually did so we learn from a reference in the Charitamrita to the fact that he recited an Oriya poem beginning with *Jagamohana Parimunda*, etc., bidding Swarupa to sing it to him. Govinda Das tells us that he addressed people in the Bombay Presidency in Sanskrit and Tamil and in another place of the Karcha it is stated that he spoke "a language of jargon" to the people in the Deccan who spoke "jargon" and adds a note further stating that travelling for a long time in the Southern India Chaitanya had

---

[1] Adwait Prakash by Ishannagar.

acquired the different popular dialects current in that country. Thus we see that he had acquired many of the Dravidian languages of Southern India during his tour. As Hindi was the *lingua franca* of India at this period, it goes without saying that he had mastered it having lived in the Upper India for six years. That he had acquired Maithili is easily observed from the fact that he recited songs of Vidyapati day and night and at his time these songs had not been yet Bengalicised. We thus find that he had not only mastered the Indian classical languages such as Sanskrit, Pali and Prakrit but also different Indian vernaculars such as Tamil, Telegu, Malayalam, Canarese, Hindi, Oriya and Maithili.

(d) Spiritual emotion and love for mother. Influence on the Vaishnava poets.

Next we come to deal with his spiritual emotion. It is because of this, as we have already stated that the charge of lacking in sanity has been laid at his door. But these emotions above many other great qualities that he possessed was the great weapon with which he conquered. If you call it a disease it must be, as I have said elsewhere, like the pearl in a pearl-fish which is also called a disease of the animal. But is it not nevertheless the most valued thing in the fish? Similarly the trances of Chaitanya were the most wonderful thing that men ever beheld in him. This emotion made his life magnificent as a great epic poem. The whole Vaishnava lyrics, masterpieces of songs, breathe inspiration of Chaitanya's emotions. True, it related to man's love for God ; but it is the most wonderful love-tale that men ever heard.

Supposing for a moment that a man can love God as a bride does the bridegroom, all the sublimities of feminine emotions become as a matter of course the attributes of such a soul. Man can be a servant in God's temple; he may even call God a father. But it seems inconceivable to many how human soul can love God as the bride does the bridegroom. We talk of duty everywhere. But when one approaches his God in love, the question of duty does not arise at all. The wife gives her all, and this ideal is lowered by restricting her scope to certain prescribed rules for the guidance of conduct. There can be no question that Chaitanya actually fell in love with One so long considered as beyond the range of all human conception. And he indulged in all the niceties of emotion relating to this romantic situation. Rupa Goswami, who was appointed by Chaitanya to elucidate the *bhakti* cult by writing dramas about Radha-Krishna in Sanskrit, wrote exhaustively about these emotions. His famous verse beginning with

"*Tunde tandavene*" was no doubt conceived from witnessing the solicitude of Chaitanya for hearing and reciting Krishna's name. The manifold emotions, so poetically conceived in *kilakinchit* of Sanskrit poetics, described by Rupa, commented upon by Jiva Goswami (who brought out the whole wealth of the subtle felicities of the soul in love in his annotations) bear the stamp of that inspiration which came from Chaitanya's love-ecstasies. How all this is possible is not for me to explain, but the sexual romance is nothing if it does not teach us to taste the higher joys of the spiritual plane. I do not know why the question of decency so often arises in respect of sexual love,—since it is the purest, the most romantic and the most beautiful of all human sentiments. If we believe in God and in our duty to love him, this sexual love purged of all its grossness should be the very type of the sentiments with which the highest of us may approach Him. Like all things of superior quality, this love is delicate and may not bear too rough a touch. Hence Chaitanya did not speak of it before the public to whom he confined himself to a mere recitation of Krishna's name. But with Swarupa and Ram Ray he revelled in the elucidations of the subtler points of love-philosophy. Swarupa, at his bidding, referred to the various stages and conditions of a lover's emotions in his private talk. He spoke of *dhira*, the maiden in love who being wronged, does not reprimand her lover but gives him a seat near her and does not express her anger, speaks sweetly and if the lover embraces, returns the embrace; of *adhira* who being wronged takes away the lotus that decorates her ears and strikes the lover with it and makes him a captive with a string of flowers, of *Dhiradhira* who being wronged speaks crooked words and cuts jokes and is sometimes full of entreaties and at others showers abuses or remains indifferent; of *Mugdha* who being wronged knows not how to be angry but covers her face with hands to hide her tears and forgets and forgives, if the lover smiles and talks pleasantly. There are also *Madâhyas* and *Pragalvas*. And there are still subtler classifications; for instance the last-named two are classified into *Mukhara*, *Mridu*, *Sama*, etc. We need not enter into this very complicated science of love, including other infinite varieties of tender emotions, which was no doubt developed during the days of the declining Hindu power, when the spirit of galantry had made it a fashion for the learned to introduce subtle classifications of feminine feelings. These were no doubt used by Rupa as materials but looked at and interpreted from an entirely new standpoint as matters of spiritual plane. How Chaitanya thought only of his God and His relation to man from the nice classifications which the pages of rhetoric and poetics supplied, is not for me to say here; but there is no doubt that his God was near him and that he revelled in the mystic delights which that exalted presence brought to his heart in all the various shades of feelings which a lover feels in this world of ours;—nay more, for the intensity of his love was much greater than that of any human lovers ever described by a poet.

It has been urged in some quarters that the object of his worship was not a fit one. But he has assured us again and again that as human language is not sufficiently adequate to denote the sort of love that a man may feel for God, the phraseology of human love was adopted under the allegorical form of the Gopis loving Krishna. One may suppose that he actually took the Brinda groves to be the abode of his God. He not only did so but he took all the shrines that he visited as abodes of his God, but not merely that, all the places at which he had stopped and through which he had travelled, were the abode of his God in his eyes. Govindadas records Chaitanya's saying, "Everywhere the image of God shines resplendently. One who has attained a clear vision is privileged to see it." He visited the shrines associated with Kali, Ganes, Shiva and Krishna, and everywhere he felt the presence of that God who pervades this universe. He visited the shrines only with the object of experiencing a heightened joy by the associations of these places with worship. For to each and all of these shrines pilgrims have travelled for centuries, sincerely seeking One who is the final stay of the world. Though on account of his peculiar bent of mind favouring the emotional side of religion, he is identified with the Vaishnavas, yet his was the universal catholic religion that made him approach every spot of prayer and worship held sacred by the devotees with reverence, and he felt equal spiritual ecstasies at the temple of Kali at Padmakot as he had done before that of Dwarakadhish at Dwaraka. He rejected nothing in the spiritual world, however low it might appear to superficial lookers on, just as science rejects nothing as useless but by machinery turns rags and bits of paper to some fine useful purpose. His faith created flowers out of filth. The house of harlots or the resorts of robber-gangs he raised to the rank of temples by his faith. He paid a visit to the image of Kali in the Ashtabhuja temple at Padmakot in 1510 A.D. and when a Brahmin brought a goat for sacrifice he approached him and said "How can you believe it, friend, that the Mother of the universe will take meat and wine like a drunkard? The scriptures have been wrongly interpreted." His ecstatic fervour in the temple and his tears had already produced an impression as usual; and the Brahmin as he heard him speak sweetly thought

RATIONALISM 301

that he heard the voice of God. He let loose the goat and worshipped Kali with simple offerings of leaves, flowers and sandal.

Though temples and shrines were helpful in awakening afresh his emotional felicities and serving as signs and reminders, he did not share at all in popular superstitions. In the Brindagroves some people came and informed him that at a certain place in the Jamuna, Krishna appeared every night towards its latter part riding the great snake Kaliya and many men bore testimony to having witnessed the wonderful spectacle. Chaitanya smiled and said "How foolish are you to believe in such a nonsense!" and he appointed some of his intelligent people to find out what had deceived the eyes of the ignorant men of the shrine. In due course the report came stating that a fisherman used to ply his boat in the Jamuna every night. He was mistaken for Krishna and the boat was taken for the snake Kaliya and the light in the boat was thought of as the red eye of the snake. In Boroch his spiritual fervour became so great that a large throng gathered to behold it. One man wickedly said "Don't you see your Krishna is in the yonder tank." Chaitanya stood up and breathed heavily. His eyes shed incessant tears at the mention of Krishna. The man again said aloud "Just see there, your Krishna is in the tank." Then Chaitanya stretched his hands as if to run into the arms of his lover and flung himself into the tank and became unconscious. He was rescued by the help of the people who began to reproach the wicked Brahmin who had said the Krishna was in the tank. On coming back to his senses, Chaitanya said "Why do you reproach the Brahmin? Where is He not —in earth, waters and in the sky above?" The all-pervading deity was the object of his worship and all things that he saw or heard bore a message to him from the Most High. This message might have been written in a language which is Hebrew or Greek to us,—one that may find a parallel in the Song of Songs, or in the song celestial of Joydev, or in the phraseology of human passion in the Dohas of Kanupad and other mystics and saints, but that he received such a message, maddening his soul with love and elevating it to a plane in which the eyes of God and of Man met and exchanged mutual glances, admits of no doubt.

But howsoever the romantic love of Krishna may have softened his nature, the Brahminic asceticism by which such love was fed and nourished was the dominant characteristic that is marked in his career subsequent to *sannyas*. We find him declining to keep Govinda Ghosh of Agradwip on the list of the ascetics of his Order as he was found to keep the remnant of a Haritaki fruit after Chaitanya had partaken of it, for use on the next day. "He stores things for the morrow like a worldly man" said Chaitanya, and sent him back to home-life. We have referred to the incident of his refusing to admit junior Haridas to his presence for the fault of begging alms from Madhabi, an accomplished woman "These men feign asceticism but have lust and worldly desire lurking in their hearts. I will have nothing to do with such men." Being refused admittance to his presence junior Haridas committed suicide after his vain attempts to have commiseration from the Master. Whenever any man took him for an incarnation of the Deity, his overwhelming humility was in evidence. He declared in all such cases that he was a poor mortal and that it would be a sin to attribute divinity to him. Though in the Nadia-accounts of his earlier life we find him described as often asserting his identity with Godhead, these accounts coming as they do from some of his followers who tried to establish that he was no other than Krishna himself, reincarnated on the earth, must be accepted for all their worth with great hesitancy. When one of his ardent admirers had said once that he was God himself and should not subject himself to any moral restraint, he replied "I am a man and belong to the Order of ascetics. Just as in a white cloth a dark spot becomes prominent, even so a flaw in the conduct of an ascetic, however small, becomes the subject of harsh comment; it is like a pitcher full of milk spoiled by a drop of wine." Instances of such spiritual meekness lie strewn all over his life as a *sannyasi* and are too numerous to be mentioned.

Though he had cruelly cut himself off from home, his love for mother never forsook him, and it was one of the most lovable features of his character. He interviewed his mother only once after his *sannyas*, and according to a doubtful authority, twice. During such interviews he showed his feeling and affectionate regard in an unambiguous language. At one of them he said "Whatever you bid me do I will do" and complying with her request he promised that as *sannyasi* he would live at Puri from which place she would have an opportunity of receiving frequent messages about him. In the last year of his life he sent the following message to his mother through Jagadananda "Mother, I left my immediate duties to you and came away as *sannyasi*. I turned mad and laid axe to the very root of all religion by discarding you. Pray excuse me for this. I am your affectionate son and am entitled to every indulgence." Whenever any one came from Nadia he asked him to tell his mother that her kitchen was the one place which he could never forget. "I have never relished any food so well as that cooked by my mother." He said often; and we have seen how Sachi one day prepared some meals liked by Chaitanya for offering to Krishna and wept saying "Who will eat these—my Nimai has forsaken me?" On one occasion when Damodara told Chaitanya that he had derived his spiritual nature from his mother, he embraced Damodara with love and said that he had spoken the truth.

All that Chaitanya said about his mother, his remorse and all, should be taken for their worth. The vision of Krishna was ever before his eyes and it attracted him to a higher world day and night, and when occasionally only he came down to the consciousness of his material surroundings, he felt temporarily as ordinary good people feel. But a moment after he beheld the vision beatific and passed into a trance forgetting all his worldly ties.

What were these trances? Mr. Underwood says that they were similar to those experienced by men during what is called Wesleyan Revival. "At a revival in 1800," he says, "at Red River, Ohio, many dropped to the ground cold and still, or with convulsive twitches of face and limbs. Others leaped and bounded about like live fish out of the water. Others rolled over and over on the ground for hours. As the excitement increased it grew more morbid and took the form of "jerking" or in others it became "barking exercise" and in yet others it became the "holy laugh." The jerks began with the head, which was thrown violently from side to side so rapidly that the features were blurred and the hair almost seemed to snap, and when the sufferer struck an obstacle and fell, he would bounce about like a ball. Men fancied themselves dogs and gathered about a tree barking and yelping—"treeing the devil." Christendom knows the psychology of this form of adolescence in the history of Quakers and other sects also. But it is a great mistake to confound these with a Vaishnava trance. We have these in India still and no one here will mistake them for Vaishnava experiences of emotion. On the day of the Charak and other Shivait festivals low-class illiterate men do nearly all the things described by Hall and James from whose works Mr. Underwood has taken his extracts. On these days people gather by hundreds, to see these wild scenes of religious excitement. One man takes an incense-pot in his hand and runs followed by drummers who beat their drums aloud and other people gather together to form a procession. At a certain stage the man with the burning incense in his hand stops and throws his head from side to side violently with twitches of the face and eyes. The jerking becomes so violent that the man seems to lose all consciousness, and his example is followed by several others who do the same thing. In Eastern Bengal they call it *Báilpará*. After doing many things much on the lines of Mr. Underwood's descriptions they become void of their senses and remain for some time as dead men. When this point is reached, the Shivaits consider it a great success of their religious exercise. I have seen women taking prominent part in these religious exercises and remember very well a woman named Karuna in the village of Suapur in the District of Dacca, doing all the wild things imaginable in the course of *Báilpara* and in religious excitement. These wild excitements, ecstatic dances and abnormal jerks seem to have come down from a very remote antiquity and are the relics of a barbarous age. They were to be found among the Greeks and other ancient people and among the Shivaits and the Dharma worshippers of this province. Only low-class men at the present day are observed to adopt these ways during their religious festivals. Christianity may have derived some of these from its contact with the religions of the East or from the heathen ancestors of the present races that dwell in Europe. I cannot say that the emotional dance and trances of the Vaishnavas have much in common with the kind of things described above. In the Vaishnavic experiences the excitement takes a far milder and more refined form and the excitement itself is brought on by subtle religious appeals conveyed by songs of great poetic and spiritual beauty and by an exposition of the emotional doctrines based on the text of the scriptures of the Bhakti cult. The barbaric action of the illiterate Shivait might have originally had some element of mysticism in it, but it has been reduced now to a mere physical display of morbid religious excitement. The Vaishnavas on the other hand have, by scholarly exposition of their subtle religious philosophy, classified all experiences of emotion in such a manner that the *Ashta Satvic Bikar* or the eight sorts of spiritual fervour according to their classifications bears now a scientific scrutiny and stands on the basis of an analytical and masterly grasp of the whole problem of human mentality in respect of tender emotions. A vast literature giving a scientific review of the *Ashta Satvic Bikar* is in existence, laying down canons for the culture of the emotional side of the mind. There seems to be hardly any affinity between the savage excesses of religious experience of the Shivaits and the cultured mysticism of the Vaishnavas in their respective forms at the present day.

The mystic trances according to the Vaishnavas are beyond the reach of an ordinary man's realisation. Chaitanya's advice to regulate one's life before one can reach the higher plane of mystic bliss is comprehensive. Some of them I give below.

"One should be kind without hostile feelings towards others. He should adopt truth to be his greatest stay and be faultless in morals, magnanimous, pure in body and mind, humble, a universal benefactor, calm, resigned to God, without desire, a controller of passions, temperate in diet, not addicted to pleasures, giving honour to others, but not wishing for any himself, dignified, full of compassion, friendly to all, not given to talking, efficient in work and of a poetic turn of mind."

In another place his advice to the religious preceptors was—

"Do not take too many disciples, do not abuse gods worshipped by other peoples and their scriptures, do not read too many books and do not pose as a teacher continually criticising and elucidating religious views. Take profit and loss in the same light. Do not stay there where a Vaishnava is abused. Do not listen to village tales. Do not by your speech or thought cause pain to a living thing. Listen to the recitation of God's name. Recollect his kindness; bow to him and worship him. Do what he wills as a servant, believe Him to be a friend and then dedicate yourself to Him."

The last advice is the quintessence of Vaishnava religious philosophy-*Atma nibedan* or self-dedication implies the absolute surrender of one's body and soul to the Deity in the spirit of a bride offering herself to the bridegroom. When this stage is reached trances become natural to the devotee. So that a mere physical display or nervousness is not mistaken by the Vaishnavas for any high degree of spiritual advancement.

The trances of Chaitanya were often the most exalted sight to those who witnessed them. The lover sees illusions at every stage of the intensity of his emotions showing his kindredness with the poet and the lunatic. Ram seeks tidings about Sita in one of such felicitous moods from the pomegranate and mango trees and Valmiki gives a pathetic interest to his unmatched poetry by describing them. Bhababhuti keeps a continuous flow of his charming poetry by a description of the illusions and trances of his hero, and Jaydev makes his Radha absorbed in her reveries with her gaze fixed at the lovely clouds which she mistakes for her dark-coloured god. These tender and romantic situations described in literature are exceedingly attractive. But when we find one who actually mistakes a *tamal* tree and a summer cloud for the god of his vision and remains for days together, unconscious of the material world lost in mystic bliss, the poetic interest that gathers round him becomes really inspiring. The creed of emotional religion lays stress on our capacity of realizing god as lover—the soul of man being his bride. If God may be obeyed as a servant, if He may be taken to be our father, where is the psychology that would draw its limits barring Him from being our lover? To the devout Vaishnava He comes to win the human heart with a thousand flowers in the spring and shows Himself in the glory of a summer cloud with the crown of rainbow on his head and in the autumn with the purple rays of the sun spreading a golden view that looks like a gorgeous apparel. He plays on his flute in the songs of the cuckoo and in the chirp of nightingale. He comes to win the human heart by presents of his sweet fruit baskets every season, and, in the thousand beauties that appear in nature, He shows us but a glimpse of His lovely form. The devotee hears the sound of the anklets of His feet in the hum of bees and in the drone of the beetle, announcing His approach.

The sight of Chaitanya's extraordinary love created a tempest of feeling in people, and they struggled to give expression to their sentiments. One poet says "Lo! there he goes driven by emotion, as a flower by storm." Another says "He looks like the glorious summit of Sumeru, trembling under hurricane." His beauteus form is the favourite subject on which many have dwelt. Brindaban Das compares his body spotted with ink, when as a lad he first went to school, to a white flower with swarms of bees on it. One poet praises the beauty of his acquiline nose and another sings of his lovely eyes that became full of tears at the sight of flowers. Radhamohan the poet says "He talks with Some One not seen by others,—his lotus eyes are tearful and they betray a strange emotion." The literature of lyrics describing the emotions of Chaitanya is considerable, and we recommend our readers to the excellent work Gaurapadatarangini compiled by Jagatbandhu Bhadra and published by the Sahitya Parishat of Calcutta which contains the largest collection of these songs.

The influence of Chaitanya on the Vaishnava songs is enormous. He turned the very tide of them from the sensuous to the idealistic course. The *Kirtana* songs after his *sannyas* were inevitably introduced by Gaurachandrikas which gave a spiritual tone to the Radha-Krishna songs much more than they had possessed formerly. The Radha-Krishna songs are divided into several classes. There are some that treat of the pastoral life of Krishna in the midst of his fellow cowherds and these are called the Gostha songs. There are besides those which describe the romantic position in which Radha and Krishna fell in love and these are the Purba Raga songs. The Doutya is the message of love sent by one to the other. Then comes the union or Milan. The stages of Milan contain the varied phases of Khandita, Kalahantarita, Bipralabdha, and Man in which Radha feels herself wronged and is full of anger because Krishna does not come to her bower as expected, while she spends the night imagining his approach at every fall of leaves. The last of all is the Mathur, where Krishna leaves her for ever and goes to Mathura, supplemented by Bhabasanmilan in which Radha realises his presence in her spirit and thus finds him really and truly, though physically separated from him. I need not dwell on these different classes of songs, which for poetic beauty, tenderness and pathos, have a quite unique place in world's lyrical literature, fed as they are by the great spiritual culture of the Hindus and by Vedantic philosophy, which give to apparent sensuous descriptions a great mystic import. The Gaurachandrikas are the songs describing Chaitanya's emotions. These songs are introduced as prologues before each class of Radha-Krishna songs is sung. Each of the above classes is sung for four or five hours, but the inevitable prologue—the Gaurachandrika must be sung first. I refer my readers to pp. 538-42 of my History of Bengali Language and Literature for a full account of the bearing which the Gaurachandrikas have on the Radha-Krishna songs. The Gaurachandrikas by alluding to Chaitanya's emotions give a realistic interest to the Radha-Krishna songs. All sensuous matters are thus purged of materialistic elements and become thoroughly idealised by the exalted allusion; and this forms a sort of comment upon the songs interpreting the whole in the light of spirituality. The audience thus become inspired by the spiritual side of these songs, which becomes so apparent and striking that the romance of ordinary love only heightens the spiritual felicity of the musical performance. In the Swapnabilas and Dibyonmad by the poet Krishna Kamal, born in 1810, we find a systematic and successful attempt on the part of the poet to portray Chaitanya's spiritual felicities in the outward form of the Radha-Krishna legend. Radha goes to Kunda and Juthi flower plants and seeks the tidings of Krishna from them, just as Chaitanya is said to have done, as described in the Antakhanda of the Chaitanya Charitamrita. The vision of clouds bearing its ever-beautiful message to the Vaishnava devotee is attributed to Radha. She trembles with joy and with joint hands offers praise to the clouds thinking them to be Krishna, for staying a while to listen to her laments. But the clouds pass away and when Krishna actually comes to her doors she weeps and says "Say, my maids, is it really He or merely the clouds? Are those the peacock feathers of his crown or the rainbow? Are those that look like strings of pearls on his breast really so or the flocks of cranes in the distant clouds? Is this his purple dress or a flash of lightning?" This is the thin line beyond which the fine frenzy —the trance of Chaitanya often steps forth. The poet began his work by saying that when the vision of God became clear, Chaitanya thought Krishna to be in the Brinda groves, but when the vision faded he thought Krishna to have gone to Mathura and so he lamented. Sometimes Chaitanya become maddened by his vision and said to Swarupa "Show me, dear friend, once more the lovely sight or else I will die" and he fell unconscious on the ground. Thus Gaurachandrika makes the burden of the Radha Krishna songs quite clear, and inspite of all that may be urged upon by hostile critics, who have but a superficial idea about Indian religion, it must be said that the atmosphere of songs in which the allegorical element becomes very prominent during a Kirtana performance is pure and elevative. If we treat the Vaishnava lyrics, as a scholar has suggested, merely as literature, it becomes divested of its whole wealth of spiritual charm and it is besides impossible in the present stage of the songs to disconnect Chaitanya's life from the Radha Krishna songs. For instance in many of the songs of Govinda Das a situation of Radha is described in which she is near Krishna, but laments as if parted from him. This is in perfect accord with the Vaishnavite belief that Chaitanya who was always with Krishna, lamented the separation in his frenzied condition only, in which the fact of his presence appeared too dearly-prized to be believed. How can this situation be explained without a reference of the bearing which Chaitanya's ecstasies had on the Radha-songs? In many places Chaitanya is described as resting on the shoulders of Narahari and Gadadhar and lamenting the pain of God in the most poetic way. Radhamohan the poet describes Radha as leaning on her maids and lamenting in the same strain. In the accounts of Abhishar after Chaitanya's *sannyas* Radha is described always in such a way as to remind us of Chaitanya's leading the Kirtana profession. There are very direct references which cannot be interpreted without their bearing on Chaitanya's life.

Those whose cry is that some of the Vaishnava songs are erotic, lose sight of the spiritual background against which the Radha-Krishna songs are set. One who attends a Kirtan performance, must be struck with the edifying effect inevitably produced on the hearers. The singers and their audience feel the inspiring presence of the spirit of Chaitanya in the Gour Chandrikas and altogether lose sight of this material world being gradually carried into the higher regions of Divine grace and love. One who has witnessed the solemnity of these performances will not doubt for a moment the exalted character of the songs when properly interpreted.

Last of all we refer to the criticism which has been made in certain quarters regarding the immoral lives of lay Vaishnavas as due to a defect in the system of emotional religion founded by Chaitanya. The immodesties complained of as existing amongst the Sahajias and Nera Neris who at the present day profess Vaishnavism, should not be attributed to anything wrong in the Vaishnava creed; since we have seen that Chaitanya and his followers from whom the religion emanated were stern ascetics of purest morals and it is not fair to suppose that from asceticism and purity immorality can spring, any more than we can expect Nim fruit from a mango tree. These Sahajias and Nera Neris were originally Buddhist Bhikkhus and Bhikkhunis (monks and nuns) amongst whom great sexual vices prevailed. Instead of being an instrument of degenerating their morals Vaishnavism has reformed them to a great extent and the work of reformation is still going on. They were celibates and their profligacy is due to a fall of the moral standard during the declining days of Buddhism. Vaishnava leaders have, however, introduced marriage system amongst them, and this has gone a great way towards reforming their character. And if sexual vices still prevail in their society, they are like the dregs in a wine bottle—the remnants of bygone depravities, and the fault of this must not be fixed on the

Vaishnavas. That their morals had been gradually but steadily improving will be proved by the fact that the markets or fairs where women used practically to be sold for Re. 1-4 per head are growing scarcer day by day. And with these people —the Sahajias and Nera Neris—the Vaishnavas had nothing to do formerly, though their leaders out of great compassion admitted the fallen people within the fold of their religion. The subject will be dealt with elaborately in Chapter II of the Supplement of this book.

We have quoted a song by the Emperor Akbar in honour of Chaitanya on the title page as our motto. In the inscriptions of Govindaji's temple at Brindaban the statement is found that Rupa and Sanatana were the Gurus of Mansingha. It is therefore quite natural that the Emperor had heard a good deal about Chaitanya from his favourite general and others, and conceived an admiration for him. Growse tells us that the Emperor paid a visit to Brindaban and was struck by the piety of the Vaishnava Gurus. His famous court-musician Tansen sang before him songs in honour of the Hindu gods and goddesses and it is well-known that both had catholic views in respect of religion though they were Mahomedans. It will be seen that the Emperor in that Hindi song uses onomatopoetic expressions much on the lines of the songs of Chandvardai.

I cannot conclude this review of Chaitanya and Chaitanyism better than by quoting the following verse by Govinda Das, the distinguished poet of Budhuri in the 16th century.

"He gives love of God to men without their seeking.
Where is the heart so magnanimous as his?
When he danced, the lame, the blind and the deaf danced with him.
When he wept, the eyes of the world were blinded with tears.
When he called 'Krishna' 'Krishna' aloud, the sound was caught by the multitude, and it reverberated in air from direction to direction.
It is for this that I believe him to be God.
And surely His spirit was in him, just as the reflection of the Sun is in the mirror."

SUPPLEMENT

CHAPTER I.

CHAITANYA'S RELIGIOUS VIEWS.

The Dwaitádwaitabád.

Chaitanya gave an elaborate account of the Vaishnava creed to Sanatan, and to this we have referred in several places in the body of this book. It is curious to observe that one who was entirely given to felicitous excesses of emotion and always carried the people by an exuberence of them, quoted scriptural texts in supporting almost all his views, when in a quiet chamber he sat with Sanatan dictating the lines on which his book of Vaishnava Jurisprudence should be written. There he appeared more like a sound scholar and theologian than a man given to devotional ardour. But with all this, it appears that he had but little regard for *Shastric* ordinances. This he explained by a parable. A poor man sought the help of an astrologer to tell him when his evil days would come to an end. He was told that his father had dug a cavity under the plinth of his sleeping-room and there stored great riches for him. But the astrologer cautioned him against seeking them in the north, south and western plinths. Only the surface of the eastern one should be superficially dug into and then the man would come to find the treasure. "If you dig in the south," he said, "bees will come out in swarms and sting you. In the north, there is an awful black snake and in the west there is an evil spirit who, if disturbed, will stand in the way of your getting the riches." The *shastras*, the heritage left by our fathers, in their different phases represented by the four directions, are not always a safeguard to rely on. By practising austerities, penances and methods of the yoga and by mortification of the body, only evil results may befall you. This is the meaning of the parable. He pointed to the direction of the light, of the rise of the sun, symbolised by the word "east" in the parable and wanted that the spiritual soul must come in direct contact with God—only a little communion with saintly men and the Guru would serve to awaken in him a religious curiosity and inspire him with devotion in his pursuit. "Superficial digging of the surface" is a caution against falling a victim to excessive book-study leading to orthodoxy in theological matters, which was the vice of the age.

He preached what has been called the *Dwaita-dwaitabád* or "non-dualism within dualism." The

Adwaitabád of Sankara advocates the theory that Universe is identical with the Deity. The line of demarcation between the human soul and the Great Soul embracing all, is more fancied than real—the origin of the fancy being the phenomenal world denominated *Maya* in the midst of which we live. The moment we attain *Jnan* or true knowledge, the phenomenal world, which is a mere illusion, passes away, and the little soul becomes merged in the Great Soul; so that all that has created the difference ceases to exist. The *Dwaitabád* or Dualism is of course the ordinary theory accepted by most people, which promulgates that God and Man are eternally different, the latter having to rely constantly on His mercy, help and compassionate grace. The *Dwaitádwaitabád* of Chaitanya advocates Dualism in religious speculation but lays stress on the devotional side, saying that when faith has reached the state of perfection, the human soul forgets its own self, the eyes see nothing but Him—the sight of all sights, the ears hear nothing but the sound of His flute, which fills all space, and every touch is His. The senses in fact instead of leading to the consciousness of *many* make the devotee aware of the presence of Him only, so absolutely, that he forgets his own existence. That is Chaitanya's non-dualism with in dualism,—only a refined form of dualism in the highest stage of devotion.

At this stage Vidyapati's *Rádhá* is thus described in the *Mathur* songs of the poet "অনুখন মাধব মাধব সোঙরিতে, সুন্দরী ভেল মাধাই" (constantly thinking and recalling her beloved—Mádhaba, the beautiful one turned herself into Mádhaba). Jaydev practically had said the same thing nearly five centuries earlier in the line "মুহুরবলোকিতমণ্ডন-লীলা, মধুরিপুরহমিতি ভাবনশীলা." Certainly the Bhagavat, the greatest scripture of the Vaishnavas, has a text, from which these poets took their idea, in which the Gopis of the Vrinda-groves so far forgot themselves in the excess of their devotion, that each of them considered herself as Krishna himself. This unity of the lesser soul with the Great Soul is a momentary experience in the excess of emotion and does not indicate the stage of man's identity with the Absolute and the Omnipotent, indicated in the non-dualistic views of Sankara, who asserts that God and man become one at a certain stage when the phenomenal world—the *Mayà*—is removed. The Brahma Sutra of Vyās hints at an emotional stage on which the "Dwaitádwaita-bád" of Chaitanya may be said to be based, in the lines "জগদ্ব্যাপারবর্জং প্রকরণাৎ অসন্নিহাতাচ্চ" and "ভোগমাত্র সাম্যলিঙ্গাৎ". This clearly indicates that a devotee in the excess of his emotions may lose consciousness of his self and become merged in God, but he cannot thereby attain the omnipotent powers of creation and destruction.

The rules of conduct,—the theory of devotion.

The codes for daily observance and for the training of the mind to devotion, preached by Chaitanya, are on the lines of asceticism and control of passions. Chaitanya advocated abstinence, wished men to avoid taking rich meals and wearing fine apparel. He was always against too much study. This is perhaps due to the fact that at his time much pedantry was rampant, which made people vain, conceited and proud. He would not allow men to listen to gossip or become news-hunters. He would not believe in morality without faith. However acute the moral sense, however whole-hearted one's work, however comprehensive one's knowledge—they are likely to lead to error and confusion, unless man makes faith his guiding star. The rules for guidance of one's actions are fully detailed by him in his instructions to Sanatan and are to be found in Chaitanya-Charitamrita (Chap.—Madhya Khanda). Lochan Das's "Durlabha Sár," and Narottam Das's "Prembhaktichandriká" also give us some of his views in regard to action (*Karma*) and knowledge (*Jnan*) as opposed to Bhakti.

From the Buddha to Sankara, till the time of Chaitanya, much spiritual and moral ground had been trodden, when the human soul realised that the principle of good action and self-control could not be its safeguard, until it fixed its anchor on God's love which leads to the unerring perception of truth, not to be attained either by '*Jnan*' or '*Karma*' divested from faith. The latter oftentime entangled the soul in the meshes of selfishness and conceit.

Chaitanya showed the force of this faith, often without any sermon or speech. It was his eyes with tears that attracted all, it was the sweet face beaming with the light of mystic trance that acted as a charm on the multitude. What country has produced such a galaxy of poets to sing hymns and melodious songs in praise of their prophets as Bengal has done in honour of Chaitanya? The whole Vaishnava literature of Bengal, rich in its twenty thousand songs, in its conception of devotion in the imagery of Radha expressed in its numberless *Padas*, is the flower-tribute to the feet of the Nadia Brahmin, a poor *sannyasi* in life, but the prince of her princes in the domain of spirituality. The compassionate and self-controlled majesty of the Buddha has faded away from this country yielding its throne to Chaitanya, whose name is now on the lips of thousands of crypto Buddhists who have embraced Vaishnavism.

The Buddha showed us the precipitous and rickety ladder of moral life unsupported by faith to scale inaccessible heights ever-lost in the summer clouds, but what of the man who actually opened the gates of the Region of Light and thus gave us some tangible good to be realised by all. Thus to-day in Bengal the blacksmith forgets his hammer, the ploughman his bulls and the good housewife of the peasant her husking, as a song on Chaitanya is sung by the peasantry, making all hearts leap forth in joy and adoration.

The Buddha had laid great stress on the control of, nay a total extinction of passions. Chaitanya looked at spiritual truths from quite another angle of vision. He perceived that passions and emotions were the great motor-powers of the soul. God has given these to men for some definite object. It is their proper use and not misuse that would help in serving their purpose. In the 'Prembhaktichandriká' by Narottam Das and in many other works of the Vaishnavas, this idea is clearly set forth. If we give a sharp weapon to a child, it will prove dangerous, but the sharp weapon is not to be destroyed because the child has cut his finger with it.

The world is not to be renounced, nor are the ties that bind us to it to be given up. These ties are sacred, and if properly understood, lead us to the realisation of permanent bliss. I have referred to the *sānta, dāsya, sakhya, vātsalya* and *mādhurya* of the Vaishnava creed of Bengal, as embodying the highest truths of their religion. I have explained some of them in a loose and general manner in the body of this book and for the sake of a clearer comprehension of this most essential doctrine of the Vaishnava, I shall crave your indulgence to recapitulate the points summed up in an article of mine entitled "The domestic element in the religious creeds of Bengal" and make the following extract from the concluding portion of the article.[1] These five-fold *rasas* of the Vaishnavas of the Chaitanya order have been described by me also in my works "Chaitanya and his Companions" and "History of the Mediæval Vaisnava Literature."

The five-fold rasas of the Vaisnavas.

"The Vaishnava theology, as I have already stated, reached its highest point and very flower in the realisation of the emotional side of religion. It boldly asserted that there was no form of higher faith among the world's religious systems which did not possess an honoured place in the scope of the Vaisnava doctrines.

First of all, the "quiet" or the '*shánta*' stage is that attained by the Buddha and other sages where the human soul is made clear of the meshes of flesh by removing the desires. The field is weeded out of wild plants and becomes fit for the sowing of the spiritual seed. The Vaishnavas say that the doctrine of a moral life belongs to this initial stage when the mind is placed under discipline and control.

[1] See Silver Jubilee Commemoration Volume of Sir Asutosh Mukherjee, Part II.

The next is "service" or "*dásya*," where the devotee, after having grown fit by bringing his restless soul under discipline is eager to establish a relation between himself and his God. This relation is that of a servant to his master; he has for his motto "duty." He considers all work holy in this stage and longs to hear the applauding word, "Well done" from his Lord after his day's labours. This stage, says the Charitāmrita, "includes the "*shánta*" or the "quiet" and is a step forward in the spiritual progress of a man, inasmuch as he has been able now to establish some definite relation between himself and his Maker."

The next stage in this progressive faith is the '*sakhya*' or "friendship." Here the devotee has gained another step and has come nearer to Him. God is now not at such a distance as the master is from his servant. The devotee feels that in this stage he has 'to play' with his brother-men of the world with a heart full of love and sweetness, and is conscious that in this play He, the Lord, is always his playmate to direct and control the play, encouraging him when he is weary and protecting him from evil at every crisis. The devotee sees the divine smile and filled with love for Him, knows how to love others. The '*sakhya*' which comprehends as the Charitāmrita says "all the attributes of '*shánta*' and '*dásya*,' has again gained a step, in asmuch as sweetness and love has been added to a mere moral sense."

In the next higher stage comes the '*vátsalya*.' The devotee realises God as the child. This may appear a mental paradox to those who have been accustomed to look upon God as Father only. But is not the sentiment inspired by the child the grandest emotion ever felt by a human being ? A little thing, it gives infinite pleasure : it shews beauty unperceived by others, the mother alone discovers it. Through a small vista the whole heaven, as it were, presents itself before the amazed eyes of the mother. How could such a wonderful thing be ever believed that a tigress that was ferocity itself, gathers up all conceivable tenderness in her eyes when beholding her cub ? The discovery of the beautiful new-born child in the midst of things rotten and decayed is a presentation to the soul of the sight of One who is ever new in the universe, and through all the wear and tear of ages keeps up the charm of the unfading smile in all that we observe in this phenomenal world of ours. And this stage comprehends, according to the Charitāmrita " all the previous phases of *shánta*, *dásya* and *sakhya*, and implies a further advance in the realisation of bliss. The devotee views the child Krishna in all that smiles and plays around as one who supplies a never-ceasing fountain of new delights to the soul.

The last stage is the '*mádhurya.*' This is typified by the love of man for woman. It includes in its scope all the attributes of '*dásya*' for here the devotee's hand is ever ready to serve; of '*sakhya,*' for he is absorbed in his 'plays' with his Divine Playfellow; of "*vátsalya*" for he discovers in his loving God all the beauty and grace which the fondest of mothers ever found in the face of her child and much more, inasmuch as every sound conveys to him a message from the Lord, every form a sense of Divine presence and every touch the warmth of divine contact. The devotee attains to a state of fine frenzy which lends the highest poetic significance to this material world, which becomes to his sense a symbol of the greatest spiritual bliss. The rustling wind is taken as indicating His approach, the dark blue sky, the sea and landscape become symbolic of the colour of the Divine Figure. The "*mádhurya*" creates emotional felicities and a longing which are but imperfectly expressed in the best worldly poems dealing with the romance of love.

Thus home-relations are gradually idealised till the highest point of emotional fervour is reached. Through the doorway of the servants' outer quarters, through the front-garden of the home where we play with our playfellows, our brothers and sisters, through sleeping-room of the baby where the mother watches through the night, and last of all through the closed door of the nuptial chamber—from the finite—the devotee's soul wends its long journey towards the Infinite. The small windows and shutters of our houses open a vista commanding the outlook of the Illimitable. The Vaishnavas believe that the Incomprehensible may be brought within the range of human realisation—nay loved a thousand times more than ever a mother or a lover loved, and as an illustration of this they point to Chaitanya's life which has been woven into a hundred songs by their poets.

This home-life is now about to be broken. The parents are no longer loved with absolute trust and devotion, and the baby itself scarcely imparts more delight to the soul than gold. How can the spiritual soul now realise the "*vátsalya*" as people did in the days when the Bhágvata was their one, scripture? How can the idea of "*sakhya*," which to be spiritualised must be universal, elevate the soul, when the idea of brotherhood has become clannish and confined to the interest of a few named a nation? How can even "*dásya*" flourish, when the ideal of loyalty to the throne seems to be swept away by the whirlwind of Bolshevic ideas? The "*mádhurya*" is now a dream far off from our realisation when sexual love has lost the saving graces of devotion and poetry and has been reduced to fleeting emotions ever delighting in new conquests. Nuptial purity has lost its sacredness and many writers are advocating a contract system in marriage. "Give up" is the cry heard all around and nowhere does anybody say, "Come unto me and I will give." The sublime teaching of "*dāsya*," which finds blessedness in work, cannot find room anywhere in the present state of society, where work has lost its holy motive and is directed to legalised robbery, and huge machines are being scientifically manufactured for the destruction of men. Who will in this unhinged state of people's mentality stand up with God's banner in his hands and say, "I will serve Thee, O Lord, as a devoted servant serves his master. I will hear Thy voice, my great Play-fellow, in my 'play' with others and listen not to party-politics which shut off Thy voice from me. I will delight in Thee as the mother delights in her babe, as a lover delights in the beloved of his dreams?" Who will rebuild the temples that have been broken and repair the Churches where the figures of Christ and Mary lie unadored, where some people in the frenzy of their excited blood even go so far as to declare that Christ came to the world with a sword in hand to support *their* cause and to declare it holy? The opposite party are also not slow in giving him the same character, and they invoke his co-operation in their destructive policy, which they also misname "righteousness."

In this state of society all around, the peaceful, sweet and all-sacrificing devotion of family-life which inspired most of our religious cults with a spirit of universal love and brotherhood, the first lessons of which were taught us by those who loved us most—is a subject that may be held as deserving of an attentive consideration for rebuilding society in the light of all that is good and holy."

CHAPTER II

THE SAHAJIAS

When a great religion with the trumpet-call of its latest culture and new ideal, proclaims its advent to the world, the old decayed creeds surrender themselves to the New-Comer and take refuge in the new temple of faith which thrusts open its portals of brotherhood to all. But the old culture and age-long conventions do not die out. The new recruits retain their old faith under the mere name of the adventurous offspring of the old wisdom represented by the new religion. Thus the Sufis amongst the Mahomedans have retained the old culture of the Buddhists, and in Christianity itself the Gaelic, Buddhist and other forms of pagan faith are found underlying the rituals of the Church.

In Bengal a hundred different forms of the Buddhist faith of the Maháyana school were prevalent, when Vaishnavism sent its trumpet-call far and near. The leaders of those creeds had already packed up and gone to Nepal and other resorts of Buddhism, leaving millions of lay Buddhists as moral and spiritual wrecks, exposed to the contumely of the revivalists of

Hinduism. In these monasteries the Bhikshus and the Bhikshunis started the the creed of Sahaj *dharma* based in some cases on romantic love, which seemed profanation, leading to sexual depravities of the grossest kind amongst them. The tenets which the author of the Vidyonmádtarangini puts in the mouth of a Buddhist leader trample on all laws of morality and shew the worst form of atheism. They did not believe in the human soul, in the sacredness of marriage-tie and in any thing beyond the pleasures of the present moment. Buddhism thus became a hated name in the country and those that still followed it, tried by all means to hide their religious societies from the public view. Even now the Sahajias (by which I comprehend the Bául, the Nerá-Neris, the Kartá Bhajás and a hundred other sects which now represent under different names the broken pieces of the great marble house of Buddhism that once stood in full majesty in this land of ours) hold their meetings in secret and have a language in circulation amongst themselves, denominated by some as the *Sandhyá Bhásá*, not understood by people outside the pale of their own members. Laxity in sexual morals is one of the features of degenerate Buddhism, but I cannot say that these societies have not in view some of the highest ideals of the decayed religion. Perverted and led astray,

<small>The degenerate Buddhism.</small>

the ancient wisdom of monastaries still lingers in some of these societies but their members take care strictly to hide from the public. They develop psychic powers in a wonderful degree. My friend Pandit Khirod Chandra Goswami, a direct descendant of the Vaisnava apostle Nityananda, tells me that his wife had been suffering from a serious disease for a long time and was ultimately given up by the best doctors of Calcutta. But she was miraculously cured by an old woman who belonged to the Kartabhajá sect. Instances of such cures have also been reported to me by others who have nothing but contempt for the people who belong to such secret societies.

I have mentioned elsewhere that when the Bhikshus and the Bhik-

The Buddhist join the Vaisnava Order.

shunis, the shaven couples of the Buddhist monasteries, were abandoned by their leaders and got nothing but contempt from the people of the Hindu Renaissance, Bir Bhadra, son of Nityananda, gave them a shelter and converted them to Vaisnava faith. This conversion, however, does not mean much. For they have retained the ancient forms of their rituals, mystic training and practices, though they call themselves Vaisnavas. They merely cry aloud the names of Chaitanya and Nityananda and there ends all their connection with Vaisnavism. They have written a large number of books propounding the

VAISNAVA AUTHORITY

doctrines they follow, often in that unintelligible language of theirs and in all these they have tried to trace their doctrines to some Vaisnava authority of the Chaitanya-cult, like Krisnadas Kaviraj, Rup and Sanatan. The doctrines of the latter-day Maháyána creed, have to be modified to a certain extent for adaptation to the texts of Vaisnava works like the Charitamrita ; when they cannot contrive to do it and their views are in direct discord with those of the Vaisnava masters, they try to explain away the anomaly by manufacturing fables. They maintain that the Vaisnava masters were themselves the originators of the theories propounded by them, but for some reason or other the masters could not find time or opportunity to put them to writing in their life-time. They, however, communicated the gospel to some of their disciples from whom the Sahajias have got them. Thus Mukunda Das, author of Vivarta Vilás, is said to have been one of the disciples of Krishna Das Kaviraj to whom are attributed many mystic views which in reality belonged to some local form of latter-day Buddhism. The Sahajias would by no means confess that they were Buddhists, nor refer to any Buddhist texts which would make it far easier to trace the doctrines to their genuine origin. In the theories themselves and in their practices, many Buddhist rites and views have left their

The process of adaptation.

indeliable marks, which my friend Babu Manindra Mohan Bose, M.A. will disclose to you, engaged as he is in making research into the various forms of the prevailing Sahajia creed in Bengal. The last man in Bengal proper who openly declared himself to be a Buddhist, was Ramananda who wrote a Ramayan in Bengali early in the 18th century. But though the student of Buddhism will find ample materials amongst the Sahajia sects, he will find none among them who openly professes that faith, unless he visits Chittagong and other border-lands of Bengal. The ethical standard raised by the Hindu Renaissance became such a complete monument of sexual purity that the corruption prevailing amongst the Sahajias was a shame which feared the exposure of day light and passed into the shade of their nocturnal societies where no outsider had access. The modern Sahajias themselves do not know that they closely follow the Buddhist tenets, their ancestors concealed the fact when they were admitted to the Vaishnava order, while following them still in their rituals; and at the present stage it is the duty of a historian and scholar to thresh out grains from the chaff and find out the true Buddhist elements in their views and practices.

These Sahajias of the various sects, who outwardly profess the Vaishnava religion, present a very large number in Bengal. Mr. Ward in his work on the Hindoos says that nearly one-fifth of the whole Bengali nation are Vaishnavas. By far the largest portion of these are the Sahajias. Their literature is very considerable. If we examine the different libraries of old Bengali manuscripts in the country, it will be seen that there is scarcely a bundle of a dozen leaflets and books, which have not in them some treatise or brochure on the Sahajia cult. It is an immense literature, far greater numerically than any one could think of ten years ago. The spiritual truths they disclose often come to us like a marvel ; it shews that the lowest classes of our community have been in touch with some of the greatest discoveries in the theological and spiritual domain. They set forth canons and theories with a boldness which is really amazing. The upper classes of our country are orthodox, but they are not at all so. They have always remained open to conviction and are ready to follow new light if an appeal on religious questions is made to them in an intelligent and feeling manner.

<small>Their activities.</small>

The proselytising work they are doing is wonderful. They do not put any stress on any special religion which would serve to limit the scope of their work. They gather recruits from all religions. There are Mahomedans, Christians and Brahmins amongst them. Very often the members of depressed castes take the

<small>The universal character of their Order ; development of occult powers.</small>

lead in their society and are accepted as Gurus; so that even a cobbler claims homage of self-surrender and utmost humility from his Brahmin disciples. In the atmosphere of this country, where stringent caste rules have such a hold on the people, the societies created by the Sahajias are free from all caste-prejudices. the Brahmins, Christians, Mahomedans and the depressed castes eat at the same table, and often the texts of their faith are furnished by the Koran and not rarely by the Bible. The Hindu scriptures of course have their due respect and attention. A Kartá-bhaja or a Baul (the different sorts of Sahajia) may be a Hindu, a Mahomedan or a Christian, but that is no bar to his enjoying perfect fellowship with the members of his sect in their secret societies. Caste, rank in society and orthodoxy of views are out of question there. They are disciples of a Guru and in that capacity meet together—ready for any sacrifice or duty which the Guru may enjoin on them. Would it be believed that those, who in the day time pass as good orthodox Brahmins, sit in the nocturnal meetings with the Mahomedans and eat beef without the least scruple. I do not mean to say that in every society of the Sahajias this is the case. These local societies under different names and forms have special codes for guidance and there are such of them where beef is freely used by the Hindus and Mahomedans alike. They put stress upon the training of the physical system in man and the psoychic powers developed by Yoga practices. Profession of religion, they hold to be merely a superficial thing. The training of body and mind is the most essential question and in that there is no Hindu, no Mahomedan, no Christian. It is curious to observe that this country rent by caste-distinction and crushed by orthodoxy has within her fold a very large number of people, possessed of a special wisdom, who entertain the utmost freedom in thought in religious and social matters. They are under the banners of a cult that has subordinated all the religions prevailing in the country to a life of training,—mystic and unknown,—and progressed towards a surprising unification of men of different creeds and conflicting religious views.

I will give here a brief account of the leaders and other particulars of the more important sects of the Sahajias.

In the village of Ula (near Santipur) there lived a man of the Bárui caste, named Mahadev. One morning in February, 1694 A.D., he happened to meet a lad, eight years old, who seemed to possess bright talents but who would by no means disclose his name or whereabouts. Mahadev Bárui brought the boy to his home where he lived 12 years. Then he sojourned for seven years in different countries and in his 27th year appeared

The Karta-bhajas.

in a place called Bejra in 1715, and here he shewed some wonderful powers by which he attracted disciples. He was called "Baba Aul." This was not his name but title, signifying "the mad father." Baba Aul preached his creed to 22 disciples, chief amongst whom were Hatu Ghosh, Ramsaran Pal, Nitai Ghosh and a few others. The current song in the countryside describing Baba Aul runs as follows.

"Oh whence has this strange man come ?

"Without anger, ever-content he always says 'Tell the truth.'

"There are twenty-two men with him—they are all one mind and soul.

"They raise their hands up and sing together—'Praise to our master' and are full of love for all.

"And he, their chief, restores life to the dead, gives back what is lost and at his word the rivers become dry."[1]

Baba Aul Chand died in 1769 at a village called Boali. Ramsaran Pal with seven other followers of Aul cremated him at Parari, six miles to the west of Chakradaha. Ram Saran became the Guru of the sect, after Baba Aul.

---

[1] "এ ভাবের মানুষ কোথা হ'তে এলো ।
    এর নাইকো রোষ, সদাই তোষ, মুখে বলে 'সত্য বল' ।
    এর সঙ্গে বাইশ জন, সবার এক মন, জয়কর্তা বলি, বাহুতুলি, কল্পে প্রেমে ঢলঢল ।
    এ যে হারা দেওয়ায়, মরা বাঁচায়, এর হুকুমে গাঙ্গ শুকাল ।"

THE INITATION

This sect admits Hindus, Mahomedans and Christians to its fold without any distinction whatever. Sexual morality is strictly enjoined, though among most of these sects, it is more honoured in breach than in observance. But we shall dwell upon this point hereafter. The ordinary rule in this respect is embodied in this couplet :—

"Let one, whether man or woman, first become an eunuch or a hermaphrodite, and then get admittance to the order of the Karta Bhajas." [1]

The rule of initiation is simple. It requires a promise on the part of the initiated to conform to what is laid down in the following conversation between the Guru and his disciple.

> *The Guru* (called Mahásay by this sect).—
> "Will you be able to act in conformity with the doctrines of our creed ?"
> *The disciple* (called Barati).—"Yes, Sir."
> *The Guru.*—"You must give up lying, you must not steal, you must not commit adultery, you must not also mix too much with women.
> *The disciple.*—"No, Sir, I will not do any of these things."
> *The Guru.*—"Say to me—'You are true, your words are true.'"
> *The disciple.*—"You are true, your words are true."

---

[1] "স্ত্রী হিজরে পুরুষ খোজা, তবে হবি কর্তাভজা।"

Then the Guru gives him a certain *mantra* for recitation enjoining strict privacy in regard to it.

The *mantra* is to this effect.—

"Oh my Guru, Baba Aul, I am always in thy company, not a moment I am without thee, I am always with thee."

The desciple is enjoined to observe the following rules:—

In respect of body—to avoid adultery, theft and murder.

In respect of the mind—to avoid a wish for adultery, a wish to steal and a wish to murder.

In respect of the tongue—to avoid lie, unpleasant talk, vain talk and talking a good deal.

There were many Mahomedan Gurus in this sect and good Brahmins eat refuse from the plates of these Gurus. This is what Babu Akshoy Kumar Datta wrote 50 years ago, and I believe the state of things continues to this day. The principal seat of this sect is at Ghoshpárá—a village near Calcutta. Here thousands of disciples meet every year on the occasion of the Grand Melá that sit there in April. The Guru is believed by his disciple to be his God. They believe Aulchand to be an Incarnation of Chaitanya.

THE VIEWS OF THE BAULS

The Neras and the Bauls. The Neras and the Bauls do not shave; they seldom wash themselves. They behave like mad men outwardly. Their object in doing so is to shew that they are absolutely beyond the prejudices and conventions of the ordinary people living in society. They do not believe in images. On one occasion I had asked a Baul if he worshipped any image of Chaitanya for whom he shewed such devotion. He smiled and said " How can one worship any image of Chaitanya when he is without any form ? " He used the word " *Sunya Murti.* " Curiously the word is exactly the same as we find in the religious code of a class of Mahayanists who assert that " The Void " is to be contemplated. Their motto is " যাহা নাই ভাতে, তাহা নাই ব্রহ্মাতে " which means that what is not in the human body, exists nowhere in the universe. The body is the epitome of the whole world. Just as the tree is in the seed, so the universe lies in a state of embryo in the human body. Its powers are capable of infinite development by mystic processes of which they profess to have knowledge. They do certain things which are abominable to mention and abominable to hear, though they give their own explanation for their conduct. In fact they try to rise above prejudices and conventions of every sort and to court popular contempt as if to keep themselves in secluded glory and aloof from the rest of mankind—content with their own mystic and esoteric knowledge : One of their principles is "লোক মধ্যে লোকাচার, সদ্‌গুরুর মধ্যে একাচার." (When living among men conform to their rules—but when in the circle led by the Guru, no caste, no rule.) A class of these people totally idealise sexual love, by which, they hope to reach the highest spiritual plane. But this idea is entertained and practised by many sects of the Sahajias and we shall speak of it at some length in this discourse.

The Ramballavi sect sprang into existence as a protest against the Kartabhaja sect, to which its founders originally belonged. Krishna Kinkar Guna Sagar and Srinath Mukhopadhyay were once its leaders. They were inhabitants of Bansberia in the District of Hughli. They believe in the scriptures of the Hindus, Mahomedans and Christians and cull out their doctrines from the Gita, the Koran and the Bible alike. All classes of men, including Christians and Mahomedans sit in the circle and partake of beef and other profane food offered to their altar without caring for caste.

The Ramballavis.

Another sect the *Saheb Dhani*, called so after the name of its founder, flourished for a long time at Shaligram, Dogachia and other villages in the district of Krishnagar. They do not worship

The Saheb Dhani.

THEY ACT AS MAD MEN 347

images, and caste is no bar with them. Hindus and Mahomedans are served from the same plate in their circle and become bound up by the utmost ties of fellowship and good will under a Guru.

The Darveshis. The Darvesh sect, said to have been founded by Sanatan, includes this precept. "কেয়া হিন্দু কেয়া মুসলমান। মিলজুলকে কর সাঁইজীকি নাম" (No difference between a Hindu and a Mahomedan, let all mix together as brethren under the banner of our Guru Saiji). The curious sect of *sáddhini* is openly in revolt with all that is laid down as rules of conduct in human society. They talk like mad men in a language which appears jargon to us. They behave like mad men. And if anybody approaches them, they abuse him in a vulgar language, so that they may be left undisturbed in their course. They openly eat food served by all men, irrespective of caste. They live as celebates all their life. They will not sleep in the same place every night, entirely relying on what food or sleeping accommodation chance may bring them.

The Sahajias. The Sahajia sect is for indiscriminate mixing of men and women. In doing so, they have a great ideal before them, which they profess to follow, but is transgressed at every step. Women elect their own *Guru*. But this Guru need not be one. Living under the guidance of a Guru for the time being, she yields herself entirely to him, body and soul, and her motto is "গুরু করবি শত শত মন্ত্র করবি সার। যার সঙ্গে মন মিলিবে দায় দিবি তার ॥" ("We will make a hundred Gurus but follow one Mantra which is to be the essence of life. He who will capture our heart, we will belong to him.)"

The Khusi Biswasi sect was founded at a village called Bhaga near Devagram in the district of Krishnagar. Khusi Biswas, who was a Mahomedan, had a large following of Hindu and Mahomedan disciples by whom he was believed to be an incarnation of Chaitanya. Khusi Biswas enjoined absolute surrender of his followers to himself. His call is to this effect. "If in distress or trouble do pray unto *me*. And if *I* have any One, I will pray to that One for you."

The Khusi Biswasis.

The founder of the Balarami sect was one Balaram—a Hari by caste, which is one of the lowest in the Hindu Society. Balaram was born in the year 1785 in Malapara—a ward of the village Meherpur in the district of Nadia. He was a *chaukidar* in the employ of the well-known Malliks of the village and was once suspected of theft, which he had not committed. He gave up the post in disgust and sojourned in different parts of Bengal, and when after long years he

The Balaramis.

returned, he proclaimed himself to be God Almighty. The boldness of the illiterate man was immense. By his pithy eccentric sayings, he often hit at great truths which came as surprise to the Brahmins. It is said that no one ever heard him tell an untruth. On one occasion the Brahmins of the locality were performing *tarpan* in Ganges. This was the custom of taking handfuls of water from the river and throwing it down, by which acts they believed, the thirst of their departed ancestors would be allayed. Balaram attracted the attention of the Brahmins by taking handfuls of water like them and throwing it on the bank. When asked the reason, he said; "If your water will go to your departed forefathers who are far away, mine ought to go to my vegetable garden which is only a mile from here and certainly not so remote as the land of the dead." Balarám has left a treasure of spiritual songs, couched in the *patois* of the country. They are simple and direct home-thrusts levelled at the superstitions and conventions of the Hindus.

<small>Minor sects.</small> There are many sects in Western Bengal to which may be given the general denomination of "Sahajia" besides those mentioned above. The *Hazrati*, the *Gobrāi* and the *Pāgalnāthi* were founded by Mahomedans, though the

bulk of their followers were Hindus. *Tilakdasi, Spastabādi,* and *Darpanárayani* are also important from the point of faith they preach, Hazrat was a native of Bānsbaria, a mile to the east of Ghoshpārā, Gobrā belonged to the village of Murādpur and Pagalnāth to Nagdā, and Darpanāryan was a cobbler in Sāntipur.[1]

In Eastern Bengal there are still many such sects about whom we have got some information. In a village named Khārar Char near Rowile in the District of Dacca, there lived Panchu Fakir who had a large following of Hindu and Mahomedan disciples; the healing power

Panchu Fakiri.

possessed by this man was highly admired and appreciated, and his services were frequently required by even the enlightened and aristocratic families of the locatity. He died only lately. At a village named Mainat in the same district there is another Mahomedan Fakir who is a preacher of the mystic doctrines of the Sahajia creed, much appreciated by people, and his followers are increasing every year. In Jessore Pagla Kanai, the lyrical beauty of whose songs elicited admiration even from distinguished men of letters, died within a few decades. This man was perfectly illiterate, but the songs that he composed are

---

[1] Much of the above is taken from Babu Akshoy Kumar Datta's *Upasaka Samprodaya.*

characterised by a keen perception of spiritual truths. He has left a vast number of followers who culture mystic powers on the lines of the Sahajias.

There are hundreds of these sects silently working in Bengal, and of whom we have only a superficial idea. We have, however, secured some accounts of their religious veiws, the treatment of which is reserved for a future and fuller discourse on the subject. The educated community of Bengal have up to now, kept themselves quite aloof from these indigenous developments, but there is no doubt that some of these have attained an astoundingly flourishing condition in recent times. The other day I counted roughly the number of the prophets of Bengal who are still living or died a few years ago only, and they amounted to about fifty. Each of these prophets has a large number of followers, Hindus and Mahomedans, who are counted by hundreds and thousands. They believe in him entirely as the Christians believe in Christ and the Mahomedans, in the Prophet. The religion they propound is some phase of the old Buddhistic wisdom, the lessons of which lie deep-rooted in the soil, and which have not been forgotten by the masses. If properly enquired into, these creeds will disclose the connection which they evidently have with one

The Buddhist elements.

or the other of the different schools of Mahayanism of the Madhyamic school, founded by Nagarjoon in the first century of the Christian era. The doctrines are imbued with those of the different schools of Indian philosophy and present a hotch-potch of various elements of Indian spiritual speculations and age-long *tantric* practices.

The predominating Buddhist idea in the doctrines is apparent. The sects are generally opposed to caste. In the matter of eating cooked food, where strict orthodoxy is observed by the various sects of the Hindu—nearly all these sects are without any prejudice, and their indiscriminate behaviour at the dining table reminds one of the custom prevailing at Puri, once the greatest shrine and resort of the Buddhists. In many places the Sahajia refuses to eat the meal-offering made to Chaitanya, nor does he bow to the latter's image, though he calls himself a member of his apostolic Order.

During the Brahmanic Renaissance, *achár* or observance of rules of conduct was recognised as the first quality. The *achár* includes rules of eating and daily practices of certain religious rites. In fact *achár* was considered to be the most important of the nine qualities to be entitled to Kulinism, or a position of honour in the social scale. This was evidently laid down in view of the extreme lawlessness which characterised decaying Buddhism. The feature so prominent in the Sahajia sects is to revert to the original recklessness of decayed Buddhism and a complete upsetting of our social fabric.

One of the great merits of the *tantric* Buddhism was the curative power of those who were said to have developed certain psychic powers of the soul. At the present day, the old conventions of power by touch, hypnotism and mesmerism are gaining strength under scientific names. The different sects of the Sahajias in the countryside have this special feature that the adepts are endowed with some hidden and occult powers which they do not explain to those outside their own circle. For the purpose of bringing their body under full control and discipline, they perform many mystic rites which the followers of each of these sects take care to hide from others. The elaborate quotations I have made from the work "Jnanadi Sadhana" in my Typical Selections from old Bengali Litrature (Part II, pp. 1630—37) will clearly show the Buddhistic element in them. Though owing to these sects owning a very considerable number of Hindu population as their members, their creed appears in some essential points Hindu in character, they often in a clear and undisguised language revile the Brahmins and the Vedas (p. 1632). And curiously though they call themselves Vaishnavas, they do not believe in any image of Krishna (p. 1632) to which fact I have already made a reference. Though living in society, many of these creeds have no faith in sexual morality, nay some of them openly discard it in favour of free love, which they take to be a higher ideal in sexual matters for the culture of emotion than the marriage-bond, but this will be discussed hereafter.

In Nepal the Buddhists are called *Gubhajus*, or followers of Gurus and the Hindus *Devajus* or followers of the Devas—the gods. The one common feature of the Sahajia creeds is the implicit surrender of self to the will of the Gurus on the part of their disciples. This trust in the Guru is so great that a wife will sometimes accommodate herself to the will of the Guru without the least scruple, if the latter happens to be a bad man, even when her husband is living. This implicit faith in the Guru is the characteristic of the Buddhists of the Mahayan school. The Sahajia disciple pays an annual tax to the Guru as rent of the house he dwells in, by which term he implies his body, of which the absolute master is the Guru, formally acknowledged as such at the time of initiation. This tax the Guru gets for the permission he gives to his disciple to dwell in his body.

The ideal of love which some of the Sahajias preach is a dangerous game, as Chandidas the poet, himself a Sahajia, declares in many of his poems. The poet says that no God is to be worshipped, but Man or Woman. There is no god or goddess in heaven who can teach spiritual truths more than the person whom one loves with the whole heart. In fact this was the mandate which the poet received from the goddess Bashuli whom he worshipped. She is said to have told him "Stick to your love, she, the washer-woman, will teach you higher truths than I or a hundred gods and goddesses like me can teach you. Even Brahma, the creator will not be able to lead you to that heaven of bliss which Rami the woman will help you to reach."

The Sexual Romance.

An adept in the Sahajia-cult explained to me why the worship of images cannot elevate the heart to that heaven of bliss to which human love can lift it up. The images accept whatever is offered, at least the worshipper supposes it so. Even a decoit or thief may discover by his devotion a smile on the lips of the image, as if approving the sort of life that he may lead. But if on the throne of an image, you place a man or woman, the situation will be a complicated and difficult one. At the first sight the lover captivates the heart by unfolding many charms and seems to be perfection itself. But as you proceed and put up with him or her, the defects of the person's character will gradually become glaring and by living together a while, all novelty will pass away in most cases, often giving rise to a feeling of vexation and disgust. But a particular sect amongst the Sahajias enjoin that you should continue to love inspite of everything. Their motto is "One who loves and then leaves does not get the spiritual culture of emotion. At the outset choose your man or woman and pay your heart's homage to the person. Whatever ill you may receive from the lover, you are to bear with smile. You should not get vexed although the person may give you a hundred causes for it. That one's joy will be your joy and you will absolutely forget yourself and abide by that person's will surrendering your own will. When you have accomplished this you will be able to reach that One who pervades the whole world." My informant was an aged woman, and I asked of her. "If she be a woman and wife, and the person for whom she professes love wants the surrender of her body?" She said in reply, "When her lover is her God, she must give her all without reserve. Forget all social conventions when you deal with the ideal of the Sahajias. If the man wants her body, she must give it, but with this difference that she will delight only in the joy which she will afford to her lover, and shall absolutely be indifferent to the gratification

The philosophy of their love.

THEIR IDEAS NOT CONVENTIONAL 357

of her senses." She referred to a line of Chandidas which says "শুষ্ক কাষ্ঠ সম দেহকে করিতে হয়" (this body should be reduced to the state of a dry log) and said the body will be beyond its physical plane of pleasure or pain and it should be merely a vehicle of the spirit dedicated to the worship of her lover."

These Sahajias do not believe in the established ideals of womanhood represented by Sita, Savitri and the *suttees* who burnt themselves with their dead husbands in the days bygone—as living examples of their absolute devotion. The woman from whom I learnt the particulars, told me "These examples from your Hindu scriptures and epics fall short of the love-ideal of the Sahajias. These wives were actuated by hopes of getting rewards in the next life and praises from society in this for their chaste life. How far they were actuated by love cannot be determined in view of the complex character of the sentiments which prompted them in doing all that they did. If a woman foregoes the ties of family, receiving nothing but contempt of society and surrenders herself absolutely to her lover at the sacrifice of every other consideration—that love is admittedly pure and unalloyed gold, standing the test of all analysis. The lover may spurn her, assault and betray her and prove false in a hundred ways—but she must bear all ills and cleave, not with mere patience, but train her mind so as to consider her misfortunes and sorrows as joys—gifts from her dear lord. The devotee takes his worldly pain, as divine dispensation and bears it with joy. This should be the Sahajia-standpoint in regard to emotions of a lover. This is recommended not merely in the case of a woman but also for a man. Says Chandidas, "He that loves and breaks is not privileged to have that training which leads to one's spiritual well-being." Divorce is not recognised in the ethical code of a Sahajia. "Love first, love always" is the motto here. Love here is religion, its range is infinite patience, infinite joy out of infinite sorrow. The phraseology of society is to be changed, all foul is fair here, all pain joy.

This creed so dangerous, is not recommended for the average men and women.

The Sahajias do not mean their love-creed for all.

"In a million," says Chandidas, "there may be found one man up to the mark"—the rest will be ruined. Chandidas cautions men and women against coming to try their strength in this sphere of spiritual training, though he himself was a Sahajia. He says, "Let him come, who can make a frog dance in the mouth of a serpent or can hang a mountain by the fine thread of a cobweb." This means that it is an impossible height to scale for one who has not absolutely conquered his body. He alludes to innumerable instances where youths and maidens were attracted by the romantic creed of the Sahajias, but by far the greatest number of whom became utter wrecks and eternally damned. It appears from Chandidas' writings that this form of the Sahajia creed does not require a mere culture of emotion. The lovers are required to do some mystic practices for regulation of breath by which a control over the mind and a conquest over the flesh might be achieved. We are not conversant with the language of Yoga and therefore cannot interpret the teachings. For the culture of love without sensuality, the lover is required to sit whole nights on the bed of the object of his love for six months, without touching her, enjoying her sight; for the next six months to do so by touching her feet. At a certain stage the lovers must live apart from one another, and perfect freedom must be given to them to mix with other people and the personality of one individual must not be allowed to exert an undue power over the mind. Through all these trials the mind must be in an atmosphere of perfect freedom and face temptations. If devotion is proved inspite of all these, the next higher stages should be attempted. The Yoga practices—added to this, will facilitate and expedite the attainment of their goal—the reaching of the *Sahaja desha*—the heaven of the Sahajias, which is nothing but a stage of bliss, the region of beatitude. To the purely materialist mind, this will appear as utter nonsense,—where is the time and patience for all these absurdities for a man busy with jute-business, counting figures in an Insurance Office, or actively preparing statistics for administrative work? But here lies the difference between East and West. I might as well say that a man who sacrifices his life to attempt to discover the Arctic regions is extremely foolish! In the spiritual world, whether result be success or failure, no risk, no sacrifice has daunted the Orient, as in the physical plane, the occidental mind has followed pursuits at any risks which appear as the pursuit of phantoms to many people. The Sahajia creed is pernicious so of as it misleads and has misled hundreds of young men and women, and we must join with Chandidas in condemning those who recommend it to the youth of our society. But it should not be forgotten that it is a system which is complete with its canons and codes, based on *yoga*—which is a sealed book to us ; and if we are to hang it, we must give it a hearing, besides the judge must acquire fitness for trying his case. That some people have scaled the heights contemplated by this religion of love will be obvious from the facts in the life of the poet Chandidas, of Abhiram Swami who flourished in the 11th century, and of Billwamangal Thakur who lived about the same time. That in Bengal hundreds of men and women are attracted by the romantic nature of the creed up to this day and some of them at least have, in recent years, attained their goal will appear from the perusal of a book called the 'Sádhu Charit' by Babu Achyut Charan Chaudhury of Mayna, Kanaibazar, Sylhet. This book is the memoir of a departed Vaisnava saint of the Sahajia sect, whose home is now a shrine visited by hundreds of pious men and women.

The name of this Sádhu was Durgá Prasád Kar and he belonged to the village of Khema Sahasra in Pargana Ita in Sylhet. His father was Hari Ballava Kar and mother Shanta Dasi,—Kayasthas by caste. Durgaprasad was born in the year 1851. Achyut Babu, the biographer of Durgáprasád, relates many incidents in the life of the Sádhu, shewing his devotion and asceticism of character. He loved or rather worshipped a woman named Manomohini, with an ardour which, in its first stages, none but himself knew of. This love proved not only the essence but the motive-power of his spiritual life—and curiously even Manomohini herself knew nothing of it for many years. He implicitly carried out the least wish of the woman and delighted in eating food from the plate from which she had eaten first. This caused some scandal and Manomohini, who was a neighbour distantly related to Durgá Prasád, would not tolerate this conduct in the young

The example of a Sahajia Sádhu practising woman-worship.

man. Durgá Prasád meanwhile had taken the vow of silence, but every morning and evening he called on her to pay his *pranám*, staying for a minute there. At noon day (he took his meal only once a day) the mute Sádhu stood at the gate of Manomohini, who ate a little from the plate which he placed before her, and then he returned home and ate the remaining food. The scandal to which I have referred was not of any grave character, as every man in the village was perfectly aware of the stainless morals of both these persons. But "Why should she," the people said, "tolerate the maniac to pay his *pranám* every day to her and why should she take any food from his plate?" On a certain day the shy lady took fright and refused to come out when the Sádhu presented himself before her. I will here quote an extract from the memoir.

"Our Sádhu against the express wish of Manomohini still waited at noon that day, with a plate in his hand hoping that she would partake a little of the food, that he might afterwards eat the rest. Manmohini came out and abused him in a rough language. As he stood still mutely gazing at her, she did not stop there, but cruelly threw away the food from the plate and went her way.

"There was no reason why she should behave thus roughly, but being vexed with the scandal she had taken the vow never to tolerate this any more. She did this deliberately that day to discourage his mad excesses.

"The Sádhu (a youth 24 years old), who had taken the vow of silence, departed with the empty plate and did not touch any food that day. He looked pale and weary, and his brothers guessed from his looks and learnt on enquiry that he had not taken any food. They brought him milk and fruits but could not persuade him to eat. Three days passed in this way and Durgá Prasád continued his fast unmoved by the earnest requests of his kith and kin. His relations appealed to Manomohini and tried to bring her to him, but her reply was cut and dry. "What does it matter to me if some one eats or does not eat? What do I know of it? Do not trouble me with any request on behalf of that man." The relations of Durgá Prasád returned home in disappointment and two days more passed but the Sádhu's fast was not broken. His two brothers in great distress remembered their aunt who had a great influence on their brother. But she lived at a place which would take two days to reach from their village. The brothers, however, took him in a boat and arrived at their aunt's village on the third day. During their journey, all their attempts to make him take food failed, so that when he arrived at his aunt's, he had already fasted seven days. The brothers stayed there for three days but the good old woman's lamentations and entreaties proved of no avail. Durgá Prasád could not be induced to eat anything. In great disappointment and grief his brothers brought him back to their home and two days more passed in the way. So that Durgá Prasád had now fasted 14 days."

The biographer here says "How could this be possible? An ordinary man, if he fasts for a day, sees every thing dark around him. How could Durgá Prasád live having fasted 14 days? This seems almost inconceivable, yet it was a fact beyond all doubt, witnessed by many who are still living."

The good people of the village took alarm at this point. A youth whose morals were unimpeachable, who by great austerities and piety had already attained the fame of a saint in popular esteem, was going to die of starvation, and this they could not bear to think of. They all went in a body on the evening of the 14th day of the Sádhu's fast to Manomohini's house and appealed to her to save the life of the young man. Her heart had secretly bled at all this event, and now when the people of the village made the request she gladly went to the Sádhu's house in the following morning and partook of the meal prepared at his house and gave Durgá Prasád her plate from which he gladly ate the remaining food. For some time Manomohini was gracious, but off and on she treated him cruelly refusing him the privilege of *pranám* and not agreeing to eat the first handful from his plate. Numerous instances of this sort have been mentioned by the biographer of the Sádhu. While fully recognising the delicate position of a Hindu woman and of her repugnance to pander to the queer fancies of an outsider to her home, we cannot help feeling compassion for the great sufferings caused by his unswerving devotion and his great forbearance.

Durgá Prasád's course of spiritual training seems almost inconceivable at the present day of rationalism. For a time he accepted every man's command as the word from the Most High. At this stage he still observed the vow of silence. One evening a man named Kalicharan Tarafdar wanted to try the extent of his spiritual forbearance and patience. He brought him to his dirty cow-shed and ordered him to stand up there for the whole night. It was thundering and raining all around, and the straw-roof leaked so profusely that the Sadhu was completely drenched. The stench of the cow-dung and the buzzing sound of a thousand gnats which covered his whole body and drank his blood could not move this picture of patience in human shape; the midnight passed, and he was still standing motionless in that hell, considering the word of Kalicharan Tarafdar as divine mandate. But the heart of this man at last relented and fearing lest his conduct would bring down God's curse on him, he came to the cow-shed at 1 A.M. and released the poor Sádhu from his sad predicament.

Many miracles are related of this man, but I consider the above instances of the patience and devotion of the man as nothing short of a miracle. If ever any man performed miracles, he must have been of the type of Durgá Prasád, whose love, devotion and patience are all miraculous. If the East and the West are to be weighed in the scales, I want some one of this type from West to be balanced against our Sádhu. If we are to dismiss him as a queer man odious to modern taste, and an antiquated specimen of humanity, we will certainly do him wrong. He followed a principle, it may be urged, to folly, but our scriptures and religious systems have reserved a place for him. His life is an instance of infinite love, infinite devotion and infinite patience for a cause, and he lived a life of uniform consistency of principle. The story in one of the Buddhist Játakas has a living parallel in him and he belongs to a region of which the words are the Upanishads and the Puranas. For, in the system of his creed, one will find elements of culture from the whole Indian wisdom of the Past. The exotic air may be too stiff for an outsider; but we, Indians, must analyse the whole system before pronouncing the word of judgment. In the case of the Sádhu, it was an extreme point that the soul coveted to reach, but in the domain of spirituality the extreme step of the ladder often indicates a nearness to the gates of the Paradise.

Similar training in mystic ways is practised even now in the country-side, and it is a subject well worth being carefully investigated by our scholars.

The Sahajia concept of love itself was derived from the Buddhists. We are now in possession of definite proof of it from a Pali work called the Katha Vathu compiled in the 3rd century B.C. We find in Book XXIII of this work that the Andhras, the Vetalyaks and the Uttara Páthaks amongst the Buddhists had special sects which advocated a system of religious culture by what has been termed *Ekahhippaya* or "united resolve," *i.e.*, by a human pair who feel natural sympathy or compassion (not merely passion) and who are worshipping, it may be, in some Buddha shrine and aspire to be united throughout their future lives. The Uttara Páthaks attribute such practices even to their holy men and hold that "infra-human beings, taking the shape of Arhants follow sexual desires."

These people certainly cultured higher sexual feelings in private and gave them a religious character even as early as the third century B.C., if not earlier. But the orthodox community amongst the Buddhists were bitterly hostile to the supporters of these views, and the Katha Vathu is full of instances of their attacks on these sects, who, I believe, have since been holding their meetings in secret as their views could never bear exposure before the orthodox society."

Love for one with whom one is not bound in wedlock is the essential feature of this spiritual romance, but the baneful influence which this creed exerted on the morals of average men and women made it abhorrent in the eyes of men. Chandidas of course believed that nothing could be so sublime as this form of idealised sexual love and he attempted to arrive at the spiritual plane by practising it in his life. But as I have already stated, he did not recommend this extremely risky path to ordinary spiritual aspirants. Chaitanya's voice was more stern and decisive. He declared himself in a clear language against all sexual romance. He said that it could not be the path for salvation of men. He accepted the Rádhá Krishna legend as merely symbolical. He said "Just as the ardour of a youth is to meet his beloved, so

The Parakiyá accepted as a mere symbol by Chaitanya.

should be the ardour of the soul be to meet God; this allegory is adopted for lack of a better one to signify the earnest yearnings of the soul." True, he visited the shrines, and the figure of Krishna was ever present in his mental vision. It was a mere sign to bring to his soul the whole treasure of devotion. In his delicate vision, the material and the immaterial seem to have lost all difference, and every sight and sound threw him into a frenzied delight. The fence of the outer world proved no bar, but on the contrary only heightened his spiritual felicities. Chaitanya said "People speak a good deal about love without knowing its true character; sexual romance is not the higher love, I tell you, on the other hand if one will completely get rid of the sexual feeling and find no difference between men and women, it is *then only* that one will be privileged to taste true love." As an instance of his stern attitude towards those who wanted to cultivate a little the romantic feeling of a sexual nature, I remind you of the treatment that junior Haridas received from him. It was not merely hard but cruel.

I have already stated that the Sahajia in its various forms represents the old culture and wisdom of the Buddhists in the shape it had assumed during its declining days in this country. The higher order of monks and nuns fled from

Bengal proper when the Brahminic Renaissance asserted itself in full glory here, and it was amongst the masses that the teachings of the Mahayana were preserved in a crude form. The Buddhist laity did not receive any enlightenment from their leaders, so the occult knowledge they preserved is found mixed with great vices and superstitions. It is like gold mixed with much alloy, which requires the discriminating eye of the expert to separate for ascertaining their respective worth.

Surely the Madanotsava or the Puspotsava of the old times was in this country, before the ascendency of the Krishna-cult. We find a reference to it in the Mudra Rakshasa written in the 6th century. This festival used to be held in honour of Kamadeva—the Indian Cupid. There was an extraordinary enthusiasm amongst the masses which chiefly consisted of Non-Aryan population, on such occasions. Dance and song, flower and the red powder *fag*, swinging and playing—all these created an atmosphere of light amusements from which all sterner laws of sexual ethics were dismissed for the time being, and men and women mixed indiscriminately—the green trees wearing red apparel, as it were, owing to profuse *fag* that filled the whole atmosphere, over which the April sun threw its gaudy purple rays. Such dance and song, swinging

Marginal note: Kamdeva conquered by Krishna.

and other amusements prevail among many of the neighbouring hill-tribes even to-day. This Madanotsava was replaced by the Dolotsava, when the Krishna-cult gained ground, and the latter has retained the light pleasures and gay amusements of the former in many respects in a somewhat abated form—of course the pure moral standard of the Vaishnavas has given these festivals a far more sober character in respect of sexual freedom. Madana's throne is now occupied by Madana Mohan (Krishna) and in the Vaishnava songs there are frequent references to Krishna's power of crushing the pride of hundreds of Madanas. The victor thus exults over his fallen adversary. In order to shew the contrast clearly the Vaishnavas put a great stress upon *Kama* and *Prema*. Kamadeva is the God of *desires* and Krishna is the god of *love*. "Krishna is the destroyer of pride of hundreds of Kamadevas" is an epigraph to be met with in many songs in honour of Krishna. I think it is because Krishna had driven the older Deity of love from his established throne, and occupied it himself that his followers found an occasion for repeating every now and then that Kamadeva was no match for Krishna. There is, however, distinct evidence shewing that Krishna fulfilled all the functions that Kamadeva had done in a previous chapter of history. It is mentioned in the Bāla Khanda of the Krishna Kirtan that being unable to persuade Radha to love him by sweet words and even by threat, Krishna at last took recourse to aiming his invincible flower-arrows, five in number, at his lady-love. Now nowhere in the Vaishnava or other scriptures do we find mention of Krishna being equipped with five arrows made of flowers. These weapons belong, as is universally known, exclusively to Kamadeva, who is popularly known as " the God of five arrows." As Krishna was placed on the throne of Kamadeva in the Dolotsava, it was found necessary by his followers to give him all the traditional equipments of the rival whose throne he had usurped.

But the Vaishnavas no doubt made the situation infinitely more exalted. They idealised love and purged it of all dross of sensuality. The Chaitanya Charitamrita emphasises the point that Kama clouds the reason, but Prema is like the glorious sun, dispelling all gloom and making things appear in their true light.

The Radha-Krishna cult, I believe, had already been introduced amongst the *tantriks*, both Hindu and Buddhist, before the Vaishnava revival in the 15th century. 'Radha-tantra,' 'Radha-chakra' are familiar names in the Tantrik literature; the names " Rai-Kanu " so popular in the country, savour of a Prakritic derivation, earlier than Brahminic Renaissance. Some of the European scholars have asserted that the

Gita-Govinda itself seems to be a Sanskritized version of earlier Prakrit lyrics, as the metres and poetics used in the book conform more to the rules of Prakrit rhetoric than of Sanskrit. Radha-Krishna songs are found in Prakrit in some of the anthologies of that language. All this shews that Tantriks used the Radha-Krishna cult for their mystic practices, whereas the sexual freedom embodied in the legend was adopted by the more sensuous people as supplying a sanction for the gratification of grosser pleasures.

The Radha-Krishna cult supplied subjects for Tantrik practices.

The cult, therefore, had existed in a more or less gross form, before the higher standard of Vaishnavism gave it a symbolical interpretation, purifying the atmosphere from all sensuality.

In the secret meetings of the Sahajias, the degenerate Buddhists, the old atrocious element of sensualism is sometimes found to linger. These vices have been exposed in the most outspoken manner in a novel named "Charu Darshan" written by Kaviraj Parvati Charan Kavishekhar of Dacca. There is no doubt a great deal of exaggeration in his descriptions. His is a work of satire which always magnifies small faults into huge proportions, but that there is truth underlying his account, no one will deny. I must here repeat that the

The wickedness of some of the Sahajia Gurus.

charge of wickedness in sexual morals on the part of a section of Vaishnavas, brought by Babu Jogendrachandra Bhattacharya and Mr. Underwood is not true. The dregs of the old monkish life, the vices which brought about the overthrow of Buddhism in Bengal, is manifest in the account given by Parvaticharan. Vaishnavism, as I have just said, has been gradually improving the morals of the Sahajias—the dilapidated Buddhists of the later school in Bengal. Babu Parvati Charan himself draws a clear line of demarcation between the Vaishnava ideal and the contemptible moral standard of the Sahajias —the so-called Vaishnavas of Bengal, against whom he cries himself hoarse throughout his interesting novel. It is a tale of degraded moral virtues, of selfish and disgusting manœuvres of a class of the Sahajia Gurus with vested interests. The author saw the grim skeleton of old *tantric* practices, devoid of its mystic import of a conquest of the flesh conceived by its originators, now sunk in the utter depths of sensualism. The chapter in question of the book "Charudarshan," relates to the visit of a Deputy Magistrate, to one of the secret meetings held by a class of Sahajias who call themselves "Kishori Bhajaks" or "Worshippers of maidens." This class even now is the most degraded of all such sects. It should be stated here that the members of the society, with a Guru at their head seldom allow any outsider to enter their circles. But as the Guru in the present case was involved in a criminal suit pending before the Deputy Magistrate, he was eager to please him in every possible way, so the rules of privacy were relaxed in his favour. The following gives an account as to what happened upon the entrance of the Deputy Magistrate into the circle.

<small>A satire on the Kishori Bhajaks.</small>

"When he came to the circle of the ' Kishori Bhajaks,' he found that about 500 souls had already gathered there. Seventy-five per cent. of these people were women, amongst these 83 per cent. were widows : the number of the young amongst them was no fewer than 50 per cent. None of these women had any child in their arms. Amongst the male members, there was hardly any below 16 years of age, the number of old men also was very small. Ninety-nine per cent, of the visitors were youthful men and youthful women. There was no man seen there who had any respectable status in society. There was scarcely any judge, munsiff, pleader, zeminder, tālukdar, professor, head pundit or scholarly Brahmin in the assembly. The more respectable of them were a few *mukteers*, heads of temples, grocers and village tax-collectors. Their mean dress and coarse manners shewed that they were mostly recruits from the scum of society. Though the Deputy Magistrate was not favourably impressed with all that he saw, one point struck him as specially good in the assembly. Even the reformed Brahma Somaj of which he was a member, he thought, could not boast of an equal progress in social reformation. Though the Brahmas loudly advocated the cause of female freedom, they could not allow their women to mix with men with the same degree of unreserved familiarity, as he met here. A far greater toleration he found in this assembly than he could believe possible. Men and women had taken their seats indiscriminately without any scruple and with full freedom. The Deputy who was an enthusiast in the cause of social reformation, was so greatly rejoiced at this state of things that he forgot all the defects that had struck him in the society on his first entrance. As he was contemplating this excellent feature he observed in their function, the religious service commenced. Krishna Dasi, the woman who was implicated in the criminal suit, together with a number of other women, came near the Deputy and sang the following song :

> "Do not come, brother, to this assembly of mad men.
>
> Come not, dear brother, sit not too close to us.
>
> If you do so, once for all, your caste will go.

THE MERRY MEETING

> Here the Chandal cooks the food which the Brahmin takes.
> There was a mad man like us in the Vrinda groves.
> He acted as the policeman and made his consort (*Radha*) the queen.
> Another mad man is our great God Siva.
> He gave all to his Guru, and himself delights in ashes and dust. He sleeps in the cremation ground.
> We shall name yet another mad fellow. He is our Shambhuchand—The Guru of the Hindus, the Shiva of the Brahmins and the Shai (prophet) of the Musalmans."

(Shambhuchand who is mentioned in the colophon of this song was evidently the founder of the sect.)

When the song was finished, their Guru Kamal Das stepped forward and said something in a language known only to the people of the sect, which implied that unless hunger was appeased, their devotional fervour would be lost. On the bed that was spread there, large plates, full of eatables, were brought and men and women sat there and freely ate them. In their joy women put food into the mouth of men and the latter were not slow in returning the attention, and the house rang with merry laughter. The Deputy was greatly pleased at seeing this unceremonious display of freedom by the women. He could not conceive that the people who called themselves Hindus and belonged to so many different castes, could, without the least prejudice, sit together and eat from the same plates placed on their beds (highly repugnant to Hindu tastes and absolutely forbidden by their caste-rules). He felt as if the impossible had taken place when he witnessed the people of high and low castes vying with each other in breaking the caste-rules, eating remnants of food left by one another. Yet what wonder, they lived in the Hindu society and passed for its orthodox members! He was encouraged to hope that these people could be easily induced to accept the tenets of the enlightened Brahma Samaj, as they had already made a considerable advance towards social reform. When this new hope was kindled in his soul, the Magistrate could no longer restrain himself, but leaped up from his seat and addressed the assembly thus :—

" Dear sisters and brethern. I am not here to encroach in vain on your time. The spectacle of fraternity, freedom and friendly union, presented to me here, has given me infinite delight and I cannot suppress my desire to thank you from the bottom of my heart. Especially has your absolute disregard of the pernicious caste system filled me with wondering admiration. Hence I have risen to speak—

to pour out my sympathy with you. I hope you will excuse me for this interruption to tell you the truth, I feel almost ashamed at the thought that I am causing a delay in the discharge of your religious function by my speech. But I assure you, friends, my address will be short.

Two words more and I have done. Now you have disregarded the caste-system and shewed such noble example by dining together so freely, it would be well for you to keep the doors of your house open, so that visitors might come and see this noble sight as I am doing. If these things are done secretly, there will be no opportunity given to the world for preaching the truth. Why do you perform this function in secret, as if the freedom allowed to women is a great sin? The Bramha Samaj advocates the cause of the emancipation of women by trumpet-call and in the open daylight. It is for this reason that our cause is gaining ground. When religion has given you the strength to discard the old conventions, why then, and whom, should you fear? Who can resist the force of truth and religion? Just remember that Jesus Christ gave his life at the altar of truth, but did not swerve from its ways. One of the chief causes of the degeneracy of Hinduism is the system of Zenana. This barbarous system does not exist amongst any civilized nation. If you want to improve your community and awaken them to a call of modern civilisation, and freedom,—absolute emancipation must be given to women. Just see, if half the portion of a tree gets sunlight and the other half is in the shade, the tree will never be vigorous, its growth will remain stunted for ever. In the same way, whatever culture and high education you may give to your men, unless you give the same advantages to your women, the nation will not, and cannot, thrive. I believe every word of what I say is true. It is for this reason that our poet, with a deep insight into the problems of our society, announced with a thundering voice :—

"Awake—awake O ! Indian women.
If you awake not—our nation will not awake."

I am afraid most of you are not advocates of higher education. Still I see from your ways that there is much agreement between your views and those of the enlightened community—the Bramha Samaj. It is for this reason that I invite you to attend the meeting of the Bramha Samaj, next Sunday. I shall be present there to shew you our scheme of social reform. If you would feel any scruple or hesitancy in coming to our Samaj without a formal invitation, or a sign of earnestness on our part, as you are quite unknown there, I should gladly bring here some conveyances myself at 12 A.M. on that day and take you there. If you agree to go to our Society's Hall and grace the function with your presence, we shall be all very thankful to you."

This speech was not understood by any one in the assembly. They did not pay attention to it, nor care to listen to such teachings. The mouth of their Guru was the only fountain-source of instructions recognised by them. They did not believe that there could be any other mouth from which any advice should proceed. They believed with their whole soul that they were the only persons who knew the right path and the rest of the world had gone wrong.

They considered scholarship and wisdom to serve only to lead to the wrong way. They considered the Vedas and other scriptures to have been manufactured by worldly men for their own selfish ends. They had no regard for the Brahmins. They entertained no respect for either the priestly class, or for their elders. The women cared nothing for their husbands. They besides considered image-worship, the sound of the sacred bell and conch, the current ideas about abstinence and purity to be all vain. They only aspired for a state of beatitude, for the culture of which their societies had their nocturnal meetings. When the magistrate had finished, the "true men and women" of the sect, without heeding to his speech any way, or caring to give any reply, began to sing in chorus the following song :—

"Oh my soul, oh my bat, do not fly in the twilight.

If the black crow can trace you—it will seize you
   and bite.
Ah my foolish bat, ah my dear bat, remain as a blind
   thing in the daylight, but become clever in the night.
Why doest thou, dear bat, hang thy tail upwards?
Is not that a vile habit, induced by your bad nature?
Thou delightest in drinking the juice of the Kamranga fruit.
Thy tongue is cursed that thou ignorest the ananas
   which grows on the soil.
Now listen to the truth about the ananas. It puts
   forth eight leaves in eight directions, and in the
   midst is a red something. On the top it is covered
   with bushy leaves and outside it are numbers of
   eye-like holes—inside is its sweet juice. Alas!
   Chandi could not taste this sweet juice!"[1]

---

[1] The meaning of this song is known only to the adept. In the first portion the poet Chandi (who mentions his name in the colophon) refers evidently to the advice so commonly given by the people of this sect to remain inactive members of their societies, whether Hindu or Musalman, absolutely indifferent to the duties enjoined by the respective communities.

The bat sees in the night and hides itself in the day-time. The Sahajia also does so. His whole activities are roused in the night in the secret societies. The reference to the bat's turning its tail upwards is condemned; it probably implies the habit of speculating about higher things,—life and death,—which according to the Sahajias is quite futile. They attach a great importance to the training of the body for spiritual purposes by means of which occult powers grow in the soul. The tasting of the *Kamranga* fruit which grows on the higher branches of its tree is symbolical of higher speculation indulged in by our religious aspirants. This is condemned and contrasted with tasting the ananas, that grows on the soil, by which the Sahajias mean the body. "The eight leaves and the red something" mystically refers to certain occult powers of the physical body, revealed to one by *yoga* and *tantrik* practices. I am not an adept in these things.

THE GURU'S SERMON

The song and the repast were now both finished. They began to wash their face. The women came forward to help the Deputy to wash his. He was not, however, prepared for this queer piece of courtesy and struggled to avoid the friendly service offered. The result, however, was a bath a little later, for his person as well as his clothes were soiled. Kamal Das had expected that the song and amusements would capture the Deputy's heart. But it was quite the opposite. There is difference between men and men. What pleased the illiterate, proved repugnant to the taste of an educated man. The Deputy became quite disgusted with the shamelessness of women. So after bathing he did not allow the women the privilege which they had there, of wiping the person of a respectable man. The Guru Kamal Das at this stage came forward to give a religious character to the amusements enjoyed there. He said :—

"Contempt, shame, anger, fear, greed, envy and addiction to worldly things and a habit of blaming—these are the eight bonds. By regular training of the mind, these bonds should be cut. Unless one is free from these, one cannot attain childlike simplicity. Unless one is simple as a child, one cannot approach God."

The Magistrate could find no agreement between what Kamal Das said and the shamelessness of the women there. But Kamal Das, stopping for a while, resumed his speech in the following way :—

"There are four regions in the spiritual plane. (1) The "*Sthula*" or that of the superficial and coarse, (2) the "*Pravartaka*"—that of the beginner, (3) of the *Sadhaka*—the more advanced in spiritual training, (4) *Siddha*—of the emancipated.

There are six things in respect of each of these :—

A

(1) Desha—country, (2) Kála (time), (3) Ashray (help), (4) Pátra (subject), (5) Abalambana (ways and means), (6) Uddipana (impetus).

A. In respect of the region of "Sthula"—the coarse and the superficial :—
1. Desha (country)... The world. (Jambu Dwipa).
2. Kála (Time) ... The fleeting as opposed to eternal.
3. Ashray (help) ... The feet of parents and elders.
4. Pátra (subject) ... Brahma—The Creator.
5. Abalambana (ways and means) ... The Vedic rites.
6. Uddipana (impetus) Hearing of the recitation of scriptures.

B

In respect of the region of "Pravartaka"—(the beginner):

1. Desha ... Nadia—the birth-place of Chaitanya.

(The beginner must consider himself as a citizen of the shrine, having no connection with the rest of the world.)

2. Kála ... Eternity,—the Kali-yuga.
3. Ashray ... The feet of the Guru.
4. Pátra ... Chaitanya.
5. Abalambana ... Company of saintly man.
6. Uddipana ... Recitation of the name of Krishna.

C

In respect of the region of the Sadhaka:

1. Desha ... The Vrinda groves (the shrine of Krishna).
2. Kála ... Eternity. The Dwapara-yuga.
3. Ashray ... The Gopis of the *Vrinda-*groves (to culture tender emotions on their footsteps).
4. Pátra ... Krishna.
5. Abalambana ... The love of the *Gopis*.
6. Uddipana ... The sound of flute (reminding one of Krishna's flute).

D

The region of the Siddhas :

1. Desha ... The Vrinda groves (not the physical plane as in the preceding stage) but the eternal shrine of the soul, called the Nitya Vrindavana or the everlasting Vrindavana).
2. Kála ... 18 dandas of the great night.
3. Ashray ... Rupamanjari—one of the chief maids of Radha.
4. Pátra ... Radha
5. Abalambana ... The emotion of the milkmaids of the Vrinda groves.
Uddipana ... Loving services."[1]

---

[1] The stages are evidently taken largely from the Vaisnava doctrines. The soul rises step by step from the materialistic plane. At the first stage he is under the guidance of his parents, attends to the fleeting things around and has a simple belief in his Maker with whom his acquaintance is of a mere superficial kind. In the next plane, he owns citizenship of Nadia, the Vaisnava shrine, cuts himself from the rest of the world, the laws of which do not govern him. He tries to culture his higher emotions there with the help of his Guru. In the third stage he has dispensed with his Guru and even with Chaitanya and proceeded to realise the emotional love of the *Gopis* for Krishna. The fourth plane is entirely mystic, where the soul is the dweller of the eternal region of bliss. The references to this stage are not very clear, involved as they are in esoteric practices known only to the adept.

Then the women sang another song, mystic and unintelligible, though couched in the current language, full of simplicity, directness and force. I need not give the song here but shall resume the topics of the book.

The spiritual truths embodied in the song or its meaning were not at all clear to the Deputy, so he could not join the men and women in their appreciation of it. All of them covertly smiled in derision and the magistrate felt the insult.

The author next proceeds to denounce the immoralities indulged in by the men and women of the circle, some of whom had a fancy to play the sports played by Krishna and the milkwomen. The scene created thereby appeared revolting to our magistrate who contrived with much difficulty, to escape from the assembly. It need hardly be said that the good opinion which he had formed at first, was now completely removed and he left the circle with a feeling of disgust.

The serious Vaisnavas of the Chaitanya Order have naught but unmitigated abhorrence for the Sahajias of all classes, though the latter

---

These four stages have things more or less in common with those of the Vaisnavas but the common element is the result of an adaptation by the Sahajia Gurus of their own creed to that of the Vaisnavas, the *Modus operandi* of the former is quite different, savouring of the practices of the Buddhist tantriks of the latter day.

call themselves Vaisnavas of the same order. The author of "Charu Darshan"[1] as I have already noticed, while sneering at the faults of the Sahajias, gives a sunny and smiling sketch of the Vaisnavas of his own order. No one will, however, doubt that his account is one-sided. There are certainly good Sahajia Gurus, also good disciples, famous for the mystic powers they have developed, as well as for their ascetic life, full of noble abstinence and philanthrophy. As, however, the Sahajia-cult is professed mostly by the illiterate and the rustics, there may be quite naturally some crude and vulgar elements in it. Even in the above extracts, the Buddhistic views are in evidence in open revolt against the Brahmins, the Vedas and the Hindu society. There is, besides, the monkish disregard for the family ties, which would remind one of similar sentiments expressed in the Jnanadi Sadhana. The reader will find how a man may

---

[1] "Charu Darshan" is a Bengali romance by Babu Parvati Charan Kabishekhar published at the Moslem Hataishi Press, Dacca. Its price is Rs. 1-8 as., and it is to be had of the author, Asak Lane, Dacca. It is a remarkable book, its humours has more flashes than one finds in the 'Hutum Pechar Naksa' or 'Alaler Gharer Dulal'—it gives the most faithful picture of Bengali life and of the religious views of those unfamiliar with Western ideas. Written by one, who knows the character of his own people far better than most men, he has the gift of style which is not acquired but is natural, and his shrewd insight into human character invests his writings with a life-like and realistic vividness. If one wants to know Bengal as it is, let him read this book—it it not clouded by European ideals. The book ought to be translated into English.

worship a woman—as a course of his spiritual training. Though such a thing may appear queer to us, yet the instance of Durga Prasad clearly shews that it is quite possible for a man to accept the doctrine and follow it.

Though most of the songs of the Sahajias *Sahajia Songs.* are written in the *Sandhya bhásá* which none but the adept can penitrate yet there are some which are intelligible to us. They touch the heart by their naive and simple charm. The songs of Lal Sashi, from which I have given copious extracts in my Typical Selections (Vol. II.) are mostly difficult of comprehension. I will quote here a few of the songs written by other authors, to shew the lucid charm of these spontaneous songs, which burst forth from the heart, like the *Kundi* and the *Malati* flowers from our soil.

1. "A great storm is breaking in; the eyes see water everywhere—lands are submerged. O! boatman, ply thy oar steadily. Whoever has a boat, must face the storm, don't you know this boatman? Wait a while, O boatman and listen! Spread the sail of truth and ply the boat slowly over the rough waters. Look at and see the One who is at the helm. Why dost thou look at the storm?"[1]

---

[1] তুফান আসছে কষ্টে, জলে জল যাবে মিসে, মাজি হাল ধর কষ্টে।
আর বাঁধ নৌকা, তাহা তুফান, নৌকা রাখ কি কারণ, ওরে মাজি দাঁড়িয়ে শোন।
মাজি সত্য বাদাম লও, ধীরে ধীরে বাও, তুফান পানে কেন চাও, হাল ধরেছে নিরঞ্জন।

2. My Guru is a mad fellow, thrice-blessed is he, oh ! what excellent qualities has he ! He is without qualities they say ;[1] it is false, there is a perfection and harmony in them, that I find in Him. He throws away sandal perfumes and covers himself with ashes. Talk not of his possessions. A mere rag and torn mantle, are all he has. He teaches truths to the poor and lowly—nay, it is an empire that he gives them. He casts his quick glance around and there is no place where he does not go. He is here now and everywhere, and where is it that he is not ?"[2]

A curious couplet of the Ramballavi sect of the Sahajias, embodying their tenets runs thus :—

"Kali and Krishna, God and Khoda—a mere fight with names. When combatants fight, these names throw them into a puzzle. Do not be a party to these disputes. Oh! my soul! sing Kali, Krishna, God and Khoda—the names of the One."[3]

---

[1] The Brahman is without qualities according to Sankara's spiritual philosophy.

[2] "ধন্য গুরুরে পাগল গোঁসাই, আহা মরি মরি গুণের লইয়া বালাই।
নাহি কিছু গুণ লেশ, সকল গুণের শেষ, চন্দন ছাড়ি আবেশে অঙ্গে মাখেন ছাই।
কি কব ধনের কথা, নেংটী আর ছেঁড়া কাঁথা, গোলামে এলেম দাতা, সবে বাদসাই।
চঞ্চল লোচনে চায়, কে বুঝিবে অভিপ্রায়, কোথা থাকে কোথা যায়,
কোথা আছে—নাই।"

[3] "কালী কৃষ্ণ গাড খোদা, কোন নামে নাহি বাধা, বাদীর বিবাদ দ্বিধা, তাতে নাহি টলোরে। মন কালী কৃষ্ণ গাড খোদা বলোরে।"

I do not quote too many of these couplets because I cannot understand them but from their exceedingly simple language, and homely references to the familiar things of village-life, they seem to have a great influence upon those who understand the technicalities of the Sahajia theology ; the songs are all about boats trades, mortgages, farming and a hundred other topics of rustic interest, evidently used with such appropriate and direct reference to religious experience, and strung in such rhythmical harmony that they have the power to charm and please, though most of the higher truths conveyed are unfamiliar to us.

Though the majority of the recruits are from the lower ranks of society, there is a respectable minority of higher class people amongst them, having talent and education of no mean order. Their number is immense. At Ghoshpara and other centres, many thousands of people, mostly women, gather during the religious festivities of the sect in April.

Even outside Bengal there are these Sahajia sects under various names. In the town of Dhenkanal in Orissa there is a temple of Mahaprabhu, where special religious festivals are held thrice every year, in February, April and November. Many thousands of people attend these festivals. The Guru is an "up-country" man. He has a large number of

Buddhist adopt other creeds in Orissa.

Bengali disciples besides a considerable number of the Madrasis, known as the 'Telengas' or Telegu-speaking people. There is amongst these a sprinkling of the Kurmis of the Northwestern Provinces. The temple lies at a place 24 miles distant from Jonepur—a station on the B. N. Railway. The Mahaprabhu worshipped in the temple is not Chaitanya, but the Sungod. The name of the Guru is Mani Das Babaji. Though of an "up-country" extraction he is a domiciled resident of Jajpur. The people of the sect are prohibited to eat in a house where the *srad* ceremony is going on. Besides they would by no means eat in the house of a Brahmin or the food cooked by him. The more advanced members of this sect are said to be endowed with marvellous powers of healing.

Though this is not a quite relevant topic, as these people do not belong to the Chaitanya cult, I have introduced it here to show that in various parts of India, the Buddhists, after the Brahminic Renaissance, took shelter under different forms of prevailing Hindu religion, retaining much of their original creed of Mahayanism. As the Vaisnava sects opened their doors of brotherhood to all, irrespective of creed and colour most of these Buddhists incorporated themselves with that community, and what could be a greater proof of their having once been Buddhists than the fact that some. of these sects refuse to take food cooked by a Brahmin up to this day, though they call themselves Hindus? The Brahmin was the great enemy of the Buddhist who was eventually crushed by him. The Sunya Puran of the Bengali Buddhists cries itself hoarse in its last chapter against the Brahmins and announces that it was for vengeance of the wrongs done by the Brahmins to the Buddhists, that the Mahomedans were commissioned by the Most High to destroy the Brahminic temples. The Bathuris and some other tribes of Orissa, who outwardly profess Vaisnavism were at one time Buddhists. They have preserved much of the older creed in their theology and scriptures under the disguise of Vaisnava religion. Rai Sahib Nagendra Nath Vasu has proved this fact beyond all shadow of doubt in his book called "Buddhism in Orissa."

The Sahajias have composed many songs on Radha-Krishna. Unfortunately these have not yet been collected or published. These songs deal with the loving sports of the Divine cowherd and his consort the princess,—the adventurous boat-trip of the lover—called the Noyka Khanda,—*the mān* or Radha's jealousy and her outward indifference to Krishna's entreaties, however much she was gratified by them,—the *abhisār* or the secret meetings—the *māthur* or separation and many other still nicer

<small>The Radha-Krisna songs of the Bauls as contrasted with those of the Vaisnavas.</small>

classifications of tender emotions. The Sahajia Vaisnavas, the Bauls and others, also deal with these topics as the genuine Vaisnavas do. But one can clearly see a difference between the modes of treatment of the two different schools. The Baul takes a very ordinary view of matters in his songs and cannot for a moment forget that Krishna is the Lord of the Universe and Radha is a devoted worshipper. This brings in the phraseology of Divine Service and prayers in his attempts to describe sports. For instance when the ferry-boat of which Krishna is at the helm is tossed by the waves of the Jumna under a storm, Radha, in the Baul-songs of Noyka Khanda, offers a regular prayer like a devotee fallen in distress. The human interest flags as the spiritual element gets the upper hand. Every now and then the Baul in his songs introduces Dehatatta, or the physical principles for development of our occult powers—the goal of the Buddhist *tantriks*. Vaisnavism is a creed of joy and Buddhism of misery. In the Baul-songs reference to decay, death, and transitoriness of life and body is frequent. But the true Vaisnavism makes an essential departure from viewing such an aspect of life; it is all sunny and even in its pain, it seizes the golden moments of love, and delights in dying the death of a love-martyr. In the pure Vaisnava-songs the theological ideas do not find a place. The love songs are pure love-songs and if they bear a high spiritual significance, it is only because this love appears in such an idealised and platonic form, that, though it is born in human heart, it points to the divine element in human feelings. The intensely human— the selfless absorption of one's self in love—is intensely spiritual as well. The Baul and the pure Vaisnava thus offer a contrast, one modelling the new creed according to age-long conventions of a different character, the other offering all the freshness of a new ideal in poetry and spiritual domain which essentially emanated from Chaitanya. Sir Rabindranath Tagore is more indebted to the Baul than to the Vaisnava, so far as the spirit of his songs is concerned, though he has frequently borrowed the sweet language of the Vaisnava masters. The Bauls have appealed to him, as in their faith there is no place reserved for image-worship and there is more of philosophy in their creed than ardour of devotion. The Bauls aim at that 'quiet' of the souls which is purely Buddhistic. But Rabindranath has not accepted their pessimistic outlook of life nor their speculation of physical training—the Dehatatta.

I invite the students of the vernacular songs to apply themselves to finding out the difference, and analyse from the standpoints of the different creeds of the Baul and the Vaisnava, the lyrical literatures of both the cults which professing the same religion, yet differ so largely in some of their essential features.

Babu Parvaticharan has given the sketch of a Sahajia Guru. Under the shade of the Radha-Krishna legend, he is depicted as practising all kinds of sexual immoralities. But the genuine Vaisnava, however wicked he may be, will never forget the sacredness of the Radha-Krishna legend and defile it. Even the bad women of the city purify themselves by touching the Ganges water and changing their clothes, when they have to appear in the *ashar* of the Kirtan songs. They enter the house for this purpose in the frame of mind in which one enters the church. When a song is finished and the name of the poet is to be mentioned in the colophon, they join their hands and bow, and offer their respect to the songs, as if they are sacred as mantras. What greater refutation can there be of the charge of sensuousness in the Radha-Krishna songs? The audience invariably return as better people, with a spiritual awakening in the soul. These songs have been thoroughly idealized in the country by the faith, austerities and renunciation of the Vaisnava saints, whose interpretation has filtered down to the lowest layer of our social life. But not so always with the pseudo-Vaisnavas—the Sahajias. Their point of strength is *tantrikism*, *yoga*, and a hundred ways to attain a mystic stage of *jnan*, in which control of self, not the beatitude reached by emotions, is the aim. They adopted the Vaisnava creed merely for expediency's sake in order to have some status in the country which had rejected them altogether. Hence the Radha-Krishna cult was in some cases vitiated by the more wicked of the Sahajia Gurus.

CHAPTER III.

I cannot conclude this book without pointing out the duties of our young graduates who have taken up the Indian vernaculars as their subjects of study. My appeal is to all educated men of my country, specially to these students, as they are the more immediately interested. Buddhism has not passed away from this country; it lives not amongst a few but amongst thousands to-day. Is it not curious that we should always await messages from Europe to satisfy our intellectual curiosity even in matters that are Indian, nay purely Bengali? Shall we sit quiet like Buddhist gods in stone and put forth our energies only to copy, when a Max Müller, a Rhys Davids, a Sylvain Levi or an Oldenburg has brought us new facts? We boast of our intellectuality but completely ignore the large field that is before and around us in our immediate neighbourhood, which we can approach for research and interpret as no foreigner can do. It is true that for the purposes of excavations and other expensive measures required for research, European officers who can easily command help from the Government and from their own communities, have a distinct advantage over us. Yet if we learn the lesson of organised action, pecuniary resources may be open to us in a hundred ways. We must not forget that the race that has made the Germans, the Japanese, the English and even our neighbours, the Marwarees, rich, remains poor to-day through not knowing the principles of organised labour.

But in respect of a research into the ways and manners of the various sects living in Bengal no money is required. We should only mix with our own men, not despising our rustic neighbours. The proud Europeans mix with them when they want jute and other products of our land—but we do not care to do so, even for the sake of the truths of our own religion, philosophy and literature which they have preserved and we have lost. Vaisnavism is making itself accepted more intimately in the ranks of these pseudo-Vaisnavas and, I am afraid, after some years the Buddhist wisdom amongst them will dwindle away. It is, therefore, time that we should make researches in these fields, which are so near to us. Europeans want to be intimately acquainted with the truths of Indian wisdom from educated Indians. What they acquire from our old scriptures and literature is good enough, but about the phases of genuine Indian religious culture and rural literature, at present the educated Indians will mislead and disappoint them. They will only re-echo the sentiments of Europeans in a feebler voice, but this they do not expect from Indians. We do not know our own country. In the pride of western culture we have so long kept aloof from the more genuine sources from which we could learn much. Within the last half a century education on Western lines has made rapid strides to the utter destruction of our own ideals of culture. If any European scholar seeks the old Indian wisdom, born anew amongst our multitude, let him go to the villages even as some of his European countrymen go seeking jute and other agricultural products. There are even to-day many Gurus who preach the old cults. They are not guided by the spirit of Hindu renaissance but proceed in the catholic manner of the ancient teachers laying no stress on caste or convention. And though some of them may interpret the scriptures wickedly, as already shown by us in this chapter, surely there are others whose teachings represent the flowering faith of the Mahayana Buddhists. They have a very vast literature, only a portion of which has been published by the Presses of Bat-tala, but by far the greatest portion of which is lying in the shape of manuscripts, uncared for and not at all noticed by the educated community. In these religions, there is a constant tendency to rebuild the social fabric on the basis of amity and brotherhood and unify

SAHAJIA AN ALL-EMBRACING CREED

the divergent elements into one homogeneous whole. There are Mahomedans and Christians and in some parts of the country, there is also a sprinkling of population professing other creeds, such as the Sikhs. It is therefore very interesting to observe that many of the Sahajia creeds have included not only the Bible and the Koran in the list of their holy books, but have also, as the Ramvallabhis have done, reserved a place for the Grantha Saheb of Guru Nanak. Though attending thus to the scriptures of all religions prevailing in this land in a truly cosmopolitan spirit, they have yielded their own views to none, but have subordinated all of them to their own special creeds which contain the old wisdom of the Tantrik Buddhists. They have not been able to declare war against the Maulavi, the Missionary and the Hindu Guru, but in an unassuming way they have contrived to have large followings from all these great religious sections of the population of Bengal, making them their own in the fullest sense. For, the Christian Sahajia, the Mahomedan Sahajia and the Hindu Sahajia pay by far a greater respect to their Sahajia Gurus than the conventional leaders of their own respective societies. The Sahajia will give up his life and property at the bidding of his Guru, though outwardly he seems to cling to his community. The song quoted on page 380 says that the Sahajia remains like one blind in the daylight, his eyes are opened in the night and his true life begins in the night. In the day-time he has to do conventional things, to observe the rules of caste and pay respect to the Mollah, the Missionary or the Brahmin as the case may be and abide by their orders, but he becomes the true man at night in the secret societies, when his real work begins, and so great is the attraction of these societies which sit every night, that men and women of the Sahajia cult consider it their greatest misfortune if they cannot attend them. There they perform their mystic rites, promulgate the doctrines of their creeds, indulge in songs for the culture of emotion, and pay no heed to the rules of caste and other social restrictions. There is much that is very good mixed with the vulgar and bad, as I have already stated, but in many such societies only good things are done where the Guru is really a good and pious man.

The catholicity of soul and the brotherhood of men that are cultivated in these circles together with a high spiritual training, have only been possible in Bengal because all these different classes of men can gather together under the banner of Chaitanya. It was he who preached an all-embracing brotherhood and showed that the portals of heaven with all its treasures of beatitude might be open to men by culture of tender emotions and by discarding scriptural rites, and hence it is that the Sahajias have flourished under the protection of his name up to now. The creeds require thorough investigation, and their mystic writings in the Sandhya Bhasa should be made clear by research.

INDEX

A

Abalambana...384, 385, 386.
Abhiram Lilamrita...98.
Abhiram Goswami...7.
Abhiram Swami...360.
Abhisar...316, 393.
Achar...352.
Achyuta...38.
Achyatcharan Choudhury...361.
Adhaksaja...38.
Adbira...298.
Addikhanda...73.
Adiparva...108.
Adaitya...107
Aditi...107.
Adwaitabad...322.
Adwaitacharya...16, 46, 47, 49, 61, 64, 101, 102, 106, 107, 109, 110, 133, 144, 151, 157, 163, 167, 173, 175, 187, 239, 244, 245, 284, 291
Adwaita Prakasa....66, 98, 118.
Aghasura...34, 36.
Aghore Panthis...171, 275.
Agradwip...302.
Aiswarya...41, 42.
Ajitnath Nayaratna...108.
Akshoykamar Datta...344
Alalnath...211, 212, 248.
Alandi...63.
Allah...153.
Allahabad...227, 228, 230, 241, 242
Amarda...177.

American tourist...236.
Amina Khatoon...62.
Amjhora...277.
Amlaki...124.
Amogha...66.
Amritabatika...187.
Amritabazar Patrik.a ..60, 88.
Ananta...76.
Ananta Shayya...76
Aniruddha...38.
Annakut...227.
Anta Khanda...314.
Anuragballi...92, 98.
Arati...288.
Arctic regions...360.
Arhants...361.
Arjuna...203.
Aryan...14.
Ashar...262, 263, 396.
Ashta Sastreo Bikar...308.
Ashray...384, 385, 386.
Asiatic Society Journal...267.
Assam...125, 242.
Assamese...242.
Assulatwin...23.
Astavingsati Tatva.. 100.
Almanepadi...118.
Atmanibedan...309.
Atulchand...344.
Aul...342.
Avangas...211
Ayodba...220.

B

Ballava Bhatta...239, 241, 242.
Ballare...239, 240, 241, 248, 256.
Baiba Aul...342, 344.
Ba disingha...121, 293.
Bataranri...177.
Baisakh ..191, 211.
Bailpara...306, 307.
Baniantree...53.

Bandhu...62.
Banipati...236, 237.
Baikuntha...203.
Baraha...88.
Basudev Ghosh...192.
Basu Ghosh...97, 159, 291.
Basudeva Sarbabhaum...100, 190, 179, 180, 185, 213, 239, 244.

INDEX

Basudeva Datta...187, 233.
Batsayana Gotra.. 101.
Ballal Sagar...112.
Ballavi Sect.. 122.
Banamali Acharyya...122, 123.
Banamali...123.
Banana plant...270.
Basuli...24, 25, 26, 30, 355.
Bataalya...27. 170.
Balaram...33, 64, 88, 348, 349.
Balaram Das...152, 282, 283.
Bharati Dera...169.
Bhilpantha...201.
Bhikshus...10, 335, 336.
Bhikshunies.. 10, 335, 336.
Bhadra...202.
Bhargadev...12, 193.
Bhagavata...31, 32, 35, 36, 51, 69, 76, 77, 111, 118, 136, 182, 232, 240, 241, 252, 254, 256, 289, 323, 331.
Bhagavat Acharya...233, 252.
Bhaktiratnakara...42, 92, 98, 155.
Bhaga...348.
Bhakti-Cult...1, 42, 44, 46, 47, 180, 229, 230, 232, 244, 288, 290, 291, 294, 296, 310.
Bhugarva...49.
Bhakta ..47, 66, 91, 138.
Bhagan Acharya...238.
Bhubaneswar...178.
Bhakti...51, 73, 135, 147, 231, 244, 324.
Bharati Gossami...12.
Bhaktirasamrita Sindhu...78, 183.
Bhabasanmilan...313.
Bhababhuti...310.
Bhowanisankar...177.
Bhakta Mal...204.
Bipralabdha...312.
Bijoynagar...184.
Bijoy Gupta...54.
Bibhisana...83.
Bishnudev...116.
Bijli Khan...228, 229.
Birudhamati...121.
Bisarad...179.
Birbhum...16.
Bikrampore...39.
Bisranti Ghat...227.
Bidyapati...252.
Birabhadra...284, 336.
Billamangal...252.
Bible...346, 401.
Balya Lila Sutra...98.
Bakasur...34.
Baka...36.
Baroda...200.

Barmukhi...43, 205, 206, 207, 208.
Bankol...45, 201, 202.
Barai...341.
Baul...340, 345, 394, 395.
Barati...343.
Balaji...206.
Baladev Bhattacharya...224, 228.
Baladeva...224, 225.
Bateswar...194.
Bala Khrnda...371.
Baroda...200.
Bakreshwar...239.
Bashudev...159, 180, 181, 182, 183, 185, 239, 246.
Balagopal...242.
Baninath...246, 247.
Battala Press ..259, 400.
Bangabasi Press...259.
Bay of Bengal...261.
Baid Pashara Buddhism...256, 267, 285.
Bataalyarasa...272.
Balasore...177.
Basanta Ranjan Ray...17.
Baranagar...233.
Benapole...56.
Betasak...124.
Betal...125.
Bel...167.
Bengal...1-3, 21-23, 32, 37-39, 41-45, 51, 52, 56, 95, 100, 142, 172, 219, 220, 223, 233, 237, 244, 245, 267, 276, 278, 279, 280, 284, 285, 286, 287, 291, 325, 326, 334, 338, 348, 351, 360, 391, 399, 401, 402.
Beveridge...267, 275, 276.
Begum...19, 21.
Bengali...2, 19, 32, 33, 35, 37, 42, 43, 54, 64, 71, 97, 103, 143, 204, 222, 237, 259, 338, 339, 392, 393, 398.
Benares...57, 120, 225, 226, 230-232, 201.
B. N. Railways...392.
Beshar...71.
Bishanath...233.
Bidagdha Madhaba...238.
Bishwarup...104, 106, 110, 141, 161, 175.
Bishnupriya...24, 103, 128, 166, 174, 204.
Bireswar Sen...177.
Bombay Presidency...294.
Boroch...301.
Balshevic...331.
Boali...342.
Bagula...197, 201.
Brahma Kshatriyas...125

INDEX

Brahmin...11, 17, 26, 27, 31, 47, 48, 53, 54, 55, 57, 64, 71, 75, 105, 111, 112, 123, 124, 126, 129, 140, 147, 15, 162, 199, 210, 214, 218, 222, 226, 228, 235, 249, 250, 254, 256, 279, 281, 282, 286, 300, 302, 325, 339, 340, 344, 349, 353, 377, 381, 388, 392, 393, 402.
Brindabandas...11, 55, 65, 73, 74, 77, 78, 81, 82, 94, 95, 97, 99, 110, 113, 118, 120, 141, 170, 179, 246, 311.
Brahminic...26, 28, 48.
Brahmanic Renaissance..34, 352, 370, 372.
Brahmandabhandodasa...66, 73.
Brindaban...74, 77, 90, 94, 122, 178, 189, 221-224, 227, 228, 234, 254, 262, 318.
Brindagroves...77, 80, 131, 163, 223, 224, 299, 301, 315.
Brahman Krishna Das...87.
Brihaspati...118.

Brahma...384
Brahmas...37.
Brahma Sntra...323.
Brahma Samaj...376, 378, 379.
Buran...49.
Burdwan...145, 176.
Budha...61, 62, 222, 276, 324-327.
Buddhist...8, 10, 13, 184, 193, 284, 334, 335, 337, 338, 354, 367, 368, 369, 370, 372, 373, 374, 392, 393.
Buddhimanta Khan...128, 157, 187.
Buddhism...2, 11, 13, 14, 256, 267, 285, 317, 335, 336, 353, 374, 394, 398.
Buddha Gan-o-Doha...10.
Buddha Doha-o-Gan...4.
Buddhist Sangha...268.
Buddhist Bhikkas...317.
Buddhist Bhikkhunis...313.
Buddhist tantrics
Budhuvi...319.

C

Canarese...295.
Calcutta...262, 312, 336, 344.
Carfestivities...96, 246, 263.
Chaitanya...2, 12, 16, 23, 24, 29, 31, 32, 36, 40-43-47, 52, 53, 56, 58-64, 67-72, 74-80, 82-85, 87-97, 99-102, 105-109, 115, 129, 135, 139, 141, 145, 146, 151, 169, 170, 172-174, 177-183, 185-200, 202-205, 207, 209, 210, 211-216, 217-246, 248, 249-255, 252-268, 274, 276-280, 282, 284-287, 289, 290, 292-295, 302, 303, 305, 308, 310, 312, 314-320, 322-327, 331, 336, 344, 345, 348, 368, 369, 385, 387, 392, 395, 402.
Chaitanya Bhagavata...11, 36, 37, 40, 42, 43, 50, 72, 73, 77, 87, 90, 95, 97, 101, 107, 108, 115, 116, 119, 124, 137, 144, 151, 156, 158, 159.
Chakra...6, 87, 194.
Chandal...6, 171, 275, 377.
Chandidaa...9, 10, 14, 16-22, 26-30, 32, 35, 36, 40, 69, 126, 143, 145, 146, 252, 266, 354, 357-360, 368.
Chandipore...12, 193.
Chaitanya Chandradoya Natak 12, 84, 97, 159.
Chaitanya Mangal...23, 55, 57, 77, 81, 88, 89, 95, 97, 115, 259, 262, 263.
Christ...28, 70, 141, 268, 269, 332, 350.
Chaitanya Charitamrita...38, 45, 63, 66, 77, 79, 86, 87, 90, 94, 95, 97, 101, 178-180, 183-185, 213. 217, 219, 221, 230, 231, 247, 251, 289, 290, 292, 314, 324, 372.

Charitamrita... 44, 225, 231, 233, 241, 242, 243, 246, 252, 257, 259, 261, 275, 277, 279, 294, 328, 329, 337
Charak... 306.
Chaitanya and His Companions... 49, 68, 101, 126, 186, 209, 216, 238, 243, 327.
Chaitanya Deva... 58, 246, 290, 292.
Chaitanya Charitam... 60, 61, 67, 84, 94, 126, 159,.
Chaitanya cult... 69, 337,.
Chitralata... 127,.
Champaka... 80,.
Chaitanya Chandrodaya... 84, 95, 103, 158, 179, 184, 244.
Chaitanya Charit... 90, 97, 103, 259.
Chandrasekhar... 145, 150, 157, 171, 225, 230.
Chaipalli... 202,.
Chandrakala... 235,.
Change Charana... 247.
Chang... 248.
Christian... 268, 339, 340, 343, 346, 351, 352, 401.
Christianity... 307.
Charu Darshan... 377.
Chandvardai... 318.
Chakradaha... 342.
Chaukidar... 348.
Chaudarshan... 374, 388.
Chittagong... 44.
Chitralekha... 90.
Choranandi... 197.

INDEX 407

D

D. R. Bhandarkar... 211.
Daivaki... 107.
Daman... 200.
Daaya... 27, 326, 328, 329, 330, 331, 332.
Dasaratha... 27, 37.
Damodara...58, 60, 64, 66, 67, 176, 188, 190, 192, 289, 292, 305.
Dacca...71, 139, 307, 350.
Dacca College...71.
Dakha Daksin...99, 125.
Dorbhanga...120.
Dacca muslin...146.
Daitya...107.
Dabirkhas...219.
Damodar Swarup...239.
Dandas...262.
Dande...273.
Darpanarayan...350.
Darvesh...347.
Deva Sarma...17.
Deccan...52, 63. 65, 86, 88, 184, 192, 204, 209, 211, 294.
Delhi ..120,.
Desha...384, 385, 386.
Dehatatta...394, 395..
Deva gram...348.

Devajus...354.
Dharma cult...2.
Dharma-literature...5.
Dharma Mangal...5, 32.
Dhundi Ram Tirtha...12.
Dhamrai.. 71.
Dhuti...110, 112, 131, 141.
Dhira...298.
Dhiradhira...298.
Dharma Worshippers...307.
Diamond Harbour...278,
Dibyonmad...314.
Dom...9, 279,.
Dolotsava...371,372.
Dohas...302.
Dontya...312.
Dogachia ..346.
Dohi...8.
Dravidian languages...295.
DurgaPrasad Kar...361.
Durlabha Sar... 324.
Durga Prasad...361.
Dwaitadwaitavada...41, 321, 322, 323.
Dwaraka...204, 205, 211.
Dwarakadiab...300.
Dwarulla...300.
Dwaitabad...322.

E

Eastern Bengal...39, 118, 125. 127, 238, 294.
Eclal...129.
Ekchaka...36.
Ekahhippaya...367.

Emperor Akbur...318.
English...71, 220, 399.
Emperor of Gou...52,53, 57, 148.
Europe...268, 269.
European...61, 268, 272, 279, 285.

F

Fag...143, 370.
Fakir...350.
Falgun...109.

Faridpur...62, 126.
Ferdausi...21.
Fraser...278.

G

Gadigaccha...152.
Gangetic Valley...14.
Ganges...15, 53, 99, 104, 111, 119, 123, 130, 135 140, 165, 166, 168, 170, 189, 230, 249, 277, 299, 349, 396.
Gakul Gossain...122.
Gangadhar Pandit...24, 135, 293.

Ganga Das...90, 102, 114, 115, 118, 144, 162.
Gayatri...26.
Ganes...41, 89, 120, 154.
Gangadhar...49, 50, 117, 127, 131, 139, 144, 159, 316.
Gaya...90, 91, 128, 129, 187

Garanhati...146.
Gandas...248.
Gauriya Vaishnabs...225.
Gathali...227.
Garur...237.
Gavinda Ghosh..240, 291.
Gaurapadatarangini...312.
Ganrachandrika...312, 313, 315, 316.
Gaelio...334.
Germans...399.
George Fox...267.
Geru...112.
Ghat...155.
Ghora...204, 205, 209,.
Ghoshpara...344, 350, 391.
Girishwar...202.
Gita...31, 111, 346.
Gobra...350,
Govinda Charan Basu.,.204.
Goraksha Nath...23, 4.
Goraksha Bijoy...3.
Govinda Charan...204, 205, 277.
Gopi Chandra...4, 64.
Gopel bhoga...176,
Godavari...26, 210, 235, 273, 281.
Govinda Das...31, 63, 87-89, 95-97, 107, 117, 165, 168, 179, 186, 194, 200, 204, 210, 225, 234, 352, 377, 282, 283, 294, 299, 315, 319.
Goknl ..35.
Govinda...38, 87, 123, 165, 168, 171, 177, 187, 194, 201, 210, 213, 253, 256, 275.
Gonr...52, 56, 178, 217, 219.

Gostha-Songs...312.
Gonra Emperor...57, 178.
Gourapada tarangini...88.
Gopinath...96, 117, 181, 247, 248, 249, 260, 265.
Govinda Ghosh...97, 116, 144, 302.
Gopal Basu...97.
Gobrāi...349.
Govinda Karmakar—106, 124, 168, 171, 191, 204, 277.
Gopinath Acharyya...116, 145, 185, 244.
Gopi Chandra...288.
Godhuli...143.
Gohardhan Das...214.
Gopal Bhatta...225, 290.
Goswami...225, 284.
Gopinath Ray...246.
Gobardhan...255.
Gouridas...263.
Gopis...299, 323, 385.
Goraj...149.
Greek...61, 302, 307.
Growse...318.
Grantha Saheb...401.
Guzrat...120.
Gurjari...145, 203.
Guru Saiji...347.
Guru...285, 288, 318, 321, 340, 342, 343, 344, 346, 347, 348, 354, 374, 375, 377, 383, 385, 390-392, 400-402.
Gurjari Rag...253.
Gubhajus...354.
Gyasuddin...17.

H

Haripa...2.
Harisiddha...3.
Harihara-Baity . 5.
Hafiz...23, 177.
Hari...38, 348.
Haridas...47, 48, 49, 115, 142, 144. 150, 151, 157, 193, 212, 242, 243, 249, 250, 280, 281, 282, 292, 303, 369.
Harichandra. 218, 248.
Haribhakti Bilas...222, 289.
Hallam...268.
Haritaki...302.
Hari Ballava Kar...361.
Hall...306.
Hatu Ghosh...342.
Hazrati...349.
Hebrew...302.
Hira...4.

Hindu...8, 14, 17, 23, 27, 32, 52-57, 145, 204, 220, 221, 278, 282, 298, 313, 318, 338, 340, 343, 346-350, 352-354, 372, 377, 378, 388, 392, 393, 400, 401.
Hindu Renaissance...11, 336, 338.
Hinduism...11, 27, 335, 379.
Hiranya Das...214.
Hindi...295, 318.
Hindu Jurisprudence...287.
History of Bengali Language and Literature...313.
History of the Mediæval Vaishnav Literature...327.
Haribola ..211.
Homer...273,
Hrishikesa...38.
Hussain Shah...52, 53, 55, 56, 57, 178, 214, 218, 219, 221.

INDEX

I

India...3, 27, 31, 44, 62, 63, 99, 119, 141, 163, 169, 190, 210, 211, 222, 239, 292, 293, 294, 306, 392.
Indian History...222.
Indian Vernaculars. 398.
Indian Cupid...370.
Indira Devi...202.

Indradyumna Sarobara...256.
Insurance office...360.
In toto...242.
Ishan Nagar...98, 116, 294.
Islam...13, 32, 284.
Iswar Bharati...293.
Iswar Puri...44, 50, 53, 54, 115, 116, 117, 129, 131, 181, 193.

J

Jagannatha...7, 76, 96, 102, 154, 181, 186, 187, 235, 256, 260, 262, 263, 265.
Jaksha...12.
Jamuna...17, 26, 33, 40, 69, 75, 168, 172, 173, 227, 230, 243. 255, 257, 301, 394
Jayananda...24, 88, 95, 97, 100, 102, 109, 115, 125, 127, 132, 154, 178, 186, 187, 233, 262, 264.
Jasoda...34, 143.
Janardana...38, 101, 154.
Jagannath Misra...99-101, 103-106, 113, 115, 136.
Jagabandhu Bhadra...88, 312.
Jay Gopal Goswami...88, 89.
Jajpur...101, 178, 392.
Jayaram Chakrabartty...125.
Jagai...153, 154, 155, 194.
Jaleswar...177.
Jagannath Ballav...186, 238.
Japa...112, 288.
Jaumasthami...289.
Jangal...218.
Jagadananda...239, 242, 254, 354.
Jaganath...264.

Jati-nasha...285.
Jaigir...249.
Jadunandan Acharya...282.
James...306.
Jambu Dwipa...384.
Japanese...399.
Jehangir...21.
Jessore...47, 282, 350.
Jesus...61, 62.
Jemeswar...177.
Jewish...105, 268.
Jesus Christ...379.
Jharikhanda...227.
Jiva...99.
Jizuri...202.
Jiva Goswami...290.
Jnan...244, 322, 324, 325, 397.
Jnanadi Sodhana...353, 388.
Job...105.
Joydev...7, 8, 19. 30, 31, 143, 146, 252, 253 302, 310, 323.
Jonepur...392.
Junior Hari las...243.
Jnthi...252, 314.

K

Kanair Natsala, 135, 217, 218.
Kalipa, 2.
Kanchi, 120.
Kannpa, 2.
Kanchannagore, 167, 168, 176.
Kamalkumari, 196.
Kalu Dom, 5.
Kalinga, 7.
Kanaraka, 8.
Kali, 10, 11, 55, 299, 300, 301, 390.
Kapalika, 13.
Kanaraka, 178.
Kanis, 23.

Kansalya, 27, 107, 174.
Kalia, 34, 301.
Kansa, 36.
Kamallochan, 178.
Kaustuva, 45.
Kalatirtha, 202.
Kamalakshya, 46.
Kazi, 48, 54, 114, 149, 152, 153.
Kafir, 48.
Kashinath Ghattak, 128.
Karcha, 82, 86, 87, 88, 94, 95, 97, 107, 191, 192, 193, 204, 209, 225, 277, 294.
Katwa, 92, 165, 167, 168, 171, 179.

410 INDEX

Kavikarnapur, 130, 158, 180, 196, 197, 234, 235, 244, 246, 259, 291.
Kantaknagore, 167.
Kasiawar Nayaratna, 171.
Kanpin, 174.
Kapila, 174.
Kashi Misra, 176, 214.
Karpurknpi, 187.
Karnat, 234.
Kasiahwar, 239.
Kanchrapara, 244.
Kamal Das, 277, 283.
Karuna, 307.
Kalidas, 279, 280.
Kayastha, 279, 280, 285, 361.
Kanai, 280.
Kavyaprakasha, 294.
Kahahantarita, 312.
Kamranga, 382.
Karta-Bhajas, 335, 336, 340, 343, 346.
Karma, 324, 325.
Kanaibazar, 36!.
Kala, 384, 385, 386.
Kalicharan, 365.
Kalicharan Tarafdar, 366.
Kali Yuga, 385.
Katha Vathu, 366, 367.
Kamdeva, 370, 371, 372.
Kama, 371, 372.
Kaviraj Parvaticharan Kavishekhar, 373.
Kanupad, 302.
Keshava, 38, 167.
Keshava Bharati, 44, 161, 168.
Keshab Basu, 56, 219.
Keshab Kasmiri, 119, 293, 294.
Keshab Samanta, 177.
Khadija, 134.
Khanjanacharya, 212.
Khob, 172.
Khandava, 202.
Khardaha, 283, 284.
Kheturi, 285.
Khandita, 312.
Khoda, 390.
Khusi Biswas, 348.
Kharar Char, 350

Khemasahasra, 361.
Kirnabar, 126.
Kirtan, 50, 139, 145, 146, 150, 151, 154, 155, 162, 175, 186, 240, 260, 312, 315.
King Pratap Rudra, 234.
Kilakinchit, 297,
Kishori Bhajakas, e74, 376.
Kotalipar, 126.
Kowri, 147, 248.
Koran, 346.
Krishna Keli, 123.
Kranabhanga, 121.
Krishna, 9, 17, 19, 28, 29, 32-34, 36-39, 42-44, 47, 63, 64, 66, 68, 69, 71-77, 80, 83, 86, 88, 94, 97, 105, 110, 111, 117, 118, 130-132, 143, 154, 155, 157-160, 163, 164, 166, 168, 172, 176, 181, 193-195, 198, 199, 202, 203, 206, 207, 208, 213, 214, 218, 220, 221, 225-228, 223, 239, 242, 251, 252, 254-258, 267, 276, 289, 297, 298, 301-303, 305, 312, 313-315, 319(16), 323, 329, 353, 369, 371, 372, 385, 387, 390, 393, 394.
Krishna Kirtan, 9, 17, 18, 19, 22, 20 30, 35, 371.
Kahnadhamalisa, 9, 17, 30.
Krishnapada, 143.
Krishnacharn, 143.
Krishna Das, 46, 97, 212, 213, 228, 237, 283.
Krishna Das Kaviraj, 94, 179, 183, 210, 225, 230, 231, 337.
Krishna Lilamrita, 117.
Krishna Dasi, 374.
Krishna Kamal, 314.
Krishna Kumar Gunasagar, 346.
Krishnanagar, 346, 348.
Krishna-cult, 370.
Kunda, 133, 252.
Kumarhatta, 131, 233.
Knlia, 170, 233.
Knmaries, 392.
Kumbha Mela, 228.
Kuoran, 401.
Kuliniam, 352.
Kusha, 140.

L

Lakshman Sen, 7, 8.
Lakhan, 212.
Laksmi, 22, 90, 122, 126, 127, 157.
Laur, 46, 47.
Lauri Krishna Das, 98.
Lalita Devi, 71.
Lalita Bistara, 81.

Lanka, 84.
Lakhibai, 195.
Lakhi, 196.
Lalita Madhab, 238.
Lalsaahi, 389.
Life of Akbar, 54.
Ligna-franea, 295.

INDEX

Lion-gate, 255, 256.
Lochan Das, 60, 81, 94, 97, 125, 132, 259, 263, 264, 324.
Lochan, 82, 159.

Lokenath Goswami, 86.
Lord Carmichael, 103.
Lokenath Lahiri, 125.
Luther, 267.

M

Mahanadi, 177.
Madabukara Misra, 101.
Mayniamati 3, 6, 5.
Mailn, 7, 109, 157, 168.
Madhuri, 153-156, 194.
Manasa Devi, 9, 11.
Mahayana, 10, 13, 14, 331, 334, 337, 354, 370, 400.
Mathuranath, 12.
Mahaprasad, 12.
Madhuryya, 27, 326, 330.
Mala Dhar Basu...36.
Madhab...38, 42, 341, 343.
Madhabi...242, 303.
Madhusudan...38.
Mahamahopadhya Ajitanath Nayaratna...153.
Madhavendra Puri...40, 227.
Magha...92, 165, 213, 228.
Madhyacharya...41.
Mathur Lila...42.
Mathur...393.
Mathura...42, 313, 315, 323.
Madhavendra...44, 45.
Madras Presidency...45, 277.
Mahratta...46, 203, 211, 225, 226, 230.
Mandira...152, 172.
Mahomedan...46, 48, 53, 56, 142, 178, 212, 218—221, 228, 229, 249, 250, 281, 282, 286, 290, 318, 334, 339, 340, 343, 344, 346—351, 393, 401.
Manashar Bhashau...54.
Mayapur...55.
Maya Devi...61.
Mary...61, 62, 332.
Mahomed...62.
Mahamahopadhya...103.
Mahabharat...103, 104, 156.
Madhyas...298.
Mac Nichol...122.
Markandeya Chandi...126.
Mandar...129.
Mahomet-khadija...134.
Manahar Shai...144, 146.
Madhumukhi...149.
Malayalam...295.
Magnas Opus...222.
Mahabir...222.

Maithili...295.
Maharajas...236.
Madhuryarasa...273.
Mantras...289, 344, 348.
Madhab Barui...341.
Maya...322, 323.
Mainat...350.
Man...312, 393.
Mahayanism...352, 392.
Mansingha...318.
Madhyakhanda...324.
Mahasay...343.
Malati...389.
Manidas Bahaji...392.
Manindramohan Bose...338.
Madrasis...392.
Mahayanist...345.
Max Muller...398.
Malapara...348.
Malliks...3.
Madhyamic School...352.
Mayna...361.
Manomohini...361, 362, 363, 364, 365.
Maulavi...401.
Madanotsava...370, 371.
Mahaprabhu...391, 392.
Madan...271.
Madan Mohan...371.
Marwarees...399.
Maharsi Devendranath Tagore...236.
Mediæval Vaisnava Literature of Bengal...286.
Mela...228, 344.
Meherpur...348.
Minanatha...2, 3, 4.
Minachetana...4.
Mithila...15.
Middhi...41.
Mira...206, 207.
Mirhabool...56, 221.
Misra...102.
Milan...312.
Moslem Emperor...20.
Modus Operandi...54.
Mooharghanta...124.
Mongoraj...218.
Mother-cult...269.
Mollah...402.

Mirdu...298.
Munindra...90.
Murari...37, 59—62; 90, 103, 112, 114, 118, 126, 192, 202, 239.
Mukunda Datta.. 49, 50, 214, 246, 263.
Mukunda Sanjaya...116, 135, 233.
Mukunda...50, 116, 117, 118, 164, 181, 189, 239, 240, 246.
Mula...200.

Murari Gupta...57, 59, 64, 94, 97, 116, 144, 159, 187, 212.
Munna...194, 197, 277.
Mukhara...298.
Mugdha...298.
Muchi...279.
Mukti...244.
Muradpur...350.
Mudra Rakshasa.
Musalmans...377.

N

Nahabatarchestra...214.
Narmada...200.
Nasik...200.
Nath-cult...2, 3, 4.
Nath-creed...2.
Nathism...2, 3.
Nath-literature...3.
Nath-leader...3.
Nath...4, 8.
Narada...36, 137, 157, 158.
Nagar...202.
Narattam Bilasha...10, 98.
Nadia...12, 54, 56, 59, 60, 63, 65, 68—71, 73, 75, 83, 84, 91, 92, 94, 99, 100, 102, 103, 108, 114, 116, 118—120, 122—126, 129, 131, 139, 141, 142, 150—156, 161, 163—165, 170, 173, 179, 186, 189, 190, 192, 194, 226, 232, 233, 243, 244, 282, 293, 303, 304, 325, 348, 385.
Narahari Chakrabarti—98.
Nagarjuna...13, 352.
Nagendranath Gupta...15.
Narahari Sircar...16, 68, 97, 285, 293.
Narahari...29, 32, 49, 68—70, 72, 73, 81, 92, 97, 113, 138, 141, 144, 145, 155, 159, 212, 291, 316.
Nanoor...16.
Naoroji...197, 201.
Nawab...19, 53.
Nakul...29.
Narayan...38.
Narayanpur...177.
Nandanacharya...141.
Naimisharanya...75.
Navaji...204.
Navadwip...82, 90, 119.
Nanda...75, 143, 202.

Narayani...90, 109.
Narendra Sarobar...256, 290.
Naihati...244.
Naradiya Puran...279.
Narottam Das...285, 324, 326.
Narottam...286.
Nayanananda...97.
Narasingha...286.
Nagda...350.
Nanak...401.
Neras...284, 345.
Neria...284.
Nera-Neris...284, 317, 318, 335.
Nepal...354.
Nilambar...106, 136.
Nim...110, 317.
Nimtree...255.
Nityananda...36, 37, 64, 97, 125, 141, 144, 150, 151, 154, 159, 165, 173, 176, 189, 190, 239, 240, 243, 245, 246, 278, 283, 284—287, 291, 336.
Nilambar Chakrabarty...100, 103, 179.
Nimai...109—136, 147, 150, 138—141, 144, 145, 151, 152, 153, 154, 156—170, 305.
Nityananda Das...98.
Nimai Pandit...116, 117, 120, 121, 124, 129, 146, 154, 159.
Nitai Ghosh...342.
North Bengal...9, 17, 18.
Nolak Babaji...71.
Noyka Khanda...393.
Non-Aryan...370.
North Western Provinces...392:
Nrishinghananda...217.
Nrishingha Chaturdasi...289.
Nurpur...125.

O

Ohio...305.
Ojhas...127.
Okra...111.
Oldenburg...398.
Old Testament...105,

Orient...295.
Orissa...32, 44, 52, 54, 56, 90, 101, 145, 184, 210, 213, 219, 261, 291, 391, 393.
Oriya...295.

INDEX

P

Panna Nara Singha...202.
Padmini...6, 7.
Pargana ..145.
Padmavati...7.
Parvati...8, 9, 41.
Pabanaduta...8.
Pal Kinga...11, 38.
Pali...113, 293, 295, 367.
Pada Kalpataru...15.
Panchanan Vedantik...171.
Padma...125.
Pandit Gangadhara...91.
Padmanava...38.
Padavali...44, 258.
Pathan...52, 53, 54.
Pal Rajas...64.
Papahara...178.
Parameswar Das...97.
Pandit Ganga Das...113.
Pandit Sanatan...128.
Pardanga...152.
Pandit...32, 103, 135, 137, 151, 234.
Panchahati...200.
Pandas...221, 325.
Panjab...293.
Pathan Nawab...228.
Panchatattyakhyan...231.
Panihati...233.
Puramananda Sen...244.
Padodak...255, 256.
Pakkhas...263.
Padmakot...300.
Pandit Khirodchandra Goswami...336.
Parari...342.
Pagalnathe...349, 350.
Pagal Kausi...350.
Pargana Ita...361.
Parvaticharan...374, 396.
Patra...384, 385, 386.
Patvis...349.
Peshwar...205.

Pedo...187.
Persian...220.
Pingal's Prakrit Grammar...293.
Pinda...128, 129.
Pirili Brahmins...54, 90.
Pitri Matri...26.
Pirulla...52.
Pichilda...218.
Poona...31, 63, 202.
Pragalvas...298.
Prince Lousen...5.
Pradyumna...38.
Prahlad...134, 137.
Pratap Rudra...52, 145, 184, 185, 186, 210, 221, 234, 235, 236, 246, 247.
Prabhu Jagatbandhu...62.
Premabilasa...92, 98, 246, 252.
Prakasananda...225, 230, 231, 232, 293.
Prakrit...295.
Prachyavidyamaharnava Nagendranath Basu...262.
Prembhakti Chandrika...324, 326.
Pranam...362, 365.
Premadas...97.
Prema...371, 372.
Prakritic...372.
Pravartaka...384, 385.
Punuruktabadbhasa...121.
Puri...7, 8, 12, 44, 60, 83, 84, 96, 145, 176, 178, 180, 184, 186, 188-190, 191, 192, 202, 211, 212, 213, 217, 219, 220, 221, 223, 224, 233, 234, 235, 237, 238, 239, 240, 243, 244, 245, 248, 253, 254, 257, 260, 280, 281, 286, 304, 352.
Purushottama...38, 125.
Pundarik Vidya Nidhi...44, 49.
Purandara...102.
Puri Raja...235.
Purba Raga...312.
Purana...366.
Puspostava...370.

Q

Quakers...306.

R

Ramgiri...193, 197.
Rameswar...9, 211.
Ratnagarha...136.
Rangpore...9.
Raghunath Das...213, 216, 238, 279, 292.

Radha...9, 28, 29, 40, 68, 90, 157, 267, 310, 312, 313-316, 323, 325, 372, 377, 386, 393, 394, 397.
Raja...15, 193, 209, 210, 234, 235, 248.
Rami...16, 20, 22, 24, 25, 26, 29, 355.

414

INDEX

Radhakrishna...17, 312, 313, 314, 315, 316, 368, 372, 373, 393, 396.
Ramananda...36, 205, 277, 338.
Ramananda Basu...204.
Ramanuja...37.
Raghu...216.
Ram...37, 84, 86, 174, 220, 289, 310.
Ram Das...37, 212.
Ram Rai...184, 186, 210, 218, 235, 238, 242, 244, 245, 248, 257, 281, 287, 297.
Raja Pratap Rudra...52, 178, 184, 213, 217, 218, 257, 265.
Ramchandra Khan...52, 177, 178.
Ramkeli...56, 178, 218, 234.
Ramkrishna Paramahmsa...62.
Ramkrishna...62, 296.
Raghunath...67, 153, 154, 214, 215.
Ravana...83.
Rakshasa...84.
Rajendranath Ray...62.
Raja Bhramarabara...101.
Raghunandan...100.
Raghunath Siromani...100.
Rai Sekhar...97.
Rajshahi...285.
Rajput...228.
Ragbab Pandit...233.

Ramananda Ray...239, 246, 256, 291, 292.
Rathajatra...240.
Ramnabami...289
Rasa...270, 327.
Raja of Pakkapalli...286.
Radhamohan...312, 316.
Radha songs...316.
Ramayan...338.
Ramsaran Pal...342.
Ramaballavi...346, 390.
Radha-tantra...372.
Rai-Kanu...372.
Rai Sahib Nagendranath Vasu...393.
Rabindranath...395.
Ramvallabhins...401.
Remnna...44,
Remiti...146.
Red River, Ohio...305.
Rhys Devid...398.
Rishi...75, 130.
Rissa-Culla...212.
Rowile...250.
Rupanarayan...15.
Rupa...42, 219, 220, 222, 237, 254, 280, 291, 292, 294, 297, 298, 318, 337.
Rupa Goswami...44.
Rudrapati...209.

S

Saivism...2.
Sandhya-bhaosha...4, 245, 335, 389, 403.
Sarbat...187.
Sevadasi...7.
Santipur...49, 88, 108, 173, 176, 178, 179, 189, 282, 284, 350.
Sahitya Parisat...8,19,262, 312.
Sandhi,tirtha...202.
Sahaya Dharma....10, 335,
Sanyasis...12, 13. 86, 104, 105, 106, 125, 141, 162, 164, 165, 167, 169. 170, 171, 173,-175, 181, 184, 185, 188, 197, 202, 205, 209, 210, 217, 218- 220, 225, 228, 231, 234, 242, 275, 282. 304, 325.
Sanskrit...12, 29, 37, 44, 57, 84, 103, 104, 113, 114, 117, 125, 130, 132, 204, 220, 238, 244, 291, 294-297.
Sarvats...13.
Sarbabhaum...66, 179, 180, 246, 291, 293.
Samsuddin II...22, 23.
Samsuddin Bhengara...22.
Sachi Devi...23, 99, 102, 104, 105, 106, 122, 123, 126, 128, 132, 161, 162, 165, 166, 167, 173, 233.
Sari...9, 26, 204.
Saraswati...26.

Sakhya...27, 226, 228, 229, 230, 231, 326, 328, 329, 330, 331.
Subarmarekha...177.
Sarap...192.
Saptagram...214, 279.
Saka...46, 60, 103, 109, 134, 137, 168, 211, 213, 259, 262, 263.
Sadhu...197, 204, 211, 249, 361, 362, 363, 364, 365, 366, 367.
Sankirtan...56, 144, 162.
Sanatan...56, 79, 128, 219,-222, 230, 237, 249, 254, 281, 282, 287, 288-292, 318, 320, 324, 337, 347.
Sachi...63, 75, 84, 106, 109, 112, 132, 133, 134, 167, 175.
Satirmata...66.
Satyabai...195.
Sanyasa...70, 82, 83, 92, 94, 104, 106, 108, 161, 168, 170, 171, 181, 191, 192, 211, 245, 275, 302, 304, 312.
Sarupa Damodar...216.
Sandipani...75.
Sakutabbanjana...76.
Sarpuria...187.
Sashi mukhi...96, 167.
Sadananda Puri...202.
Sankararanga Puri...104.

INDEX 415

Sastri...188.
Sakar Mallik...291.
Sama...298.
Sankara...242, 244, 256, 322, 323, 324.
Sambhuchand...377.
Sadbaka...285, 384.
Santa...326, 327, 328, 3.9.
Samaj...380.
Sahajia cult...339, 355, 368, 402.
Sahajias...317, 318, 335, 337, 338, 339, 340, 341, 346, 347, 349, 350, 351, 352-360, 361, 367, 369, 373, 374, 387, 388, 390, 391, 393, 394, 401, 403.
Sastric...320.
Sastras...321.
Saheb Dhani...346.
Saddhini...347.
Sahajia gurus...396, 397.
Sabitri...357.
Sahaja Desha...359.
Sadhu charit...361.
Santa Dasi..361
Sekhara...235.
Sen kings...37, 125.
Sevadasi...7, 253.
Shivadi ghrita...132.
Shah...57.
Shekha—Subhodaya...7.
Shaiva...204.
Sher Afgan...21.
Shakespeare...274.
Shai...377.
Shaivat...306, 307, 308.
Shivgram...346.
Siveswar...178.
Siddha...2, 3, 384.
Sir R. G. Bhandarkar...36.
Siva...8, 9, 11, 41, 64, 297.
Sisir Kumar Ghosh...88.
Sita...109, 111, 157, 175, 310, 357.
Sikhi—Mahiti...242.
Sibananda Sen...244.
Sivananda...283, 377.
Sir Rabindranath Tagore...395.
Sikh...401.
Skanda...32, 35, 36.
Sloka...45, 136, 238.
Somnath...209.
Sotuhern India...12, 31, 37, 39, 87, 89, 189, 190, 193, 203, 209-211, 234, 252, 294, 295.

Sonoria Brahmin...227.
Solomon...268.
Songs of songs...302.
Spastabadini...350.
Srikhanda...50, 68, 212, 285.
Sriman...157.
Sriman Pandit...49, 131, 133.
Srivas...49, 109, 110, 133-135, 139, 141, 144, 146, 157, 158, 162, 163, 166, 174, 187, 233, 240, 252, 263, 285.
Sridhara...38, 49, 147, 150, 241.
Sriparvat...45.
Sri Ramkrishna...62.
Sridhar Swami...241.
Srad...392.
Srinath Mukhopadhyay...346.
Stewart...23.
St. Paul...61, 81.
Sterling...184.
St. John...81.
St. Juan of the Cross...268
St. Teresa of Foligno...268.
St. Angelo of Foligno...268.
Stula...384.
Subhananda Ray...153.
Sumeru...169, 311.
Sultan Mahmud...21.
Sultan Gayasuddin...23.
Sultan Assalatwin...23.
Subuddhi Ray...57.
Sudarsan...113.
Sukta...124.
Subarnagram...125.
Suklambar Brahmachari...133.
Suklambara...133.
Sudra...279, 282, 286.
Subarnabanik...283.
Suapur...07.
Sufis...304.
Sunya Puran...393.
Sunya Murti...345.
Sungod...392.
Sutteee...357.
Svarup Damodar's note...97.
Swarup Damodar,...210, 239, 257.
Swami...241.
Swarupa...248, 252, 253, 256, 259, 294, 297, 315.
Swapnabilas...314.
Sylhet...99, 106, 114, 125, 361.

T

Tabor...50, 152.
Tamal...41, 310.
Tamil...204, 211, 294, 295.

Tansen...318.
Tantric..6, 7, 10, 13, 171, 352, 353, 372, 374, 396.

INDEX

Tantricism...6, 11.
Tantricks...275.
Tapar. Misra...225, 230.
Tapti...200.
Tarpan 349.
Telegu...120, 295, 392.
Telegus...392.
Tennyson...71.
Tibel...120.
Tilakdasi...350.
Tirodhan...260, 263, 264.
Tirtharam...194, 195, 196,
Tithi...262 263, 264.
Tol...113, 115, 116, 118, 122, 125   135,

136, 163, 233, 294.
Tole...75.
Trichinopoli...202.
Trimanda...193.
Trinabarta...34.
Tajpadi...12.
Tripatra...12, 193.
Tritya Pruahar...263.
Trivancore...209.
Tukaram...211.
Tulsi...53, 58, 80, 132, 207, 208, 288.
Tundetandubani etc....238, 297,
Typical Sebctions from old Bengali Literature...353, 319.

U

Uddharan Dutta...283 292.
Udisi...41.
Ula...341.
Ulluka...13.
Undestood...267, 305, 306, 307 374,
Upakarika...173.
Upanishads...181, 226, 366.

Upendra...36.
Upendra Misra...106, 126.
Upper India...223, 224, 234, 244, 295.
Urbashi...84.
Uriya...235, 236, 239, 246, 247.
Uriya Raja...218.

V

Vaidya...145, 225.
Vaisnava...7, 16, 17, 23, 24, 27, 29, 30, 40, 41, 45, 47, 48, 60, 77, 78, 79, 80, 81, 85, 109, 116, 125, 133, 135. 138, 143, 145, 146, 151, 161, 172, 196, 203 204, 216, 300, 305, 307, 308, 309, 311 312, 314 315, 316. 317, 318, 323.
Vaishnab...224, 225, 227, 229, 236, 238, 244, 245, 251, 258, 260, 261, 262, 264, 270, 271, 272, 273, 279, 283, 285, 286 287, 288, 389, 290, 296.
Vaishnab goswamis...
Vaishnava gurus ..318 377.
Vaishnava Jurisprudence...320.
Vaishnavism...6, 31, 37, 46, 50, 95, 142, 184, 219, 221, 222, 242, 249, 282, 286, 287, 325, 334, 373, 374, 393, 399.
Valadev Bhattacharya...63.
Vali...130.
Valmiki...27, 273, 310.
Vamana...39.
Varonch...200.
Vashu Derv...38, 54, 844, 212.
Vashndev-Sarbabhaum...54.
Vasbughosh...165.

Vatsalya...326, 329, 330, 331.
Vedanta Philosophy...182, 294, 313.
Vedas...353, 388.
Vedic age...269.
Vedic Aryans...249.
Vedic Brahmin...101
Vetoria...23.
Vidyapati...15, 16, 17, 23, 69, 143, 145, 266, 295,
Vidyabachaspati...54.
Vidya Nagar...116.
Vidyasagar...115, 118, 294.
Vidyonmadtarangini...335.
Visurad...54.
Vishnu...36, 37, 83, 84, 86, 88, 93, 128, 130, 132, 156, 194, 203, 213.
Vishnu priya...82.
Visnu Pundit...113.
Vitadra...125.
Vivarta-Vilas...337.
Von Meor...54.
Vrindaban...237, 396.
Vrind groves...33, 42, 43, 57, 173, 323, 377, 386 385.
Vyas...137. 323.

INDEX

W

Ward...338.
Weslyan Revival ..305.

Western Asia...21.
Western Bengal...53, 349.

Y

Yoga...4, 6, 341, 359, 360.
Yogi...4, 5, 97.

Yogini...29.

Z

Zemindar...23.

Zoroaster...61.

OPINIONS
"HISTORY OF THE BENGALI LANGUAGE AND LITERATURE" (IN ENGLISH)

By
RAI SAHIB DINESH CHANDRA SEN, B.A.
Published by
CALCUTTA UNIVERSITY

Price—Rs. 12.   Demy 8vo, pp. 1030, with illustrations.

HIS EXCELLENCY LORD HARDINGE OF PENSHURST in his Convocation Address, dated the 16th March, 1912, as Chancellor of the Calcutta University :—

"During the last four years also the University has, from time to time, appointed Readers on special subjects to foster investigation of important branches of learning amongst our advanced students. One of these Readers, Mr. Sen, has embodied his lectures on the History of Bengali Language and Literature from the earliest times to the middle of the 19th century in a volume of considerable merit, which he is about to supplement by another original contribution to the history of one of the most important vernaculars in this country. May I express the hope that this example will be followed elsewehere, and that critical schools may be established for the vernacular languages of India which have not as yet received the attention that they deserve."

HIS EXCELLENCY LORD CARMICHAEL, GOVERNOR OF BENGAL, in his address on the occasion of his laying the Foundation stone of the Romesh Chandra Saraswat Bhawan, dated the 20th November, 1916 :—

"For long Romesh Chandra Dutt's History of the Literature of Bengal was the only work of its kind available to the general reader. The results of further study in this field have been made available to us by the publication of the learned and luminous lectures of Rai Sahib Dineschandra Sen. * * In the direction of the History of the Language and the Literature, Rai Sahib Dineschandra Sen has created the necessary interest by his Typical Selections. It remains for the members of the Parishad to follow this lead and to carry on the work in the same spirit of patient accurate research."

SIR ASUTOSH MOOKERJEE, in his Convocation Address, dated the 13th March, 1909, as Vice-Chancellor of the Calcutta University :—

"We have had a long series of luminous lectures from one of our own graduates, Babu Dineschandra Sen, on the fascinating subject of the History of the Bengali Language and Literature. These lectures take a comprehensive view of the development of our vernacular, and their publication will unquestionably facilitate the historical investigation of the origin of the vernacular literature of this country, the study of which is avowedly one of the foremost objects of the New Regulations to promote."

SYLVAIN LEVI (*Paris*)—" I cannot give you praises enough—your work is a *Chintamani*—a *Ratnakara*. No book about India would I compare with yours......Never did I find such a realistic sense of literature......Pundit and Peasant, Yogi and Raja, mix together in a Shakespearian way on the stage you have built up."

BARTH (*Paris*)—" I can approach your book as a learner, not as a judge."

C. H. TAWNEY—"Your work shows vast research and much general culture."

VINCENT SMITH—" A work of profound learning and high value."

F. W. THOMAS—" Characterised by extensive erudition and independent research."

E. J. RAPSON—"I looked through it with great interest and great admiration for the knowledge and research to which it bears witness."

F. H. SKRINE—" Monumental work—I have been revelling in the book which taught me much of which I was ignorant."

E. B. HAVELL—" Most valuable book which every Anglo-Indian should read. I congratulate you most heartily on your very admirable English and perfect lucidity of style."

D. C. PHILLOT—" I can well understand the enthusiasm with which the work was received by scholars, for even to men unacquainted with your language, it cannot fail to be a source of great interest and profit."

L. D. BARNETT—" I congratulate you on having accomplished such an admirable work."

G. HULTZUH—" Mr. Sen's valuable work on Bengali literature, a subject hitherto unfamiliar to me, which I am now reading with great interest."

J. F. BLUMHARDT—" An extremely well-written and scholarly production, exhaustive in its wealth of materials and of immense value."

T. W. RHYS DAVIDS—" It is a most interesting and important work and reflects great credit on your industry and research."

JULES BLOCH (*Paris*)—" Your book I find an admirable one and which is the only one of its kind in the whole of India."

WILLIAM ROTHENSTEIN—" I found the book surprisingly full of suggestive information. It held me bound from beginning to end, in spite of my absolute ignorance of the language of which you write with obviously profound scholarship."

EMILE SENART (*Paris*)—" I have gone through your book with lively interest and it appears to me to do the highest credit to your learning and method of working."

HENRY VAN DYKE—(*U. S. A.*)—" Your instructive pages which are full of new suggestions in regard to the richness and interest of the Bengali Language and Literature."

C. T. WINCHESTER —(*U. S. A.*) " A work of profound learning on a theme which demands the attention of all Western scholars."

From a long review in the TIMES LITERARY SUPPLEMENT, London, June 20, 1912—" In his narration, as becomes one who is the soul of scholarly candour, he tells those, who can read him with sympathy and imagination more about the Hindu mind and its attitude towards life than we can gather from 50 volumes of impressions of travel by Europeans. Loti's picturesque account of the rites practised in Travancore temples, and even M. Chevrillon's synthesis of much browsing in Hindu Scriptures, seem faint records by the side of this unassuming tale of Hindu literature—Mr. Sen may well be proud of the lasting monument he has erected to the literature of his native Bengal."

From a long review in the ATHENÆUM, March, 16, 1912—" Mr. Sen may justly congratulate himself on the fact that in the middle age he has done more for the history of his national language and literature than any other writer of his own or indeed any time."

From a long review in the SPECTATOR, June 12, 1912—" A book of extraordinary interest to those who would make an impartial study of the Bengali mentality and character—a work which reflects the utmost credit on the candour, industry and learning of its author. In its kind his book is a masterpiece—modest, learned, thorough and sympathetic. Perhaps no other man living has the learning and happy industry for the task he has successfully accomplished."

From a review by MR. H. BEVERIDGE in the Royal Asiatic Society's Journal, Jan., 1912—" It is a very full and interesting account of the development of the Bengali Literature. He has a power of picturesque writing...his descriptions are often eloquent."

From a long review by S. K. RATCLIFFE in "India," London, March 15, 1912—" There is no more competent authority on the subject than Mr. Dineschandra Sen. The great value of the book is in its full and fresh treatment of the pre-English era and for this it would be difficult to give its author too high praise."

From a long review by H. KERN in the *Bijdragen of the Royal Institute for Taal* (translated by Dr. Kern himself)—" Fruit of investigation carried through many years...highly interesting book...the reviewer has all to admire in the pages of the work, nothing to criticise, for his whole knowledge is derived from it."

From a review by DR. OLDENBERG in the *Frankfurter Zeitung*, December 3, 1911 (translated by the late Dr. Thibaut)—" It is an important supplementation of the history of modern Sanskrit Literature. The account of Chaitanya's influence on the poetical literature of Bengal contributes one of the most brilliant sections of the work."

From a review in DEUTSCHE RUNDSCHAN, April, 1912—" The picture which this learned Bengali has painted for us with loving care of the literature of his native land deserves to be received with attentive and grateful respect."

From a review in LUZAC'S ORIENTAL LIST, London, May-June, 1912—" A work of inestimable value, full of interesting information, containing complete account of the writings of Bengali authors from the earliest time...It will undoubtedly find a place in every Oriental Library as being the most complete and reliable standard work on the Bengali Language and Literature."

From a review in the INDIAN MAGAZINE, London, August, 1912—" For Mr. Sen's erudition, his sturdy patriotism, his instructive perception of the finer qualities in Bengali life and literature, the reader of his book must have a profound respect if he is to understand what modern Bengal is."

From a long review in the MADRAS MAIL, May 9, 1912—"A survey of the evolution of the Bengali letters by a student so competent, so exceptionally learned, can hardly fail to be an important event in the world of criticism.

From a long review in the PIONEER, May 5, 1912—" Mr. Sen is a typical student such as was common in mediæval Europe—a lover of learning for learning's sake...He must be a poor judge of characters who can rise from a perusal of Mr. Sen's pages without a real respect and liking for the writer, for his sincerity, his industry, his enthusiasm in the cause of learning."

From a review in ENGLISHMAN, April 23, 1912—" Only one who has completely identified himself with the subject could have mastered it so well as the author of this imposing book."

From a review in the EMPIRE, August 31, 1918—" As a book of reference Mr. Sen's work will be found invaluable and he is to be congratulated on the result of his labours. It may well be said that he has proved what an English enthusiast once said that ' Bengali ' unites the mellifluousness of Italian with the power possessed by German for rendering complex ideas."

From a review in the INDIAN ANTIQUARY, December, 1912, by F. G. PARGITER: " This book is the outcome of great research and study, on which the author deserves the warmest praise. He has explained the literature and the subjects treated in it with such fulness and in such detail as to make the whole plain to any reader. The folk-literature, the structure and style of the language, metre and rhyme, and many miscellaneous points are discussed in valuable notes. The tone is calm and the judgments appear to be generally fair."

BANGA SAHITYA PARICHAYA.

OR

TYPICAL SELECTIONS FROM OLD BENGALI LITERATURE.

BY

Rai Sahib Dineschandra Sen, B.A.

2 vols, pp. 1914, Royal 8vo, with an Introduction in English running over 99 pages, published by the University of Calcutta.

(*With 10 coloured illustrations. Price Rs. 12.*)

SIR GEORGE GRIERSON—" Invaluable work......That I have yet read through its 1900 pages I do not pretend, but what I have read has filled me with admiration for the industry and learning displayed. It is a worthy sequel to your monumental History of Bengali Literature, and of it we may safely say "*finis coronat opus.*" How I wish that a similar work could be compiled for other Indian languages, specially for Hindi."

E. B. HAVELL—" Two monumental volumes from old Bengali Literature. As I am not a Bengali scholar, it is impossible for me to appreciate at their full value the splendid results of your scholarship and research, but I have enjoyed reading your luminous and most instructive introduction which gives a clear insight into the subject.

I was also very much interested in the illustrations, the reproduction of which from original paintings is very successful and creditable to Swadeshi work."

H. BEVERIDGE—" Two magnificent volumes of the Banga Sahitya Parichaya......I have read with interest Rasa Sundari's autobiography in your extracts."

F. H. SKRINE—" The two splendid volumes of Banga Sahitya Parichaya I am reading with pleasure and profit. They are a credit to your profound learning and to the University which has given them to the world."

From a long review in THE TIMES LITERARY SUPPLEMENT, London, November 4, 1915—" In June, 1912, in commenting on Mr. Sen's History of Bengali Language and Literature, we suggested that work might usefully be supplemented by an anthology of Bengali prose and poetry. Mr. Sen has for many years been occupied with the aid of other patriotic students of the mediæval literature of Bengal in collecting manuscripts of forgotten or half-forgotten poems. In addition to these more or less valuable monuments of Bengali poetic art, the chief popular presses have published great masses on literary matter, chiefly religious verse. It can hardly be said that these piles of written and printed matter have ever been subjected to a critical or philological scrutiny. Their very existence was barely known to the Europeans, even to those who have studied the Bengali Language on the spot. Educated Bengalis themselves, until quite recent times, have been too busy with the arts and sciences of Europe to spare much time for indigenous treasures. That was the reason why we suggested the compiling of a critical chrestomathy for the benefit not only of European but of native scholars. The University of Calcutta prompted by the eminent scholar Sir Asutosh Mookerjee, then Vice-Chancellor, had already anticipated this need it seems. It had shrunk (rightly, we think) from the enormous and expensive task of printing the MSS. recovered by the diligence and generosity of Mr. Sen and other inquirers and employed Mr. Sen to prepare the two bulky volumes now before us. The Calcutta Senate is to be congratulated on its enterprise and generosity."

From a review in The ATHENÆUM, January 16, 1915—" We have already reviewed Mr. Sen's History of Bengali Language and Literature and have rendered some account of his previous work in Bengali entitled *Banga Bhasa O Sahitya*. Mr. Sen now supplies the means of checking his historical and critical conclusions in a copious collection of Bengali verse......Here are the materials carefully arranged and annotated with a skill and learning such as probably no one else living can command."

From a review by Mr. F. G. PARGITER—in the Royal Asiatic Society's Journal—" These two portly volumes of some 2,100 pages are an anthology of Bengali poetry and prose from the 8th to the 19th century and are auxiliary to the same author's History of Bengali Language and Literature which was reviewed by Mr. Beveridge in this Journal for 1912......The Vice-Chancellor of the Calcutta University who was consulted, decided that the best preliminary measure would be to make and publish typical selections. The University then entrusted that duty to Babu Dinesh Chandra Sen; this work is the outcome of his researches. There can be no question that Dinesh Babu was the person most competent to undertake the task and in these two volumes we have without doubt a good presentment of typical specimens of old Bengali literature......The style of the big book is excellent, its printing is fine, and it is embellished with well-executed reproductions in colour of some old paintings. It has also a copious index.

The
VAISNAVA LITERATURE OF MEDIÆVAL BENGAL
[Being lectures delivered as Reader to the University of Calcutta.]
BY
RAI SAHIB DINESH CHANDRA SEN, B.A.
Demy 8vo. 257 pages
WITH A PREFACE BY
J. D. ANDERSON, Esq., I.C.S. (*Retired*)

Price Rs. 2 only

SIR GEORGE GRIERSON.—Very valuable book......I am reading it with the greatest interest and am learning much from it.

WILLIAM ROTHENSTEIN.—I was delighted with your book, I cannot tell you how touched I am to be reminded of that side of your beloved country which appeals to me most—a side of which I was able to perceive something during my own too short visit to India. In the faces of the best of your countrymen I was able to see that spirit of which you write so charmingly in your book. I am able to recall these faces and figures as if they were before me. I hear the tinkle of the temple-bells along the ghats of Benares, the voices of the women as they sing their sacred songs crossing the noble river in the boats at sunset and I sit once more with the austere Sanyasin friends I shall never, I fear, see more. But though I shall not look upon the face of India again, the vision I had of it will fill my eyes through life, and the love I feel for your country will remain to enrich my own vision of life, so long as I am capable of using it. Though I can only read you in English, the spirit in which you write is to me so true an Indian spirit, that it shines through our own idiom, and carries me, I said before, straight to the banks of your sacred rivers, to the bathing tanks and white shrine and temples of your well remembered villages and tanks. So once more I send you my thanks for the magic carpet you sent me, upon which my soul can return to your dear land. May the songs of which you write remain to fill this land with their fragrance ; you will have use of them, in the years before you, as we have need of all that is best in the songs of our own seers in the dark waters through which we are steering.

The Vaisnava Literature of Mediæval Bengal. By Rai Sahib Dineschandra Sen. (Calcutta :—The University.)

Though the generalisation that all Hindus not belonging to modern reform movements are Saivas or Vaisnavas is much too wide, there are the two main divisions in the bewildering mass of sects which make up the 217,000,000 of Hindus, and at many points they overlap each other. The attempts made in the 1901 Census to collect information regarding sects led to such unsatisfactory and partial results that they were not repeated in the last decennial enumeration. But it is unquestionable that the Vaisnavas—the worshippers of Krishna—are dominant in Bengal, owing to the great success of the reformed cult established by Chaitanya, a contemporary of Martin Luther. The doctrine of Bhakti or religious devotion, which he taught still flourishes in Bengal, and the four lectures of the Reader to the University of Calcutta in Bengali here reproduced provide an instructive guide to its expression in the literature of the country during the sixteenth and seventeenth centuries. The first part of the book is devoted to the early period of Vaisnava literature, dating from the eleventh century.

The Rai Sahib is filled with a most patriotic love of his nation and its literature, and has done more than any contemporary countryman to widen our knowledge of them. His bulky volume recording the history of Bengali Language and Literature from the earliest times to the middle of the nineteenth century is accepted by Orientalists as the most complete and authoritative work on the subject.

There is refreshing ingenuousness in his claim, " my industry has been great," and the " forbearing indulgence " for which he asks if he has failed from any lack of powers, will readily be granted in view of the enthusiasm for his subject which somewhat narrows the strictly critical value of his estimates, but does not impair the sustained human interest of the book.

Chaitanya clearly taught, as these pages show, that the Krishna of the Mahabharata, the great chieftain and ally of the Pandava brothers, was not the Krishna of Brindaban. The latter, said the reformer, to Rupa, the author of those masterpieces of Sanskrit drama, the Vidagdha Madhava and the Lalita Madhava, was love's very self and an embodiment of sweetness : and the more material glories of Mathura should not be confused with the spiritual conquests of Brindaban. The amours of Krishna with Radha and the milkmaids of Brindaban are staple themes of the literature associated with the worship of the God of the seductive flute. But Mr. Sen repeatedly insists that the love discussed in the literature he has so closely studied is spiritual and mystic, although usually presented in sensuous garb. Chaitanya who had frequent ecstasies of spiritual joy ; Rupa, who classified the emotions of love in 360 groups and the other authors whose careers are here traced were hermits of unspotted life and religious devotion. The old passionate desire for union which they taught is still dominant in modern Bengali literature not directly Vaisnava in import. As Mr. J. D. Anderson points out in his preface, the influence of Chaitanya's teaching may be detected in the mystical verses of Tagore.

From a long review in the Times Literary Supplement, 26th April, 1918 :—

" This delightful and interesting little book is the outcome of a series of lectures supplementing the learned discourses which Mr. Sen made the material of his " Baisnava Literature of Mediæval Bengal " reviewed by us on August 2, 1917.

It is an authentic record of the religious emotion and thought of that wonderful land of Bengal which few of its Western rulers, we suspect, have rightly comprehended, not from lack of friendly sympathy but simply from want of precisely what Mr. Sen better than any one living, better than Sir Rabindranath Tagore himself, can supply.

It is indeed, no easy matter for a Western Protestant to comprehend, save by friendship and sympathy with just such a pious Hindu as Mr. Sen, what is the doctrine of an *istadevata*, a " favourite deity " of Hindu pious adoration. In his native tongue Mr. Sen has written charming little books, based on ancient legends, which bring us very naer the heart of this simple mystery, akin, we suppose, to the cult of particular saints in Catholic countries. Such for instance, is his charming tale of "Sati," the Aryan spouse of the rough Himalayan ascetic God Siva. The tale is dedicated, in words of delightfully candid respect and affection, to the devoted and loving wives of Bengal, whose virtues as wives and mothers are the admiration of all who know their country. Your pious Vaisnava can, without any hesitation or difficulty, transfer his thoughts from the symbolical amorism of Krishna to that other strange creation-legend of Him of the Blue Throat who, to save God's creatures, swallowed the poison cast up at the Churning of the Ocean and bears the mystic stigma to this day. Well, we have our traditions, legends, mysteries, and as Miss Underhill and others tell us, our own ecstatic mystics, who find such ineffable joy in loving God as, our Hindu friends tell us, the divine Radha experienced in her sweet surrender to the inspired wooing of Krishna. The important thing for us, as students of life and literature is to note how these old communal beliefs influence and develop that wonderful record of human thought and emotion wrought for us by the imaginative writers of verse and prose, the patient artists of the pen.

When all is said, there remains the old indefinable charm which attaches to all that Dinos Chandra Sen writes, whether in English or his native Bengali. In his book breathes a native candour and piety which somehow remind us of the classical writers familiar to our boyhood. In truth, he is a belated contemporary of, say, Plutarch, and attacks his biographical task in much the same spirit. We hope his latest book will be widely (and sympathetically) read."

J. D. Anderson, Esq.—retired I.C.S., Professor, Cambridge University :—I have read more than half of it. I propose to send with it, if circumstances leave me the courage to write it, a short Preface (which I hope you will read with pleasure even if you do not think it worth publication) explaining why, in the judgment of a very old student of all your works, your book should be read not only in Calcutta, but in London and Paris, and Oxford and Cambridge. I have read it and am reading it with great delight and profit and very real sympathy. Think how great must be the charm of your topic and your treatment when in this awful year of anxiety and sorrow, the reading of your delightful MS. has given me rest and refreshment in a time when every post, every knock at the door, may bring us sorrow.

I write this in a frantic hurry the mail goes to-day—in order to go back to your most interesting and fascinating pages.

HISTORY OF THE BENGALI LANGUAGE AND LITERATURE :

Extract from a long review by Sylvain Levi (Paris) in the "Revue Critique" Jan. 1915 ;—(translated for the Bengalee).

"One cannot praise too highly the work of Mr. Sen. A profound and original erudition has been associated with a vivid imagination. The works which he analyses are brought back to life with the consciousness of the original authors, with the movement of the multitudes who patronised them and with the landscape which encircled them. The historian, though relying on his documents, has the temperament of an epic poet. He has likewise inherited the lyrical genius of his race. His enthusiastic sympathy vibrates through all his descriptions. Convinced as every Hindu is of the superiority of the Brahmanic civilization, he exalts its glories and palliates its shortcomings, if he does not approve of them he would excuse them. He tries to be just to Buddhism and Islam ; in the main he is grateful to them for their contribution to the making of India. He praises with eloquent ardour the early English missionaries of Christianity.

The appreciation of life so rare in our book-knowledge, runs throughout the work; one reads these thousand pages with a sustained interest; and one loses sight of the enormous labour which it presupposes; one easily slips into the treasure of information which it presents. The individual extracts quoted at the bottom of the pages offers a unique anthology of Bengali. The linguistic remarks scattered in the extracts abound in new and precious materials. Mr. Sen has given to his country a model which it would be difficult to surpass; we only wish that it may provoke in other parts of India emulations to follow it."

THE FOLK LITERATURE OF BENGAL, BY RAI SAHEB DINESH CHANDRA SEN, B.A., published by the Calcutta University. Demy 8vo, pp 362. With a foreward by W. R. Gourlay, M.A., I.C.S., C.I.E., C S.I., from a long review in the TIMES LITERARY SUPPLEMENT, MAY 13, 1920.

"Those who are acquainted (we hope there are many) with Mr. Sen's other works, the outcome of lectures delivered to Calcutta University under-graduates in the author's function as Ramtanu Lahiry Research Fellow in the History of the Bengali Language and Literature, will know exactly what to expect of his present delightful excursion into Bengali Folk-lore. Mr. Sen thinks in Bengali, he thinks Bengali thoughts, he remains a pious Hindu, though his Hindu ideas are touched and stirred by contact with many kindly and admiring English friends. He is the better fitted to explain Bengal to the outer world, for he loves his native province with all his heart. He has no doubts as to the venerable origins, the sound philosophy, the artistic powers, the suggestive beauty, all the many charms of the Bengali Saraswati, the sweet and smiling goddess, muse and deity alike, the inspirer and patron of a long line of men of literature and learning too little known to the self-satisfied West.

A Hindu he remains thinking Hindu thoughts, retaining proud and happy memories of his Hindu childhood and of the kind old men and women who fed his childish imagination with old-world rhymes, with the quaintly primitive Bengali versions of the stately epics of Sanskrit scripture, with tales even more primitive handed down by word of mouth by pious mothers, relics perhaps of a culture which preceded the advent of Hinduism in Bengal. What makes Mr. Sen's books so delightful to us in Europe is precisely this indefinable Hindu quality specifically Bengali rather than Indian, something that fits itself with exquisite aptness to what we know of the scenery and climate of the Gangetic delta, where Mr Sen was born, and where he has spent the life as a schoolmaster in Eastern Bengal, a land of wide shining mires and huge slow-moving rivers where the boatman sings ancient legends as he lazily plies the oar and the cowherd lads on the low grassy banks of Meghna and Dhaleswari chant plaintive rhymes that Warren Hastings may have heard as he "proceeded up country" in his spacious "budgerow."

All these pleasant old rhymes and tales Mr. Sen loves with more than patriotic emotions and admiration and this sentiment he contrives to impart to his readers, even through the difficult and laborious medium of a foreign language."

JULES BLOCH—" I have just finished the romantic story of Chandravati (given in the Bengali Ramayanas). May I congratulate you on the good and well deserved luck of having disc vered her after so many others and having added that new gem to the crown of Bengali Literature.

I cannot speak to you in detail of your chapters on the characteristics of the Bengali Ramayanas and on Tulsidas, I had only to learn from what you say and thank you for helping me and many others to get a little of that direct understanding and feeling of the literary and emotional value of those poems in general and Krittivas in particular. I hope your devotion to Bengali Literature will be rewarded by a growing popularity of that literature in India and in Europe ; and also that young scholars will follow your example and your direction in continuing your studies, literary and philological."

SIR GEORGE GRIERSON—" I must write to thank you for your two valued gifts of the " Folk Literature of Bengal " and " The Bengali Ramayanas." I delayed acknowledging them till I had read them through. I have been greatly interested by both, and owe you a debt of gratitude for the immense amount of important information contained in them.

I add to this letter a few notes which the perusal of your books has suggested to me. Perhaps you will find them useful.

I hope that you will be spared to us to write many more such books."

DR. WILLIAM CROOKE, C.I.E., EDITOR OF "FOLK LORE"—" I have read them ("Folk Literature of Bengal" and "The Bengali Ramayanas") with much interest. They seem to me to be a very valuable contribution to the study of the religion and folk-lore of Bengal. I congratulate you on the success of your work and I shall be glad to receive copies of any other work which you may write on the same subjects."

H. BEVERIDGE—" Of the two books I must say that I like best the Bengali Ramayanas. Your book on Bengali folk lore is also valuable " (from a letter of 12 pages containing a critical review of the two books).

FROM THE TIMES LITERARY SUPPLEMENT, APRIL 7, 1921.

" The Bengali Ramayanas " by Rai Saheb Dinesh Chandra Sen (published by the University of Calcutta).

The Indian Epics deserve closer study than they have hitherto received at the hands of the average Englishmen of culture. Apart from the interest of the main themes, the wealth of imagery and the beauty of many of the episodes, they are storehouses of information upon the ancient life of India and a key to the origin of customs which still live. Moreover they show many curious affinities to Greek literature which suggest the existence of legends common to both countries. The Ring of Polycrates is reproduced in other conditions in the " Sakuntala " the *Alcestis* has its counterpart in the story of Savitri, and the chief of Pandavas descends into hell in the manner of Odysseus though on a nobler errand.

The main theme of these lectures is the transformation of the old majestic Sanskrit epic as it came from the hands of Valmiki to the more familiar and homely style of the modern Bengali versions. The Ramayana, we are told, is a protest against Buddhist monasticism, the glorification of the domestic virtues, proclaiming that there is no need to look for salvation outside the home. The Bengali versions, which reducing the grandeur of the heroic characters, to the level of ordinary mortals, bring the epic within the reach of the humblest peasant ; they have their own virtues, just as the simple narrative of the Gospels has its own charm, though it be different in kind from that of Isaiah's majestic cadences. Thus in the Sanskrit poem "Kaucalya" Rama's mother is sacrificing to Fire when she hears of her son's exile; she does not flinch, but continues the sacrifice in the spirit of Greek tragedy, merely altering the character of her prayer. In the Bengali version she becomes a woman, giving vent to lamentations, such as one hears every day in modern India. In the Nibelungenlied one sees the same kind of transformation from the old Norse sagas to the atmosphere of mediæval chivalry.

The author approaches his subject in that spirit of reverence which is the due of all great literature, and to him, Valmiki's Ramayana is the greatest literature in the world. The fact does not blunt his critical faculty ; rather does it sharpen it, for, as he says in the preface, "historical research and the truths to which it leads do not interfere with faith," neither do they stand in the way of admiration. He sees more in the Ramayana than the mere collection of legends into a Sanskrit masterpiece from which various versions have been made from time to time. He shows us how, as the centuries proceeded, each successive version was influenced by the spirit of the age, how the story became adapted to the purposes of religi us propaganda, how in the interests of the Vaisnaba cult the hero Rama became the divine avatar of Vishnu, even at the risk of absurd situations. He takes us through the age of the Sakti influence, of Ramananda's philosophy and its revolt against Mahomedan iconoclasm, of the flippant immorality of the eighteenth century. "These Bengali Ramayanas," he says, "have thus quite an encyclopædic character, comprising, along with the story of Rama, current theologies, folk-tales and the poetry of rural Bengal of the age when they were composed." To him the Ramayan is a yellow primrose, but it is something more, * * * * To the student of folk-lore these lectures are to be recommended as an earnest and loving study of a fascinating subject."

From the "Revista Trimestrale di studi Filosofici e Religiosi—
Rai Bahadur Dineshchandra Sen's Folk Literature of Bengal.
"The University of Calcutta continues with every alacrity, the fine series of its publications thus testifying to the high scientific preparation (issuing out) of those indigenous teachers. This volume devoted to the popular tales of Bengal also constitutes a contribution of the first rank to such a subject. The tracing of the History of the Bengali language and literature in this University is one of the most well deserved studies of Bengal. To it is due, in fact, the monumental and now classical History of the Bengali Language and Literature (1912);—in which, so far as our studies go, we value most the accurate estimate of the influence of Chaitanya on that literature—accompanied by the grand Bengali Anthology Banga Sahitya Parichaya, 1914, and then above all the pleasing and erudite researches on Vaishnab literature and the connected religious reform of Chaitanya.

A world wholly legendary depicted with the homely tenderness in most secluded locality of Bengal and half conceived in the Buddhistic epoch with delicate phantasy and fondness; the world in which Rabindranath Tagore ultimately attained his full growth is revived with every seduction of art in the luminous pages of this beautiful book. The author came in touch with this in his first days of youth when he was a village teacher in East Bengal and he now wishes to reveal it by gathering together the most secluded spirit and also the legend collected in four delicious volumes of D. R. Mazumdar, yet to be translated.

A spirit of renunciation in the devotion of wives in the love of tender and sorrowful ladies, in eagerness for patient sacrifice carry us back, as we have said, to the Buddhistic epoch of Bengal; it rises as an ideal of life and is transmitted to future generations traversed by the Mussalmani faith which also is pervaded by so many Buddhistic elements. Malancha, the sublime female incarnation of such an ideal—whose legend is translated in the last pages of this volume—the Lady wholly spiritual, a soul heroic in its devoted renunciation, mistress of her body who reveals in herself qualities that essentially belong to idea, a creature of the soul, shaped by the aspiration to come into contact with the external world. Malancha loses her eyes and her hands, but so strong is her desire to see her husband that her eyes grow again and such is her desire to serve him that her hands also grow again.

In the popular narration the prose often assumes a poetic movement and metrical form. The archaic language that reminds us of remote antiquity is converted into lyric charm and becomes knotty in the prose, making us think pensively of the Vedic hymnology that entered the epic of Mahavarat.

[Translated from the Original Italian.]

Extract from the Times, dated the 7th April, Thursday, 1922.

EPICS OF BENGAL.

THE BENGALI RAMAYANAS. BY RAI SAHEB DINESHCHANDRA SEN. (Published by the University of Calcutta. Rs. 14 2a.)

The Indian epics deserve closer study than they have hitherto received at the hands of the average Englishman of culture. Apart from the interest of the main themes, the wealth of imagery and the beauty of many of the episodes, they are storehouses of information upon the ancient life of India and a key to the origin of customs which still live. Moreover, they show many curious affinities to Greek literature, which suggest the existence of legends common to both countries. The Ring of Polycrates is reproduced in other conditions in the "Sakuntalá," the *Alcestis* has its counterpart in the story of Savitri, and the chief of the Pandavas descends into hell in the manner of Odysseus, though on a nobler errand.

The main theme of these lectures is the transformation of the old majestic Sanskrit epic as it came from the hands of Valmiki to the more familiar and homely style of the modern Bengali versions. The Ramáyana, we are told, is a protest againt Buddhist monasticism, the glorification of the domestic virtues, proclaiming that there is no need to look for salvation outside the home. The Bengali versions, while reducing the grandeur of the heroic characters to the level of ordinary mortals, bring the epic within the reach of the humblest peasant; they have their own virtues, just as the simple narrative of the Gospels has its own charm, though it be different in kind from that of Isaiah's majestic cadences. Thus in the Sanskrit poem "Kauçalya" Rama's mother is sacrificing to Fire when she hears of her son's exile; she does not flinch, but continues the sacrifice in the spirit of Greek tragedy, merely altering the character of her prayer. In the Bengali version she becomes an ordinary Bengali woman, giving vent to lamentations such as one hears every day in modern India. In the Nibelungenlied one sees the same kind of transformation from the old Norse sagas to the atmosphere of medieval chivalry.

The author approaches his subject in that spirit of reverence which is the due of all great literature, and to him Valmiki's Ramayana is the greatest literature in the world. The fact does not blunt his critical faculty; rather does it sharpen it, for, as he says in the preface, "historical research and the truths to which it leads do not interfere with faith," neither do they stand in the way of admiration. He sees more in the Ramayana than the mere collection of legends into a Sanskrit masterpiece from which various versions have been made from time to time. He shows us how, as the centuries proceeded, each successive version was influenced by the spirit of the age, how the story became adapted to the purposes of religious propaganda, how in the interests of the Vaishnava cult the hero Rama became the divine avatar of Vishnu, even at the risk of absurd situations. He takes us through the age of the Sakti influence, of Ramananda's philosophy and its revolt against Mahomedan iconoclasm, of the flippant immorality of the eighteenth century. "These Bengali Ramayanas," he says, "have thus quite an encyclopædic character, comprising, along with the story of Rama, current theologies, folk-tales, and the poetry of rural Bengal of the age when they were composed." To him the Ramayana is a yellow primrose, but it is something more; and if some of his theories seem over-fanciful, at least they have the merit of sincerity. To the student of folklore these lectures are to be recommended as an earnest and loving study of a fascinating subject.

FROM A REVIEW IN THE "FOLK LORE."

FOLKLORE IN BENGAL.

THE BENGALI RAMAYANS: LECTURES DELIVERED AT THE CALCUTTA UNIVERSITY IN 1916. BY RAI SAHIB DINESHCHANDRA SEN, B.A. Published by the University of Calcutta. 1920.

THE FOLK-LITERATURE OF BENGAL: LECTURES DELIVERED AT THE CALCUTTA UNIVERSITY IN 1917. By the same Author. Published by the University of Calcutta. 1920.

It is a matter of congratulation that the author of these two volumes of lectures, an eminent Bengali scholar and author of an important work, *The History of Bengali Language and Literature*, has devoted his attention to the folklore of his country, and that a lectureship on this subject has been founded in the University of Calcutta. In the first series of lectures he considers the questions connected with the Bengali versions of the great Indian epic, the "Ramayana" the work of Valmiki. The first result of his analysis of the poem is that, as might have been anticipated, the poet used much of the current folk-tradition. Many incidents in the epic closely resemble tales in the Buddhist Jātaka. The second theory suggested is that originally the cycle of legends connected with the demigod Rāma and the demon Rāvana were distinct, and that it was left for the poet to combine them into one consistent narrative.

The second course of lectures deals with a series of folk-tales current among Musalmans in Bengal, which evidently embody early Hindu tradition. The influence of women in preserving these tales, and particularly the scraps of poetry embodied in them, is illustrated in an interesting way, and he makes an important suggestion that tales of the Middle Kingdom, or the Upper Ganges Valley, were conveyed by the crews of ships sailing from the coast of Bengal to Persia, and thus were communicated to the people of the West long before any translations of collections like the Panchatantra or Hitopadesa were available.

The learned author of these lectures is doing admirable work in a field hitherto unexplored, and the University of Calcutta deserves hearty commendation in its efforts to encourage the study of Indian folklore.

TIMES LITERARY SUPPLEMENT MAY 13, 1920.

THE FOLK-LORE OF BENGAL.

THE FOLK-LITERATURE OF BENGAL: BY RAI SAHIB DINESHCHANDRA SEN. (Calcutta University Press.).

Those who are acquainted (we hope they are many) with Mr. Sen's other works, the outcome of lectures delivered to Calcutta undergraduates in the author's function as Ramtanu Lahiri Research Fellow in the History of the Bengali Language and Literature, will know exactly what to expect of his present delightful excursion into Bengali Folk-lore. There is some humour, to begin with, in the odd fact that he should be lecturing to Bengali lads on Bengali nursery tales in English. Mr. Sen is not, and does not profess to be, one of those remarkable Bengalis who, like Sir Rabindranath Tagore, for example, are perfectly bilingual to the extent of being able to think with equal ease, and write with equal felicity and justness of expression, in both languages. Let not this be regarded as a sin in the Ramtanu Lahiri Fellow. He thinks in Bengali, he thinks Bengali thoughts, he remains a pious Hindu, though his Hindu ideas are touched and stirred by contact with many kindly and admiring English friends. He is the better fitted to explain Bengal to the outer world. For he loves his native province with all his heart. He has no doubts as to the venerable origins, the sound philosophy, the artistic powers, the suggestive beauty, all the many charms of the Bengali Saraswati, the sweet and smiling goddess, muse and deity alike, the inspirer and patron of a long line of men of literature and learning too little known to the self-satisfied and incurious West.

A Hindu he remains, thinking Hindu thoughts, retaining proud and happy memories of his childhood and of the kind old men and women who fed his childish imagination with old world rhymes, with the quaintly primitive Bengali versions of the stately epics of Sanskrit Scriptures with tales even more primitive, handed down by word of mouth by pious mothers, relics, perhaps, of a culture which preceded the advent of Hinduism in Bengal. What makes Mr. Sen's books so delightful to us in Europe is precisely this indefinable Hindu quality, specifically Bengali rather than Indian, something that fits itself with exquisite aptness to what he knows of the scenery and climate of the Gangetic delta, where Mr. Sen was born, and where he has spent the whole time of his busy life as a student of his native literature. He began life as a village school master in Eastern Bengal, a land of wide shining meres and huge slow-moving rivers, where the boatman sings ancient legends as he lazily plies the oar, and the cowherd lads on the low grassy banks of Meghna or Dhaleswari chant plaintive rhymes that Warren Hastings may have heard as he "proceeded up country" in his spacious "budgerow."

All these pleasant old rhymes and tales Mr. Sen loves with a more than patriotic emotion and admiration, and this sentiment he contrives to impart to his readers, even through the difficult and laborious medium of a foreign language. We can imagine his lectures to be pleasant by conversional than eloquent in the academical fashion. He tells the lads before him what life-long pleasure he has taken in the hereditary legends he shares with them. But in the present volumes, for example, he is driven to assume from time to time the austerity of a professional student of a comparative folk-lore, and so strays (unwittingly, we may be sure) into the region of heated controversy. Mr. Gourlay, distinguished administrator and student of the History of Bengal, has given Mr. Sen a friendly fore-word. It is evident that this professional element in Mr. Sen's work has a little frightened his kindly sponsor. "When I read the author's enthuasiastic appriciation," he says, "of Bengali folk tales, the thought crossed my mind that perhaps the Rai Sahib's patriotism had affected his judgment; but after I had read the translation of the beautiful story of Malanchamala, I went back to the first lecture, and I knew that what he said was true."

Mr. Gourlay has expressed a hope that Mr. Sen will make a collection of Bengali folk tales. It must be admitted that the late Rev. Lalbehari Dey's tales may well be supplemented. But surely Mr. Gourlay knows Daksina Ranjan Mazumdar's four wonderful and wholly delightful volumes, one of them with a preface of appreciation by Sir Rabindranath Tagore himself. Mr. Mazumdar may well claim to be the Grimm of Bengal, and Mr. Sen has repeatedly acknowledged his debt to his unwearied diligence in collecting Bengali folk-tales. The wonder is that no one has yet translated the marvels of "Thakurdadar Jhuli," "Thakurmar Jhuli," "Thandidir Thale" and "Dadamahasayer Thali." Appropriately illustrated, sympathetically rendered, they may yet be the delight of Western nurseries, and form the best, the most natural and easy of introduction to Indian thought and literature. There are other admirable works for the nursery in Bengali, such as Miss Sita Devi's "Niret Gurur Kahini" and the volume of Hindustani Fairy tales translated by her and her sister. But there is only one Majumdar, and we heartily hope that Mr. Sen's version of his Malancha Mala in this volume will draw the attention of European students of Indian folk-lore to the four excellent collections we have mentioned. Their style, subtlety, archaic yet colloquial, may well puzzle the translator, for not every one of us has the pen of a Charles Perrault. But the task is well worth attempting. Meanwhile Mr. Sen does well to remind us that two of the best of La Fontaine's Fables are taken from the "Panchatantra."

BENGALI RAMAYANS by D. C. Sen, from a review in the Journal of Royal Asiatic Society by Sir George Grierson—

This is the most valuable contribution to the literature on the Rāma-saga which has appeared since Professor Jacobi's work on the Rāmāyaṇa was published in 1893. The latter was confined to Vālmīki's famous epic, and the present volume, from the pen of the veteran author of the *History of Bengali Language and Literature*, carries the inquiry on to a further stage, and throws light both on the origins of the story and on its later developments.

The subject covers so wide a ground, and its treatment exhibits so wide a field of Indian learning that, within the limited space available, it is impossible to do more than indicate the more salient points adduced by the author, and, perhaps, to add a few new items of information.

It has long been admitted that the core of the Sanskrit Rāmāyaṇa—the portion written by Vālmīki himself—consists (with a few interpolations) of the second to the sixth books. The first and the seventh, in which Rāma is elevated from the stage of a heroic mortal to divinity, are later additions. The Rai Saheb, accepting these conditions, has been able to dispel part of the darkness which has hitherto enveloped the sources of Vālmīki's poem, and to trace its origin to three distinct stories, which the great poet combined into a single epic.

The oldest version is that contained in the Dasaratha Jātaka,[1] in which Sītā is said to be Rāma's sister. Rāma is banished to the Himālaya, being accompanied by her and Lakṣmaṇa—under much the same story of palace intrigue as that told by Vālmīki,—and returns to reign after twelve years. He then marries his sister Sītā, and they live happy ever afterwards. She is not abducted by anyone, and there is no mention either of Hanumān or of Rāvaṇa.

The second strand of the epic belongs to Southern India, where there grew up a cycle of legends[2] about a grand and noble Brāhmaṇa.[3] Most of these stories are said to be collected in the Jaina Rāmāyaṇa of Hēmacandra, a work which I have not seen, and which is described by our author as far more a history of Rāvaṇa than of Rāma. On the other hand, a Buddhist work—the Laṅkāvatāra Sūtra—narrates a long discourse which Rāvaṇa held with the Buddha, and claims him as a follower of Mahāyāna Buddhism! He was thus revered by Hindūs, Jainas, and Buddhists alike.

The third strand was the floating group of legends related to ape-worship once widely current in India. In these Hanumān was at first connected with Śaivism, and there are still extant stories telling how Śiva made him over to Lakṣmaṇa for service under Rāma. Even at the present day it is not only the devotees of Viṣṇu who adore him, and Śaivas, but the crypto-Buddhists of Orissa claim him as a powerful divinity.

From materials taken from each of these three sources Vālmīki welded together his immortal poem. He refused sanction to the ancient legend that the Sītā whom Rāma married was his sister, but gave no hint as to her parentage. This was supplied in later works, such as the Adbhuta Rāmāyaṇa—a wonderful collection of old and fantastic traditions—in which she is described as the daughter of Mandōdarī, the wife of her abductor.[4]

After thus discussing the origins of the Rāma-saga, and its development by Vālmīki, the Rai Saheb proceeds to the main subject of his work—the Rāmāyaṇas of Bengal. None of them are translations of the Sanskrit epic. Like the celebrated *Rāma-carita-mānasa* of Tulasī Dāsa, each author tells his story in his own way, weaving into it his own thoughts and ancient traditions current in his neighbourhood. They secured their general popularity by the thorough Bengalization

[1] This was long ago recognized by A. Weber. See *Indian Antiquary*, Vol. i, p. 121.
[2] We find much of this in that portion of the *Uttara Kāṇḍa* which Jacobi calls the *Rāvaṇeïs*.
[3] Numerous temples in Southern India are said to have been founded by Rāvaṇa (see *Bombay Gazetteer*, I, i, 190 454, n. 1 ; XV, ii, 76, 290 ff., 341). He is said to have performed his celebrated austerities at Gōkarna, in Kansra (Bombay Presidency), a district which abounds in legends about him. Some of these have spread to very distant parts of India. For instance, the story of the loan to him of Śiva's "self-liṅga" (*Gaz.* XV, 29C) reappears in the Kāshmīrī Rāmāyaṇa.
[4] *Vide* JRAS., 1921, p. 422. This story appears to have been widely spread. It is popular in Kashmir. According to the Jaina *Uttara Purāṇa*, quoted by our author she was a daughter of Rāvaṇa himself.

of their theme. The scenery, the manners and customs, the religions rites, the very food, although placed in Laṅkā, are all those familiar to Bengal. The most famous, and one of the oldest, of these Rāmāyaṇas is that of Kṛttivāsa (fourteenth century). All these features are already found there, but later writers, falling under the influence of the Vaiṣṇava revival of Caitanya, not only filled their poems with Vaiṣṇava doctrine and with theories about *bhakti*, but even transferred legends concerning Caitanya to pseudo-prototypes in the war before Laṅkā.[1] Space will not permit me to mention all Kṛttivāsa's successors. Each had his own excellencies and his own defects. I therefore confine myself to calling attention to the incomplete Rāmāyana of the Mymensingh poetess Candrāvatī. In one of her poems she tells her own beautiful and pathetic story, and there can be no doubt but that her private griefs, nobly borne, inspired the pathos with which her tale of Sītā's woes is distinguished. It is interesting that, like one or two other authors, she ascribes Sītā's banishment to Rāma's groundless jealousy. A treacherous sister-in-law, daughter of Kaikēyī, named Kukuā, persuaded Sītā, much against her will, to draw for her a portrait of Rāvana. She then showed this to Rāma as a proof that his wife loved, and still longed for her cruel abductor. This story was not invented by the poetess. It must have been one of those long orally current, but not recorded by Vālmīki or by the writer of the seventh book of the Sanskrit poem, for it reappears in the Kāshmīrī Rāmāyana to which I have previously alluded.

A few words may also be devoted to another curious version of the old tradition. Under various orthodox names Buddhism has survived in Orissa to the present day, and, in the seventeenth century, one Rāmānanda openly declared himself to be an incarnation of the Buddha and, to prove it, composed a *Rāma-līlā*, or Rāmāyana. I have already alluded to the fact that Hanuman was worshipped by this Orissa Buddhists. It need not therefore surprise us that Rāmānanda stated that he wrote his book under the ape-god's inspiration.

I have drawn attention to only a few features of this excellent work in the hope that my remarks will induce those interested in the subject to buy the book and study it for themselves. It deserves attention, even if we do not accept all that its author wishes to prove. As a collection of hitherto unknown facts bearing on the development of the Rāma-saga in Bengal it is unique.

[1] The Bengali version of the conversion of the hunter Vālmīki is worth noting for the light it throws on the connexion of Bengali with Māgadhī Prakrit. Nārada tried to teach him to pronounce Rāma's name, but he could not do so owing to sin having paralysed his tongue. Nārada succeeded in getting him to say *maḍā* (pronounced *marā*), meaning "dead." This is the Māgadhī Prakrit *maḍā* (Vr. xi, 15). It is peculiar to the Bengali language, the more western word being *marā*. Nārada next got him to use this western pronunciation, and to repeat the word rapidly several times,—thus, *marāmarāmarāmarā*. It will be seen that in this way Vālmīki, without his paralysed tongue knowing it, uttered the word *Rāma*, and thus became sufficiently holy to become converted. *Apropos* of the *bhakti* influence, on page 127, there is a story about Niẓāmu'd-dīn Anliā and a robber, which recalls the finale of the Tannhäuser. The robber is told that he cannot hope for forgiveness till a certain dead tree bears leaves. In process of time he does feel true repentance, and the dead trunk becomes at once covered with green leaves from top to bottom.

ImTheStory.com

Personalized Classic Books in many genre's

Unique gift for kids, partners, friends, colleagues

Customize:

- Character Names
- Upload your own front/back cover images (optional)
- Inscribe a personal message/dedication on the inside page (optional)

Customize many titles Including
- Alice in Wonderland
- Romeo and Juliet
- The Wizard of Oz
- A Christmas Carol
- Dracula
- Dr. Jekyll & Mr. Hyde
- And more...

Emily's Adventures in Wonderland

Ryan & Julia